Arabic–English–Arabic Legal Translation

I0890980

Arabic–English–Arabic Legal Translation provides a groundbreaking investigation of the issues found in legal translation between Arabic and English. Drawing on a contrastive–comparative approach, it analyses parallel authentic legal documents in both Arabic and English to examine the features of legal discourse in both languages and uncover the different translation techniques used. In so doing, it addresses the following questions:

- What are the features of English and Arabic legal texts?
- What are the similarities and differences of English and Arabic legal texts?
- What are the difficult areas of legal translation between English and Arabic legal texts?
- What are the techniques for translating these difficult areas on the lexical and syntactic levels?

Features include:

- a thorough description of the features of legal translation in both English and Arabic, drawing on new empirical research, corpus data analysis and strategic two-way comparisons between source texts and target texts
- coverage of a broad range of topics including an outline of the chosen framework for data analysis, a historical survey of legal discourse developments in both Arabic and English and detailed analyses of legal literature at both the lexical and syntactic levels
- attention to common areas of difficulty such as Shariʿah Law terms, archaic terms and model auxiliaries
- many examples and excerpts from a wide selection of authentic legal documents, reinforced by practical discussion points, exercises and practice drills to encourage active engagement with the material and opportunities for hands-on learning.

Wide-ranging, scholarly and thought-provoking, this will be a valuable resource for advanced undergraduates and postgraduates on Arabic, translation studies and comparative linguistics courses. It will also be essential reading for translation professionals and researchers working in the field.

Hanem El-Farahaty is Teaching Fellow in the Department of Arabic and Middle Eastern Studies at the University of Leeds, UK, and an Associate of the Higher Education Academy. She is also a Lecturer in the University of Mansoura, Egypt.

Arabic–English–Arabic Legal Translation

Hanem El-Farahaty

Routledge
Taylor & Francis Group
LONDON AND NEW YORK

First published 2015
by Routledge
2 Park Square, Milton Park, Abingdon, Oxon OX14 4RN

and by Routledge
711 Third Avenue, New York, NY 10017

Routledge is an imprint of the Taylor & Francis Group, an informa business

British Library Cataloguing in Publication Data
A catalogue record for this book is available from the British Library

Library of Congress Cataloging in Publication Data
A catalog record for this book has been requested

ISBN: 978-0-415-70752-7 (hbk)
ISBN: 978-0-415-70753-4 (pbk)
ISBN: 978-1-315-74589-3 (ebk)

Typeset in Times New Roman
by RefineCatch Limited, Bungay, Suffolk

To My Family

Contents

Figures

Tables

Abbreviations

AChHR	Arabic Charter of Human Rights
ChUN	Charter of the United Nations
ISESCO	The Islamic Educational, Scientific and Cultural Organization
LSP	language for specific purposes
Lit.	literally
MSA	Modern Standard Arabic
SL	source language
ST	source text
TL	target language
TR	target reader
TT	target text
UDHR	Universal Declaration of Human Rights
UIDHR	Universal Islamic Declaration of Human Rights
UN	United Nations
UNCTAD	United Nations Conference on Trade and Development

Acknowledgments

I would like to thank colleagues at the Department of Arabic and Middle Eastern Studies, University of Leeds, particularly Dr Hussein Abdul-Raof, Prof. James Dickins and Dr Mustapha Lahlali for their help and advice. Thanks are also due to Dr Alison Johnson of the School of English and Dr Serge Sharrof of the Centre for Translation Studies for their invaluable advice.

My heartfelt thanks are due to my parents who have been, all my life, encouraging, and providing enormous moral support. A word of thanks, I suppose, is not enough to express my gratitude to my husband, Mohamed Elwan, who has been there behind me caring and supporting since we were married. He has always been patient, and has given me both practical and moral support. This book would not have seen light without Mohamed's encouragement and sacrifice.

To my boys, Youssef and Ahmed, extremely wonderful kind boys, many thanks for appreciating how hard I need to work. You have sacrificed your share of time and the care I should give you for my book. I owe you a lot, sweethearts. Last, not least, I would like to thank my brothers and sisters for all their support.

Permission acknowledgments

The author and publishers would like to thank the following copyright holders for permission to reproduce extracts from the following material:

Some of the material in Chapter 3 of this book, previously published in El-Farahaty, H. (2010). 'Lexical and Syntactic Features of English and Arabic Legal Discourse: A Comparative Study.' *Comparative Legilinguistics: International Journal for Legal Communication*, Poznan: Adam Mickiewicz University, vol. 4: pp. 59–77. Used with kind permission of Poznan.

Extracts from Hatim, B., A. Shunnaq and R. Buckley (1995). *The Legal Translator at Work: A Practical Guide*, Jordan: Irbid, Dar Al-Hilal for Translating and Publishing.

Excerpts from the Arabic legal documents available at http://www.arlawfirm.com

While we have made every effort to contact copyright holders of material used in this volume, we would be grateful to hear from any we were unable to contact.

1 Introduction

1.1 AIMS OF THE BOOK

This book aims to present an account of legal translation between English and Arabic. The primary objective, therefore, is to analyse the common features of legal discourse in both languages, be they lexical, syntactic, or textual. Analysing the features of legal Arabic; contrasting them with the features of legal English is a pioneering step in the study of legal discourse. Such a comparison will help us come up with a list of the similarities and differences between both languages. This paves the way to figuring out the common difficult linguistic areas that a translator needs to consider when translating legal discourse between both languages. In undertaking this investigation the book offers a broad set of topics that will benefit many readers such as contrastive linguists, researchers undertaking contrastive English/Arabic research, researchers in the field of translation in general and in legal translation in particular, translation professionals and academics who are teaching translation modules for undergraduate and postgraduate students. These are the topics that the book offers:

- a brief account of the historical background of legal translation and its presentation in the literature
- a thorough account of the features of English and Arabic legal discourse supported by corpus-analysis
- the similarities and differences between both languages with regard to legal discourse
- the differences between the two languages; with a focus on some of the common difficult areas (for example Shariʿah Law terms, archaic terms, modal auxiliaries among others)[1]
- an investigation of how certain difficult areas have been rendered into the target text (TT).

I will adopt a contrastive approach to analyse the techniques used in translating an authentic Arabic–English–Arabic parallel corpus. The reason why I have chosen to analyse texts from both directions is two-fold: (i) to arrive at some reliable results and commonalities by looking at one element from both directions; (ii) if one looks at the translation from one direction, there is a possibility of the interference of the stylistic preferences from either language, so an attempt to avoid such a possibility is also in mind.

1.2 HYPOTHESIS AND RESEARCH QUESTIONS

The underlying hypothesis for the study is that the mismatch between the features of English and Arabic legal discourse results in some problematic areas in legal translation from and to these two languages. This mismatch at the lexical and/or the syntactic levels requires certain techniques on the part of the translator. To check the validity of this hypothesis, we will attempt to answer the following research questions:

What are the features of English and Arabic legal texts?
What are the similarities and differences of English and Arabic legal texts?
What are the difficult areas of legal translation between English and Arabic legal texts?
What are the techniques for translating these difficult areas on the lexical and syntactic levels?

By answering the above questions, the book will draw some conclusions about the nature of legal discourse in Arabic compared to English and pave the way for more empirical and corpus-based studies in this field which incidentally is under researched.

1.3 RESEARCH ON THE PROBLEMS OF LEGAL TRANSLATION: A BRIEF REVIEW

Researchers have engaged in the study of legal translation such as Šarčević (1997), Alcaraz Varó and Hughes (2002), Mayoral Asensio (2003) and Cao (2007) among others. Šarčević (1997) presents an interdisciplinary study in law and translation theory, a study that is not bound to one specific language or legal system. Cao (2007) has investigated the difficulties of translating different types of legal texts such as private legal documents, domestic legislations and international legal instruments. Alcaraz Varó and Hughes (2002) have focused on pragmatic issues, such as problems of and ambiguities resulting from lack of correspondence between two or more languages and legal systems. Matulewska (2007) has compared English and Polish statutes and contracts. She has examined the problems connected with the Polish–English and English–Polish translation of the texts belonging to a big variety of legal subtypes. Mayoral Asensio (2003) has tackled the translation of official documents from English into Spanish. In the field of English–Arabic translation, Alwazna (2013a) has written *Translating Ḥanbalī Sharīʿa Code from Arabic into English: The Books of 'Sale', 'Hire' and 'Loan' in Majallat al-Aḥkām al-Sharʿiyya by al-Qārī* (died in 1359 H/1940 AD). The book discusses issues in the Arabic source text, such as the transformation of the language of juristic Islamic texts into legal codes. It also analyses the translation problems of this particular text into English. In 2013b, Alwazna has discussed the translation of Islamic legal terms into English.

Nevertheless, the features of legal Arabic and the difficulties of legal translation between Arabic and English are under researched. Emery (1989) wrote an article on the features of Arabic legal discourse. Al-Bainy (2002) has referred, in one chapter of his Ph.D. thesis, to additions and omissions in some Arabic–English official legal texts. Lack of English/Arabic legal translation research may be attributed to the complex nature of the subject matter. It is challenging to undertake research in an area that has long been neglected. This book, however, will be considered a point of departure towards investigating this subject in a bit more depth for future research, applying more approaches and advanced tools such as corpus-based translation tools.

1.4 METHODOLOGY

As has been stated in the research questions, this study will account for the similarities and differences between English and Arabic legal language and contrastive linguistic analysis will be used as a preliminary stage leading to defining the most common lexical and syntactic mismatches. Hence, we will establish the difficult aspects of legal translation.

For the data analysis, the study adopts the Vinay and Darbelnet (1995) contrastive analysis approach. This will help in highlighting the techniques used in translating authentic Arabic–English–Arabic parallel corpus. 'Techniques of adaptation' cited in Alcaraz Varó and Hughes (2002) will be useful tools for the methodology proposed above as they have been applied for translating legal documents. Mona Baker's (1992) levels of equivalence will also add value to the method.

As the preliminary stage of the data analysis, I have presented alignment Arabic–English–Arabic tables which give the ST/TT parallel examples along with the technique of translation. The actual analysis itself, either on the lexical or the syntactic level, will be divided into two stages, the first of which is quantitative where I have provided simple statistical analysis. This helps to highlight the techniques used to translate the specified difficult areas. The second phase provides a qualitative critical analysis in which I will critically comment on the techniques used for translating the specified difficult elements and provide interpretation and/or suggestions for the problematic areas when possible. It is worth mentioning that at the end of the practical chapters that deal with data analysis, some practical exercises will be included. They will benefit postgraduate translation students, translation academics and professionals, hence will help them relate theory to practice, reflect on and discuss what they have learnt in the practical chapters.

1.5 DATA ANALYSIS

Various texts either in English or in Arabic will be used to analyse the features of English and Arabic legal discourse. For the purpose of analysing some difficult areas in Arabic–English–Arabic legal translation (for example religious, culture-specific and system-based terms; archaic terms; passivization and modal auxiliaries), I have chosen a corpus of parallel documents of three legal subtypes, namely: international (for example the UN documents) legislative (constitutions and statutes) and official documents (for example certificates).[2]

1.6 STRUCTURE OF THE BOOK

This book consists of seven chapters which are summarized below:

Chapter 1: Introduction

Chapter 1 presents an outline of the book: rationale, methodology, data analysis and finally a summary of the chapters.

Chapter 2: English and Arabic legal discourse and legal translation

Chapter 2 gives a brief account of English and Arabic legal discourse. I also attempt in this chapter to review the approaches of legal translation in the Western tradition and establish the link between legal translation and the most common approaches followed in general translation theory in the twentieth century. One can argue that there was no specific legal translation theory as such and that it was linked to the theories of the time (for example linguistic theories). There has since been a shift in approaching legal translation with the lawyers and theorists becoming more sceptical about the reliance on equivalence and linguistic-based theories of legal translation and they have attempted to introduce other function-based theories such as the skopos theory and the text type theory. The chapter concludes with listing the subtypes of legal discourse which paves the way for Chapter 3.

Chapter 3: Features of English and Arabic legal discourse

Chapter 3 investigates the semantic, grammatical and textual features of legal discourse in English and Arabic. Such an analysis is based on sample texts of different legal subtypes. These texts include authentic published documents and others obtained from law professionals such as legislations, constitutions, contracts, court reports.

The aim of analyzing the features of English and Arabic legal language is to establish the similarities and differences between them, hence, identify the difficult linguistic areas that a translator is likely to face. At the end of this chapter, some practical exercises will be included to help the readers compare, discuss and analyze the features of legal English and Arabic. This will help them figure out the commonalities and differences between both languages and prepare them for Chapter 4.

Chapter 4: Framework for data analysis

Chapter 4 deals with the methodology for the analysis of data. It falls into three parts, the first of which starts with listing the relevant translation models that will provide tools for data analysis. These models include Vinay and Darbelnet (1995), the techniques of adaptation cited in Alcaraz Varó and Hughes (2002) and levels of equivalence cited in Baker (1992). It also introduces a contrastive study of the areas of difference between English and Arabic (for example modal auxiliaries and passive structures). The second part will explain the two-stage framework (both the quantitative and the qualitative analysis). The third part lists the documents which will be investigated in Chapters 5 and 6.

Chapter 5: Analysis of Arabic–English–Arabic texts: the lexical level

Chapter 5 aims to provide a contrastive analysis of the difficult areas on the lexical level from Arabic into English and vice-versa with reference to three legal subtypes, namely: international, legislative and official. These elements include religious (for example Shariʿah Law terms), culture-specific and system-based terms (for example civil partnership terms) and archaic terms. Some practical exercises are included at the end of the chapter to help the readers practice and apply what they have learnt. It will also teach them to reflect on the above areas of difference.

Chapter 6: Analysis of Arabic–English–Arabic texts: the syntactic level

Chapter 6 is concerned with the analysis of the areas of difference on the syntactic level, namely, modal auxiliaries and passive structures from English into Arabic and vice versa.

These two areas are particularly important to investigate since they are major areas of difference between English and Arabic and they are prominent in legal discourse. Modal auxiliaries, for example, can be problematic in terms of the meaning associated to them and their negation. That is, associating the right modal with the right meaning is not an easy task and if not carefully translated into the TT, it may lead to the wrong interpretations. This is also true for the negation of modal auxiliaries since it is not straightforward due to the difference between both areas in English and Arabic and if not appropriately rendered, meaning of the TT negative message will be distorted. The passive is also an important area as it specifies the overall information structure and defines agency. As it is not straightforward between the two languages, rendition of it is worth considering in this book. Some practical exercises are included at the end of the chapter to help the readers practice and reflect on the above areas.

Chapter 7: Conclusion and recommendations

Chapter 7 discusses the conclusions and findings of the book. It also suggests proposals for further studies.

2 English and Arabic legal discourse and legal translation

2.1 INTRODUCTION

Chapter 2 gives a historical background of legal discourse and legal translation in the English and Arabic traditions. It also presents the categories of legal translation with respect to functions and categories of legal discourse. This chapter also reviews the approaches of legal translation in the Western tradition. It explains the interface between general translation theory and legal translation, hence presents different views on the most common theories which researchers have opted to use for the transfer of legal language.

2.2 WHAT IS LEGAL TRANSLATION?

Since legal translation is bound by each language's culture, it is not merely the transcoding between the SL and the TL or as Cao (2007:10) puts it 'rendering of legal texts from the SL into the TL'. It is rather 'a translation from one legal system into another – from the source legal system into the target legal system' (Šarčević, 1997:13). It involves all the legal sub-text types which are used in various legal settings, whether a court, a national or international organization, a law book, a legal report, a birth certificate, a contract, among many others.

2.3 HISTORICAL BACKGROUND OF LEGAL DISCOURSE AND LEGAL TRANSLATION IN THE ENGLISH TRADITION

English legal discourse goes back to Ancient Greece with philosophers such as Socrates and Plato advocating freedom and democracy. In Byzantium, the first bilingual encyclopaedic dictionaries were introduced for the purposes of replacing Latin with Greek (Mattila, 2006:7).

During the Celtic invasion of the British Isles before the birth of Christ, England witnessed the existence of Celtic lawyers 'perpetuating a customary law in a learned archaic language' (Mellinkoff, 1963:36). When the Anglo-Saxons invaded England in the fifth century AD, contracts and pleadings could be traced to their reign and they 'formed laws in their primitive language that was rigid in both meaning and form' (Gu, 2006:110). That is, laws were affected by 'the alliterative and rhythmical fashions of the day . . . the vein of rhythm runs through the language of the law, sometimes in traditional oral words, sometimes carried over into what is only written' (Mellinkoff, 1963:36–37).

Between 529 and 534, *Corpus Juris Civilis*[3], one of the influential Roman jurisprudence texts, was translated into numerous languages after its initial literal translation into Greek pursuant to emperor Justinian's approval. In this context, Šarčević (1997:24) comments: 'not only do the legal systems of the western world have their roots in Roman Law, but the translation activities under Emperor Justinian also leave their mark on the history of legal translation'.

During the Norman Conquest (1066), French and Latin were the languages of education. The former being the language of writing and the latter being the language predominantly spoken in the courts of Europe; it was normal for it to be used in England too (Beveridge, 2002:57). French became the language of legal proceedings for a period of 300 years (Haigh, 2004). Latin terms and word order were deliberately adopted for making the text appear more sophisticated (ibid.). The linguistic legal effects of French did not ease straightaway and they continued to have an impact for nearly a century before the real transition to using English took place when 'the domination of the law by French and Latin was over and in 1731 a new English for lawyers' law was passed' (Beveridge, 2002:59). Legal English, however, continued to borrow from other languages at the time, French and Latin being two of them, and these borrowed terms continued to be used until today. In this context, Beveridge (2002:57) comments: 'what we know today as legal English did not begin its life as English alone, but rather was predominantly French and Latin'. Bach and Cable (2002:11) mention that 'half of the English vocabulary is derived from Latin, be it directly or indirectly'.

In eleventh century France and Italy, the Justinian *Corpus Juris Civilis*, which was written in Latin, was taught in the universities by 'using monolingual glosses which expressed the whole passage through textual interpretation or commentary and it continued during the period' (Šarčević, 1997:27). A revolt against Latin was led in the thirteenth and fourteenth centuries in Germany, Italy and France.

English as the language of the court proceedings started in 1362 and with the introduction of Magna Carta which 'became the great precedent for putting legislation into writing . . . in theory at least everyone in England should have heard Magna Carta read out' (Clanchy, 1993:264). Magna Carta was so influential that other countries managed to have similar documents of their own such as the United States' Bill of Rights in 1791 (Garre, 1999:15–16). Because the educated elites, who were responsible for writing the law, were well-versed in Latin, it remained the language of the law. Following the introduction of the printing press in 1476 and the acceptance of the London Standard as the standard form of written English, statutes began to be printed in English (Beveridge, 2002:58). Middle English commonly used in the period after the Norman Conquest until 1476 is characterised by the existence of many phrases which continued to exist until now such as *thereby*, *hereinunder*, *herewith*, etc . . . The switch to or the increasing focus on English happened as a result of politics and perhaps because of a greater fusion with English culture.

Awareness of the role of legal translation increased from the nineteenth century onwards up until the advent of the twentieth century. During the first decade of the nineteenth century, Napoleon established his civil code known as the Napoleonic Code (1804) which, though not the first code, has been so successful that it has left its impact on the law of many other countries such as Germany. The second half of the twentieth century witnessed the progress in the translation movement in general and legal translation in particular. Legal translation has long been playing a vital role in communication both nationally and internationally. This role has become even more important due to globalization and the establishing of international bodies (for example the UN). Thus, the need for multilingual legal translation has increased significantly.

In the following section, we will discuss the historical background of legal discourse and legal translation in the Arabic tradition.

2.4 HISTORICAL BACKGROUND OF LEGAL DISCOURSE AND LEGAL TRANSLATION IN THE ARABIC TRADITION

The existence of legal discourse in the Arabic tradition dates back to Babylon with the establishment of the code of Hammurabi. Hence, legal translation can be traced to Babylon[4] (2001 BC) with the establishment of Hammurabi's translation centre which hired employees to work on translation. Legal translation can also be traced to the second century BC. Mattila (2006:7) comments that 'the first legal text translated from one language to another, and which has survived until today, is the peace treaty in two languages between the Egyptians and the Hittites, dating back to 1271 B.C.'.

Before the advent of Islam in the Arabian Peninsula, the law of the tribe was the only acknowledged law. It was run by custom and shaped by loyalty to one's tribe. Esposito (1998:4) argues that:

> The Arabs placed great emphasis on tribal ties, group loyalty or solidarity as the source of power for a clan or tribe. Tribal affiliation and law were the basis not only for identity but also for protection. The threat of family or group vendetta, the law of retaliation was of vital importance in a society lacking a central political authority or law.

The seventh century witnessed the rise of Islam, the Qur'an being its Holy Book and Muslims' reference, which has two main branches: 'the beliefs and the Code of Laws' as explained by Shaltout (1987:87, 119) below:

> The greater number of laws which make up the Islamic code are classified under these two headings: worship and dealings. The latter includes dealings within the Muslim Community, the family, monetary dealings, with non-Muslims both as individuals and nations. Islamic Law has clearly stated the obligations of the Muslims in all areas of life and the penalties to be inflicted for offences and irregularities.[5]

Treaties exist in the Muslim tradition after the Prophet's hijrah; in 628 (6 AH), Prophet Muhammad signed the treaty of Hudaybiyyah between the Medina Muslims and people of Quraish in Mecca. In 637 (15 AH), the Caliph, ʿumar Ibn Al-Khattab (d. 644), signed a treaty with the Patriarch of Jerusalem.

Translation in the Arabic tradition flourished in the Umayyad caliphate (661–750) and reached its peak in the Abbasid era (750–1258) as Steiner (1998:272) argues: 'translation is said to have reached its peak either in the 2nd century AD in Alexandria or in the 8th and 9th century in Baghdad'. In the Umayyad era, under the rule of Abd al-Malik Ibn Marawan (d. 705), Arabic was established as the uniform official language of the Empire, replacing Greek in Damascus, Pahlavi in Iraq, and Coptic in Egypt (Baker and Hanna, 2009:330). The Arabizing movement of that time 'involved a certain amount of translation of official documents' (ibid.).

In the eighth and ninth centuries, the Abbasid era witnessed the golden age of translation, especially during the reign of the caliph al-Mansur (d. 775) who 'commissioned a number of translations and set up a translation chamber' (Baker and Hanna, 2009:331), al-Rashid (d. 809) who 'supported translation activity and enlarged the translation chamber set up by al-Mansur and al-Maʾmun (d. 833) who founded the most celebrated centre of translation in Arab history' (ibid.). The establishment of Bayt al-Hikmah (the House of Wisdom) in the ninth century helped in the progress of the translation activities. Texts from China, Persia, Greece and India were translated from Syriac, Persian, Sanskrit and Greek into Arabic. Hunayn Ibn Ishaq (d. 873), an outstanding figure in the history of the Arabic translation theory in general and in the Abbasid period in particular translated works of Plato, Aristotle, Galen and Hippocrates from Greek into Arabic. Not only were philosophy and logic translated at that time, but also other subjects were widely translated such as 'mathematics, astronomy, medicine, chemistry and politics' (Baker and Hanna, 2009:330). Official translation activities for texts written in Syriac and Sanskrit also took place under the leadership of Hunayn Ibn Ishaq (Delisle and Woodsworth, 1995:112).

The increasing interest in translation in the Abbasid era has made scholars aware of the importance of developing translation methods and their linguistic competence. They had faced a terminological problem as a result of dealing with the 'voluminous works of Persian, Indian, Greek and Roman philosophers and scientists' (Bahumaid, 1994:135). Thus, the need for dictionaries increased and documents were to be collected. Watt maintains that 'one of the difficulties met with by the translators during the 9th century was that there was little original writing in Arabic on topics dealt with in the books they translated' (1972:32). They were very keen on introducing new terms to the Arabic language through one-to-one-word correspondence, or as Elmgrab (2011:493) puts it, *ishtiqaq* (derivation). He (ibid.:495–498) listed other methods of forming new words in Arabic which include: Arabicization (*al-taʿrib*), blending (*al-naht*) and borrowing. Bahumaid (1994:135) and Holes (2004:311) list other ways, though not so different from Elmgrab's list, for coining new terms in that era: (i) derivation / *al-ishtiqaaq*; (ii) compounding / *al-tarkiib*; (iii) analogy / *al-qiyaas*; (iv) metaphor / *al-majaaz*; and (v) Arabicization for proper names and foreign terms.

The techniques followed in the Abbasid era were not different from the techniques adopted by Western translators at that time. Al-Jahiz (d. 869) author of *Kitab al-Haywan* and other outstanding books, views the process of translation as follows:

> لابد للترجمان من أن يكون بيانه في نفس الترجمة في وزن علمه في نفس المعرفة و ينبغي أن يكون أعلم الناس باللغة المنقولة و المنقول إليها حتى يكون فيها سواء و غاية.
>
> (quoted in Salama-Carr, 2006a:124)

> The translator must demonstrate the same lucidity of expression and the same level of knowledge as the author that he translates. He must know the source language very well and the one into which he translates equally well.
>
> (Salama-Carr, 2006a:124)

Arab translators tended to use both source-oriented and target-oriented methods of translation. They aimed to achieve fidelity and naturalness at the same time. For instance, the ground rule was word-for-word translation but sometimes they moved away from this technique to that of omission, simplification, or transposition. They started at word level and moved on to sentence level but they did not go further to text level. These techniques were discussed later by Safadi (d. 1363) who described the two main methods of translation as follows:

> The translator studies each individual Greek word and its meaning, chooses an Arabic word of corresponding meaning and uses it.
>
> The translator considers a whole sentence identical in meaning without concern for correspondence of individual words.
>
> (quoted in Guttas, 1998:142; and Montgomery, 2000:122)

Endress (quoted in Guttas, 1998:146) summarizes the characteristics of translation, 'guide fossils', as he calls them as follows:

- The use of loan-words and transliterated Greek.
- The use of calques.
- The transition from pre-scientific use of Arabic equivalents.
- The formation of abstract nouns and other neologisms.
- Introductory, summarizing, transitional and connecting phrases.

Borrowing from Greek and Persian was one of the useful techniques: 'Greek philosophical and scientific works were translated into the lexicon of medieval classical Arabic' (Holes, 2004:306). Among these borrowed terms from Greek are: *faylasuf* / philosopher; *namus* / law, principle; *qanun* / law and others from Persian are *ustaz* / teacher; *sijill* / register (ibid.).

Techniques of adaptations were also followed in the Arabic tradition. This is perhaps due to the Arabic translators being fully aware of the difference between Greek and Arabic and because they aimed at achieving naturalness. Kunitzch (quoted in Montgomery, 2000:126) summarizes the main techniques of adaptations, which were apparent in the language of the Arab translators as follows:

- phonetic transcription
- transcription with added prefixes
- replacement by common Arabic
- substitution by Arabic words that are related to but do not exactly parallel Greek
- substitution to older Arabic names
- simplifications for the sake of memory
- descriptive phrases that explain a transcribed name according to the Greek myth.

Not enough literature is available about the translation activities in the period from the thirteenth century up until the sixteenth century after the disintegration of the Islamic Empire which resulted in 'the establishment of rival caliphates in Egypt and Spain' and 'a series of barbaric onslaughts by the Mongols eventually culminated in the destruction of Baghdad and the slaughter of the caliph and his officials by Hulagu in 1258' (Baker and Hanna, 2009:334).

The Ottomans ruled the Islamic Empire between the sixteenth and the twentieth centuries. Arabic continues to be the language of learning and Islamic jurisdiction. When Napoleon invaded Egypt in 1798, he brought his own foreign interpreters 'for reading out his decrees' and 'interpreting lawsuits and read out letters and statements' (ibid.). Thus, the majority of translation activities during Napoleon's three year invasion were of 'official documents and legal decrees' (ibid.). The nineteenth century witnessed a new era in translation supported by the reformer ruler Mohamed Ali and led by the school of Alsun (tongues) that Rifa'ah

Al-Tahtawi established. Translation from European languages (for example French) to Arabic and Turkish of technical, scientific, literary texts were among the translation activities at the time as well as geography, astronomy and mathematics. Students whom Mohamed Ali sent in missions to France later acted as 'interpreters for local government and foreign diplomats in the area' (Baker and Hanna, 2009:335).

Legal discourse continued to exist all over the world and it became more effective in the twentieth century with the establishment of the League of Nations in 1919 and the United Nations in 1945, and Arabic becoming one of the UN six official and working languages in 1973. Globalization has also brought all the peoples of the world together and the need for legal translation became even more pertinent.[6]

2.5 CATEGORIES OF LEGAL TRANSLATION

Legal translation can be classified according to the functions of legal discourse and in relation to the legal discourse subtypes.

2.5.1 Legal translation with respect to functions of legal discourse

Like any other special purpose texts, legal texts serve a certain function. According to Reiss (2000), on text typology,[7] legal texts serve an informative function where plain facts and information are represented (Šarčević, 1997:7). According to Halliday's functionalism, special purpose texts have a representational function. To Newmark (1982), legal texts have both directive and imperative function and for him (1988), they can have an expressive function. To Sager (1993), legal texts are informative for the general reader and directive for the specific group of people. Cao (2007:10–11) gives the following classification for purposes for legal translation:

1. Legal translation for the normative purpose.
2. Legal translation for the informative purpose.
3. Legal translation for legal or judicial purpose.

The first type includes multilingual legal instruments such as that of the UN and EU documents. They are parallel texts, authentic, legally equivalent and have the same communicative function, though the languages are different. According to Cao (2007:11) this category includes some other private text types such as contracts and other bilingual authentic documents. For instance, an Arabic birth certificate translated into English is considered to be as legally authentic as an Arabic version.

The second type refers to those texts that have descriptive or contrastive functions such as the translation of statutes, court decisions, scholarly works and other types of legal documents intended for giving information to the target readers. The ST will therefore be the only authentic legal source and the others are solely used for reference purposes. In this case, both the ST and the TT will have a different communicative function.

The third type of legal translation under Cao's classification is both informative and descriptive. It involves many legal subtypes such as court proceedings, contracts and agreements, business or personal correspondence, records, certificates, witness statements and expert reports.

According to this classification, the book will be concerned with the analysis of the international (for example the UN documents), legislative texts (for example constitutions) and official documents (for example certificates). For analysis of the legal features in Chapter 3, samples from the different legal categories mentioned above will be dealt with.

2.5.2 Legal translation with respect to categories of legal discourse

Researchers differ in categorizing English legal language. For Trosborg (1995a, 1995b), it is considered one of the fields of specialized language, or language for specific purposes, to be more precise. That is, it is listed among the medical language, scientific language, technical language, etc. English legal language is also referred to as a sublanguage (Kittredge and Lehrberger 1982; O'Barr 1982), a genre (Bhatia 1993), or a register (Kurzon 1989, 1997; Danet 1985). These different labels are given to legal English with consideration of the specific nature of legal language, be it lexical, syntactic, stylistic, or pragmatic. Kurzon (1989:284 and 1997:120) distinguishes between 'language of the law' and 'legal language'. For him, the former includes 'the language or the style used in documents that lay down the law' whereas the latter refers to 'the language that is used when people talk about the law, for example judges' opinions and legal textbooks'. Kurzon (ibid.:121) adds that 'legal language is in fact a metalanguage used to talk about the law in a broad sense and the language of the law is literally just the language in which the law is written'. Consider the following classification:

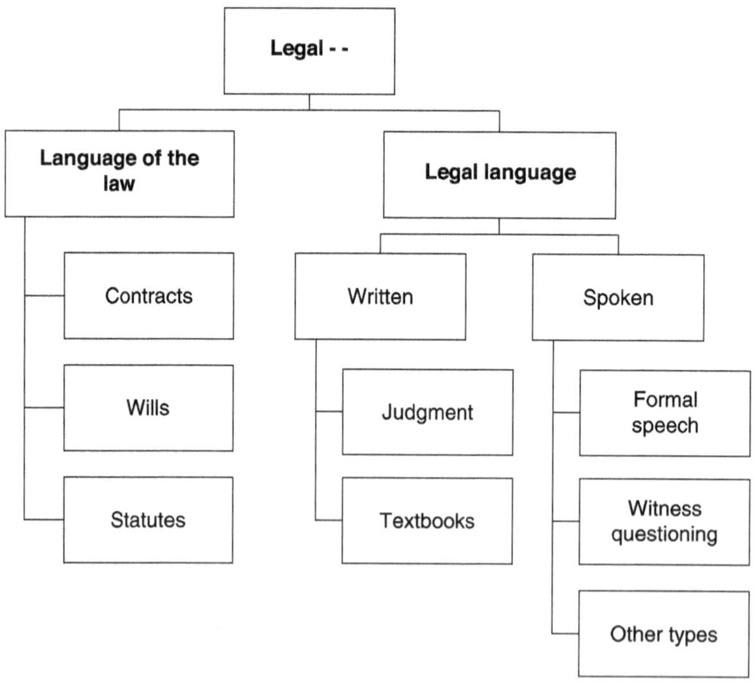

Figure 2.1 Kurzon's classification of legal discourse.

Compared to Kurzon's view, Trosborg (1997:20) views legal language as 'a superordinate', an umbrella that covers all uses in the legal context. For her, the language of the law is one of five sub-elements of legal language as follows:

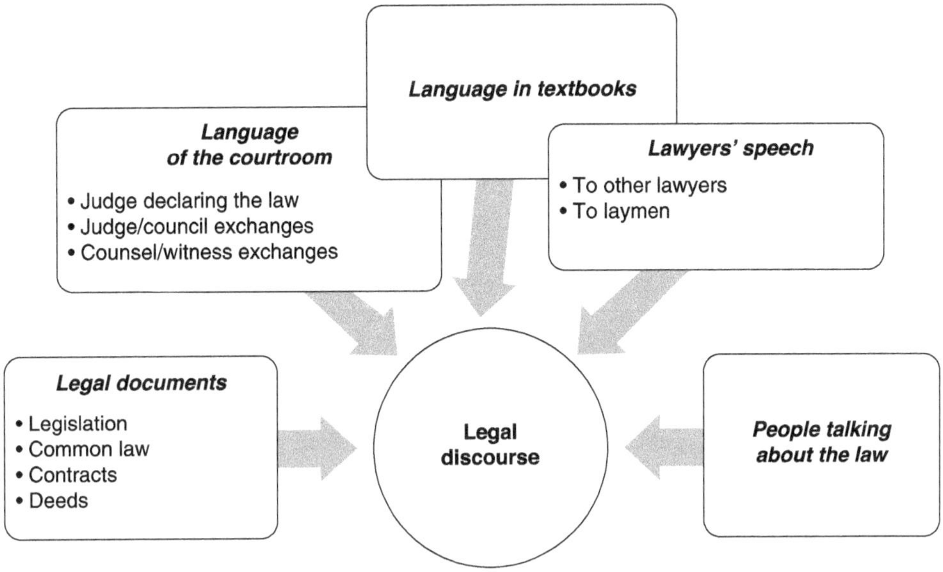

Figure 2.2 Trosborg's classification of legal discourse.

Cao (2007:9–10) gives another classification of legal texts as follows:

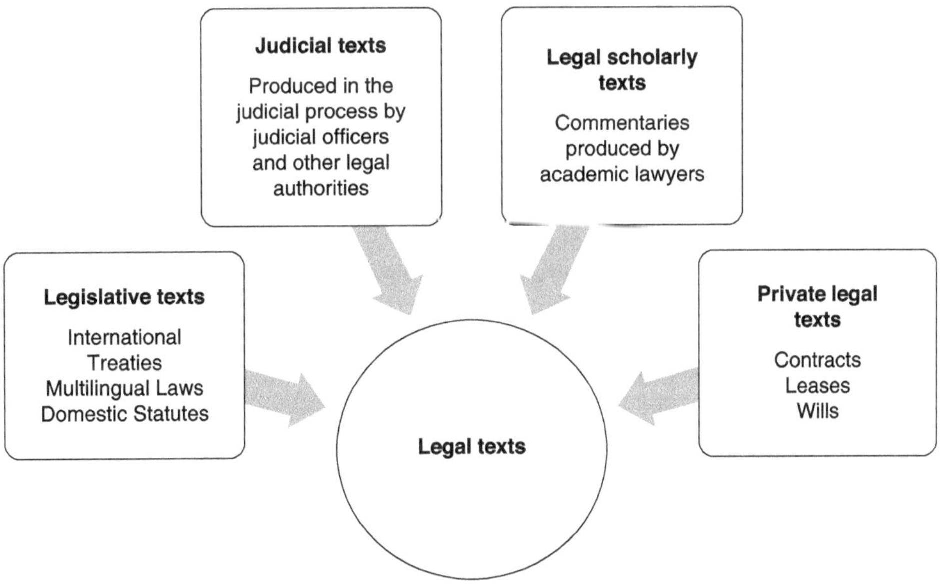

Figure 2.3 Cao's classification of legal texts.

Bouquet gives another classification of legal texts as primarily prescriptive, primarily descriptive but also prescriptive and purely descriptive (quoted in Šarčević, 1997:11). The first type includes laws, regulations, codes, contracts, treaties, conventions. This type of texts describes a course of action that an individual ought to conform to. The second type of legal texts includes judicial decisions and instruments such as actions, pleadings, briefs, appeals, requests, petitions, etc. The third group of legal texts includes legal opinions, law textbooks and articles.

Mayoral Asensio suggests dividing text types according to a continuum of 'extremely specialized → minimally specialized'. He argues that 'any attempt to draw the line between general and specialized is doomed to failure' and that 'there is not a clear frontier separating general and specialized language, communication or translation, that every text and every act of communication include, in different proportions, elements which can be characterized as general and elements which can be characterized as specialized (2007:49–50).

Mayoral Asensio (2003) classifies the private legal texts under the category of 'official documents'. He (ibid.:1) argues that 'official translation is not a well-defined activity overlaps with fields such as legal translation and court translating.' Mayoral Asensio (2007:49–53) comments on the classification of specialized translation as follows:

> Fields of knowledge are not strictly isolated from each other, science, technology, economy, law; civil law, property law, marriage law. And their categorization varies according to time and place. Even when translation is frequently divided into scientific, technical, economic and legal types, fuzzy boundaries among them are evident; furthermore, categories such as legal translation prove ill-defined.

It is clear from the previous discussion of legal discourse that classification of legal types varies and that none of the scholars has managed to provide a conclusive classification. The discussion also reveals that the boundaries between legal subcategories are fuzzy. For instance, UN documents are classified under diplomatic documents and legislative documents.

Schäffner's (1997) discussion of the *Strategies of Translating Political Texts* is a good example of such fuzziness of text types. She states that 'a political text itself, however, is a vague term. It is an umbrella term covering a variety of text types. Political discourse includes both inner state and inter-state discourse[8] and it may take various forms. Examples can be found in the form of bilateral or multilateral treaties, speeches . . .' (1997:120). She later referred to bilateral and multilateral treaties as diplomatic text types: 'quite a lot of translation is being done in the diplomatic sphere. For example, bilateral and multilateral treaties are instances of legal texts agreed and translated' (1997:121).

Legal translation types are dependent on legal discourse types. That is, certain generalizations may be made regarding the correlation between the distribution of certain syntactic patterns and a certain text type. To explain this argument, examples from the English legal arena are given. First, all English statutes employ the same performative verb: 'be it enacted'. Also, in marriage ceremonies, this declarative act is always used: 'I hereby pronounce you man and wife'. Second, English statutes have one common structure: the title, the date, the preamble, the enacting formula, the main body of parts, articles and sections and finally schedules. Third, statutes employ a declarative mode of address. Fourth, the modal auxiliary 'shall' is a very distinctive feature of English legislations as a means of expressing obligation rather than referring to the future. Fifth, the style of address in the court is highly formal so that the judge is addressed as 'your lordship' and 'your honour'.

2.6 APPROACHES TO LEGAL TRANSLATION: A BRIEF REVIEW OF TRANSLATION THEORY

> There is no one generally accepted theory of translation in the technical sense of a coherent set of general propositions . . . but there are several theories in the broad sense of a set of principles that are helpful in understanding the nature of translating or establishing criteria for evaluating a particular translated text.
>
> (Nida, 2001:108)

Legal translation comes at the periphery between translation theory and language theory. Researchers in this field often combine language theory and general translation theories in their researches. Legal documents were considered as sacred and authoritative as the Bible or the Qur'an (Tiersma, 1999:96). The goal behind this idea is attributed to the 'mysteriousness, i.e. legal texts conveyed an assumed truth not to be comprehended by the human mind but accepted on faith alone' (Šarčević, 1997:25). The stages of development of legal translation since the Roman Empire till recent time, according to Šarčević (1997:24) are given in the following continuum:

strict literal → literal → moderately literal → near idiomatic → idiomatic → co-drafting

The above continuum also represents the stages of development of general translation theory prior to or during the twentieth century.[9] As legal discourse has been considered as sacred as the Bible, translation of the law must have been affected by the approaches used for translating it. In this context, Šarčević (1997:23) comments on the link between legal translation (of authoritative texts) and Bible translation (of religious texts) as follows:

> Since both legal and religious are normative, it is not surprising that the early history of legal translation is most closely related to that of Bible translation, i.e. until the Middle Ages when the first moderately literal translations of the Bible were made into vernacular languages . . . because of the authoritative status of legal texts, legal translation remained under the grip of tradition much longer than other areas of translation.

She adds:

> Like the word of God in the Scriptures, the letter of law also demanded strict literal translation to protect it from heterodoxy. Thus, it was believed that the 'word power' of such texts could be retained only by word-for-word translation.
>
> (ibid.:25)

This shows that 'literal translation', giving the exact words of the ST in the TT, has been followed in legal translation. One of the clear examples is the translation of the *Corpus Juris Civilis* literally[10] into Greek 'to preserve the letter of the law' (Šarčević, 1997:24).

Equivalence,[11] pioneered by the American Bible translator Eugene Nida, has always been the focus of the semantic-based theory. Nida distinguishes between formal and dynamic equivalence. By the former is meant keeping the form and the content of the ST through 'gloss translation'.[12] Nida (1993:116) maintains that 'it is essential that formal equivalence is stated primarily in terms of a comparison of the way in which the original receptors understood and appreciate the text and the way in which receptors of the translated text understand and appreciate the translated text. Weisflog (1987:194) supports Nida's formal correspondence approach for translating quasi legislation or recommendations, such as the UN, UNCTAD, business contracts, license agreements, general conditions of supply and delivery (conditions of sale), among others.

Dynamic equivalence, in this context, refers to the 'principle of equivalent effect' (Nida, 1964:159). That is, the TL reader gets the same natural effect that the ST reader gets from reading the ST. This recalls Schleiermacher's (2004) 'target-oriented' approach or Venuti's 'domestication' (1995), in which the foreign features of the ST are accommodated in the TT, hence the text appears natural in the target culture. Munday (2001:146) maintains that 'domestication entails translating in a transparent, fluent, invisible style in order to minimize the foreignness of the TT'. In legal translation, Tomášek (1991:113) supports similar views. He divides the translation process into 'intrasemiotic' and 'intersemiotic'. The former refers to transferring from the first semantic level (the legal language) to the second semantic level (the legal metalanguage).[13] By the latter is meant transferring from the SL and its culture to the TL and its culture. That is, intrasemiotic translation occurs within the same sign system (within one language), whereas intersemiotic translation happens from one sign system to another (between two different languages).

In England, Newmark (1981) sees equivalence as a process of approximation between the ST and the TT and there is no absolute equivalence between languages due to their incongruity. Newmark does not question whether two texts are equivalent or not but he is more interested in the 'type and degree of translation equivalence they reveal' (1981:47). He classifies translation into two main types: semantic and communicative; the former 'attempts to render as closely as the semantic and syntactic structures of the second language allow, the exact contextual meaning in the original' (ibid.:39), whereas the latter 'attempts to produce on its readers an effect as close as possible to that obtained by the readers of the original' (ibid.).

Newmark's writings about the translation of non-literary informative translation were guided by hands-on experience and practicality. In (1982:376), he comments on the translation of authoritative texts, legal texts being one of them: 'the language of authoritative statements is likely to be literal and denotative, except where it is enforced by emotive appeal' as in the case of translating the *Preamble of the Iraqi Constitution*[14] into English. On adaptation in translation, he argues:

> I assume that the SL text is efficiently written and is specifically to the SL reader. The translator will not have to adapt the text for the TL readers; the text will more or less remain within the SL culture unless it is an international text relating to an international organization.
>
> (1982:376)

Equivalence remains a controversial issue in the Western tradition. In Germany, Werner Koller's 'Equivalence in Translation Theory' in Andrew Chesterman (1989) discussed correspondence and equivalence; the former applies to contrastive linguistics whereas the latter is more useful for translation studies. Koller supports 'foreignization':[15] keeping the foreign features of the ST in the TT in legal translation by insisting that 'full adaptation is not an accepted method of translation in legal texts as it results in semantic distortion' (quoted in Rek-Harrop, 2008:9). The issue of equivalence in legal translation remains so controversial that legal translators have failed to identify which type of equivalence to apply, although there were as many as 56 types of equivalence, but legal equivalence was not one of them (Snell-Hornby, 1988:55).

Equivalence then should not be considered a one-to-one correspondence, rather, it should be looked at from a number of variables, deviating from the rigid constraints of linguistic theories[16] to more sociocultural elements. This is when the advocates of pragmatics (for example House 1997, Halliday 1985, Hatim and Mason 1997) have their say. Pym (2010:1) comments on the Western translation theory reaction to 'equivalence' as follows:

> Newer paradigms, however, then emphasized various aspects or problems that the theories of equivalence somehow overlooked: namely, the translation skopos or purpose (challenging the dominant role of the source text), historical and cultural relativism (challenging any absolute equivalence equations), localization (deceptively blurring the divisions between translation and adaptation) and cultural translation (seeing translation in terms of processes rather than an affair of texts).

Supporters of this trend raise some issues with regard to translation: (i) to whom is the target text addressed? (ii) why is the target text being translated? (iii) what are the conventional rules in the target culture for producing texts for that particular purpose? (iv) who wrote the source text? (v) when and where was the source text written? (Šarčević, 1997:18).

House's model (1997) derives from Halliday's register analysis[17]. It focuses on comparing the ST and the TT to highlight the mismatches between them. The comparison is based on three main pillars: lexis, syntax and the textual aspect, or to put it in House's words, 'theme-dynamics, clausal linkage and iconic linkage' (1997:66). Theme-dynamics refer to the text's thematic structure: cohesion; clausal linkage may be additive, or adversative; and iconic linkage forming the parallelisms of structure (ibid.:67). She distinguishes between overt and covert translation: the former is ST-directed and the latter is TT-directed. Chesterman and Wagner (2002:50) argue that 'overt translation preserves the stylistic indicators of the ST whereas covert translation is too fluent, natural to sound not as translation'.

Functional theories[18] to translation are neglected in legal translation. That is, skopos-oriented theory initiated by Vermeer (2000) focuses on the purpose of the text which, in Vermeer's view, is more important than the semantic or stylistic aspects of the text. It determines the relationship between the ST and the TT and hence what the translation should look like (Chesterman and Wagner, 2002:40). Šarčević (1997:18) argues: 'Vermeer translation theory departs from tradition by recognizing translations in which the function of the target text differs from that of the source text . . .' For Šarčević (ibid.:236), functional equivalence is advised in case of the absence of an exact equivalent. Garzone (2000:1) asked whether they can be applied in legal translation or not: 'this question is of extreme importance: a positive answer would provide a good starting point for the construction of an all-embracing theoretical model applicable to all text-types and genres in legal translation'.

Skopos theory, however, was criticized by many theorists, such as Chesterman and Wagner (2002:40) who argue that this theory is complex and questioned its applicability. Snell-Hornby (1988:47) criticizes skopos theory on the basis that it only applies to non-literary texts, although Vermeer claims it is applicable to all translations (quoted in Šarčević, 1997:18). Munday (2001:81) criticizes it for ignoring the microlinguistic[19] features in the TT and dethroning the ST. Translators of specialized texts are still sceptical about its applicability in the language for specific purposes (LSP) translation. The reason behind this, according to Šarčević (1997:18–19), is that 'the function of the special purpose translations is usually the same as that of the source text'. She adds: 'by suggesting that the translation strategy of a legal translation can be determined solely on the basis of function, Vermeer disregards the fact that legal texts are subject to special rules governing in the mechanism of the law' (ibid.:19). Even if we agree that functional equivalence is the 'ideal method of translation' according to Weston (cf. Šarčević, 1997:236), this is only just a first step in the process of translation.

From a text linguistic perspective,[20] non-literary texts, legal texts being one of them, belong to a distinctive text type known as hybrid texts. They 'allow the introduction into a target culture of hitherto unknown and/or socially unacceptable concepts through a medium which, by its non-conformity to social/stylistic conventions and norms, proclaims the otherness of its origin' (Schaffner and Adab, 2000:325).

The interface between translation and culture is proposed by Bassnett and Lefevere (1990) who have focused on what has been referred to previously by Snell-Hornby (1988) as 'the cultural turn'. The core of Bassnett and Lefevere's ideas is that translation is governed by the dominant ideology of that time and it is an integral part of the sociocultural framework of that society. Lefevere (1992:2) believes that 'there are concrete factors that govern the reception, acceptance or rejection of literary texts, issues such as power, ideology, institutions and manipulation'.

Lefevere sees translation as a process of re-writing within which the translation function is controlled by the following factors:

Professionals within the literary system (teachers, translators and critics).
Patronage outside the literary system (economy and ideology).
The dominant poetics (literary genres and the relationship between literature and the social system).

The above factors prove useful to the translation of literary texts only and do not add much to what has been proposed by functional theories or pragmatic and discourse analysis theories. Yet, the ideological and the social aspects are also important in the translation of other discourse types.

Although advocates of the 'cultural turn' were more interested in studying the literary genre, culture and ideology are important factors in studying other discourse types, legal being one of them. Translating legal texts from English into Arabic or vice-versa is not a mere process of rendering the terminology and grammar of the ST into equivalents in the TT. A translator of such texts is transferring from one legal system that which is embedded in the SL culture into a totally different TL legal system and TL culture. That is, translation of Arabic multi-lateral treaties into English is at best a difficult task because the Arabic texts will include elements that are alien to the English culture.

To clarify the above argument there are expressions in the Arabic treaties that are purely cultural such as the Basmala (بسم الله الرحمن الرحيم – In the name of God), the formal addresses (for example حضرة صاحب الجلالة – His Majesty), the concluding religious remarks (for example و الله أكبر – God is the greatest) and reference to the Qur'an and Sunnah (the standard practice of Muhammad). Even if these expressions are translated into English, they may be meaningless to the target reader. That is why international treaties and other international documents of the UN are more secular and avoid any of the above expressions.

From this long discussion about the approaches to and theories of translating legal documents, it is worth pointing out, incidentally, that translation approaches may vary according to the legal subtypes and their functions or 'from one institution to another' (Shiyab, 2006:159). Since there is no one particular theory of legal translation, a legal translator will require hybrid tools that will enable him or her to figure out the type of the legal document, its function, its structure and its pragmatic effect. All these aspects along with the special nature of legal discourse, such lexical incongruities, syntactic complexities, textual dissimilarities and system and cultural asymmetries, make the task of the legal translator unusually challenging.

3 Features of English and Arabic legal discourse

3.1 INTRODUCTION

This chapter investigates the semantic, grammatical and textual features of legal discourse in English and Arabic. Such an analysis is based on sample texts of different legal subtypes which include authentic published documents and others obtained from law professionals such as legislations, constitutions, contracts and court reports. Discussion of the features of English and Arabic legal discourse provides examples from these different legal subtypes.

The aim of analysing the features of English and Arabic legal language is to establish the similarities and differences between both of them, hence, identify the problematic linguistic areas that a translator is likely to face. Reference will be made to media Arabic when needed and we will be occasionally referring to the University of Leeds online Arabic corpora.[21]

3.2 FEATURES OF ENGLISH LEGAL DISCOURSE

English legal discourse has been the subject of discussion of many scholars such as Mellinkoff (1963), Danet (1976, 1980), Morris (1995), Šarčević (1997), Conley and O'Barr (1998), Garre (1999), Haigh (2004) and Cao (2007), among others. Below is an account of the lexical, syntactic and textual features of English legal discourse.

3.2.1 Lexical features

Legal English, as a specialized language, has its own distinctive lexical features, its own 'legalese', just like media with its own 'journalese'. Legal vocabulary is 'a vocabulary of possibilities purportedly comprising a comprehensive system of meanings that are internal or latent within the lexicon itself' (Goodrich, 1987:177). Hiltunen (1990:84) comments on the issue of vocabulary by stating that adjectives in legal English 'are fairly scarce (because they are often imprecise and vague), nouns tend to be abstract rather than concrete (because they frequently do not refer to physical objects) and verbs are selected from a fairly small number of lexical sets'.

Alcaraz Varó and Hughes (2002:16–18) classify legal vocabulary into three subtypes: (i) purely technical terms or 'terms of art' (Mellinkoff, 1963:16) which are system specific such as 'barrister', 'court' and 'case', etc.; (ii) semi-technical, mixed terms or 'legal homonyms' as Tiersma (1999:111) calls them such as 'assessment', 'enclose', 'compensation', 'clarification', 'evidence', 'advise', 'settlement', 'instruct'; (iii) everyday vocabulary which exist in legal texts they but did not lose their meaning by occurring in the legal context such as 'record', 'access', 'repair', 'examine', 'injury', 'confirmation', 'appointment' and 'party' (A Lawyer's Letter to a Client).

3.2.1.1 Archaic terms

Legal English is characterized by its old or 'antiquated vocabulary' (Alcaraz Varó and Hughes, 2002:5). These old terms trace back to Old and Middle English.[22] Common examples of these terms are 'hereby', 'thereby', 'aforesaid', 'said', 'thereby' and 'hereof'. These adverbs often refer to the text or document in which they appear:

> I . . . <u>hereby</u> confirm that the report of . . . is true and accurate account of the injuries . . .
> (agreement confirmation)

> This contract shall commence . . . in accordance with the provisions <u>hereunder</u>.
> (partnership contract)

Old expressions do not refer to a precise meaning, i.e. a sentence including 'hereby' (I hereby certify . . .) is not more precise than a sentence without it (I certify . . .). It is not stated whether it refers to the whole document or a part of it. Meredith (1979:64) suggests the replacement of a sentence containing 'hereby' by a new sentence. He gives the following example:

> The lessor <u>hereby</u> directs that the lessee is fully authorized to . . .
>
> Meaning: the lessee may . . .

Meredith has just given a paraphrasing of the statement by using a deontic modal of possibility 'may' which implies a mood of uncertainty (Palmer, 1990). Although these old terms constitute an integral part of the language of the law, they are not as commonly used as before and they are more common in one legal text type than another. For instance, they are rare in the modern language of legislation and in international law documents such as those of the UN. Yet, they are used in private documents such as contracts, agreements and certificates. In fact, they are considered the 'daily bread' of the lawyers (Mellinkoff, 1963:13). Archaic morphological forms which are not cited in our corpus are another feature of legal English such as 'this policy witnesseth that . . .'; 'further affiant sayeth not'; and 'hear ye' (Tiersma, 1999:87).

3.2.1.2 Latin and French terms

The English law was affected by the Roman Church in the Middle Ages whose dominant language was Latin. Hence, it was the language of written texts and intellectual communication throughout Europe. An example is 'Minor', a Latin term used in English law which refers to a party in a case (Tiersma, 1999:88). Other examples include 'bona fide' (Partnership Contract, article 20), which is used in a UK legal context to mean 'in good faith'[23]; 'inter alia' (Commission on the Status of Women, Introduction, article 3) which means 'among other things' and 'ipso facto' (ChUN, article 93:1) which means 'by that very fact, as an inevitable result'.

Many legal English terms which are common today are borrowed from French. Examples of these terms include: 'purchase', 'court', 'evidence', 'jury', 'judge' and 'verdict', 'attorney general', 'tort' and 'voir dire' (Mellinkoff, 1963:58; Beveridge, 2002:59). A few French terms: 'court', 'evidence' and 'property' are cited in the Tenancy Agreement.

3.2.1.3 Formal terms

The formality of legal English stems from the use of Latin terms that are more formal than Germanic-root words (Alcaraz Varó, 2009:185). Formality is also reflected in the special nature of legal English expressed by fixed linguistic aspects: modals (for example use of shall) and enactment formulas; certain utterances in marriage ceremonies; formal expressions used in different contexts such as 'your honour', 'your majesty' (in courts), 'royal' (in a Decree by the Queen), 'master' (of a Minor in a Report to the Court).

Oaths and swearing include highly formal expressions. For instance, a witness in a court utters this statement: 'I do solemnly swear to tell the truth, the whole truth and nothing but the truth'.

3.2.1.4 Religious, culture-specific and system-based lexis

According to Matulewska (2007:130–1), English legal discourse is said to have religious words: (i) acts of God, (ii) . . . in the name of our Lord . . . , (iii) in the year of our Lord one thousand nine hundred and eighty-four. Nevertheless, such elements are not cited in the corpus of English documents investigated. English legal language has many words that are dependent on the culture and legal system (for example boilerplate and backbenchers). Some more examples of these terms are given below:

> 'Returning officer' and 'Acting returning officer'
>
> (formula for announcing the election results, UK)[24]
>
> 'Civil partnership', 'same-sex couples', 'same-sex marriage'
>
> (Civil Partnership Act 2004, UK; UN: CEDAW/C/UK/6)[25]
>
> 'Privy Council'
>
> (UN: E/C.12/GBR/5)[26]

3.2.1.5 Other lexical features

Certain words such as 'any' recur in legal documents 'any child or children', 'any living children', 'any deceased children', 'any grandchildren', 'any interest and penalties', 'any debt or charge' (Last Will and Testament).

The above discussion of lexical features shows that legal language is complex and it has been criticized for that from the sixteenth century up to recent time (Triebel, 2009). A tendency to use plain language has already begun and modern legislation has been rewritten in a way that appeals to the layman. For the purpose of clarity, many Common Law words and structures have been replaced by familiar words. Some of these words are given by Triebel (2009:153, 159–161) as illustrated in the following table:

Table 3.1 Examples from the Plain Legal English Campaign

Common Law Words	*Plain Language Words*
save	except
avoid	cancel
joint and several	together and separately
instrument	legal document
provided that	if, except, however, in any event

of course	as a matter of right
with reference to	about or concerning
prior to	before

3.2.2 Syntactic features

The syntax of legal English is characterized by complex structures, multiple subordination, with main verbs of the sentence coming late in the sentence, as well as other distinctive features that will be discussed below:

3.2.2.1 Nominalization

A nominalization is 'a noun phrase that has a systematic correspondence with a clausal prediction which includes a head noun morphologically related to a corresponding verb' (Quirk et al., 1985:1288). Examples of these nominalized forms are 'assessment', 'inspection' and 'movement' which are common in the syntax of legal English. Nominalization is reduced in the sense that the meaning one gets in a sentence is missing a tense, hence no indication of the timing of the process, modality, or often an agent and/or a patient. It is 'a radical syntactic transformation of a clause, which has extensive structural consequences and offers substantial ideological opportunities' (Fowler, 1991:80). Below are examples of nominalization:

> No one shall be subjected to torture or to cruel, inhuman or degrading <u>treatment</u> or <u>punishment</u>.
>
> (UDHR, article 5)
>
> The Contractor shall implement and maintain appropriate technical and organizational measures so as to prevent the <u>destruction</u>, <u>damage</u>, <u>loss</u> or <u>alteration</u> of the Data . . .
>
> (Partnership Contract, article 45)

Although nominalization obscures the agent (subject) and the patient (object), it is useful in cases where laws are 'to be stated as broadly as possible' (Tiersma, 1999:78).

3.2.2.2 Passivization

Passive transformation includes a shift of positions of the left-hand and right-hand noun phrases (Fowler, 1991:77). As a result, the patient (object) occupies the agent (subject) position. Passivization is chosen for some reasons: (i) to obscure the agent, (ii) to focus on a part that the author sees as more prominent and (iii) to foreground a fact by leaving it unspecified. Both nominalization and passivization are attributes that 'often obscure the identity of the actor; whether done intentionally or not, it can only reduce precision' (Tiersma, 1999:75). For example, the first person is avoided in an order, so 'it is ordered . . . rather than I order'. The following are examples of the passive cited in the legal texts analyzed:

> 'will be based', 'can be accepted', 'has been approved', 'the court will need to be satisfied'
>
> (A lawyer's letter to a client)

Although English is said to make abundant use of the passive verb, especially in scientific texts, according to Rosenhouse (1988:92), we can also argue it is not less common in English legal discourse. However, we can claim that it is more common in one legal subtype than the other. For instance, it is less common in contracts than in statutes as contracts require clear identification of the agent/patient whereas statutes can be drafted as broadly as possible.

3.2.2.3 Wh-deletion

Wh-forms deletion is one of the distinguishing features of English legal discourse, although it is not as common as other features. By wh-deletion is meant dropping the word initiated by 'wh' such as 'which', 'what' in a clause and the past participle of the verb is given. This notion is illustrated by Danet's example: 'agreement . . . herein (which is) contained or implied' (1985:280). It is not explained why wh-deletion occurs in English legal discourse; it can be considered a means of stylistic variation. These grammatical forms are repeated in contracts such as, 'premises made available', 'notices given', 'risks assumed', 'obligations assumed', 'the times required' and 'assistance required' (Partnership Contract).

3.2.2.4 Conditionals, prepositional phrases and restrictive connectors

Complex conditionals and hypothetical formulations which are presented as parenthetical clauses are commonly used in legal English. Examples of the syntactic indicators of condition and hypothesis are: 'if', 'where', 'whenever', 'provided that', 'assuming that', 'so long as', 'should', and 'whereas'. 'Whereas' is a Middle English word which is vague in the language of the law (Mellinkoff, 1963:321–2). It is commonly used in the opening paragraphs of preambles and it sometimes means 'the fact is' or 'in spite of'. Meredith (1979:64) believes that, 'it is no longer acceptable and should be replaced by 'since' or 'as'. The following instances are quoted from the corpus of documents:

> The ministry can put off the employee's annual vacation provided that the procrastination is not more than 5 months of the employee's new contract.
>
> (Employment Contract: article 1)

> The Council's agreement to its grant of the Lease(s) is subject to and in all respects conditional on the Contractors agreement pursuant to Section 38(4) of the Landlord and Tenant Act 1954.
>
> (Partnership Contract: article 25)

Prepositional phrases are common in legal English such as, 'pursuant to' (Marriage Certificate), 'without prejudice' (Report to the Court), 'in accordance with' and 'prior to', 'in respect of', 'subsequent to' (Partnership Contract).

Similarly, legal English utilizes restrictive connectors like 'notwithstanding', 'under', 'whereas' and unique determiners such as 'said' as in 'aforesaid', 'such' as in 'a penalty as such' and 'subject to' as in 'subject to clause 7 overleaf, to keep the drains, gutters and pipes of the property clear . . .' (Tenancy Agreement: article 2).

3.2.2.5 Complex sentences

English legal language is known for its long and complex sentences. An English legal sentence is twice as long as the scientific English sentence (Danet, 1985:281). The longer the sentences, the more complex they are, the higher the number of subordinating clauses and phrases. Here is an example of a long complex sentence:

> The Contractor shall implement and maintain appropriate technical and organizational measures so as to prevent the destruction, damage, loss or alteration . . . and the Contractor shall provide the Council with such information as it may require to satisfy itself that the Contractor is complying with such obligations . . . .
>
> (Partnership Contract, article 45)

The underlined verbs in the above excerpt show the approximate number of clauses included in the sentence whether (i) independent, for example 'The Contractor shall implement and maintain appropriate technical and organizational measures', (ii) dependent, for example 'that the Contractor is complying with such obligations', (iii) or infinitival, for example 'to prevent the destruction'. There is also a high frequency of nominalized forms such as: 'destruction, damage, loss . . .' and the long lexical chains: '. . . to prevent the destruction, damage, loss or alteration'. This variety of clauses results in a compound complex sentence which consists of a mixture of coordinating conjunctions such as 'and', 'as', 'so as to' and subordinating conjunctions such as the relative pronouns 'that' and 'which'. It should be noted that this sentence, though long as it appears, compared to modern English sentences of other text types, is shorter than old legal sentences.

3.2.2.6 Performative verbs and modals

Language used in the law performs certain acts, mainly, declaring a right, making a prohibition, or giving permission. Maley (1994:21) argues that 'performativity and modality are the linguistic means which express the institutional ideology of the role relationships involved in legislative rule-making'. Austin (1962) classifies performatives as explicit and implicit. Explicit speech acts are expressed through a speech act verb (for example certify, declare, confirm, enact) as in the frozen formula used in: 'be it enacted that by the king's most Excellent Majesty . . .' The following are some clarifying examples:

> I . . . hereby authorize the following marriage certificate
>
> (Marriage Certificate)

> I confirm that insofar as the facts in my report are within my own knowledge I have made clear which they are and I believe them to be true . . .
>
> (Report to the Court)

> We the people of the United States, in order to form a more perfect union, establish justice, . . . , provide for the common defense, . . . do ordain and establish this Constitution for the United States of America.
>
> (Preamble of the American Constitiution)

The first example above contains a combination of the performative verb 'authorize' and the archaic term 'hereby' in which case the latter guarantees the legal act that the verb 'authorize' assumes. In this context, Tiersma (1999:105) notes that 'only where it is unclear that a verb is a performative does it make sense to add hereby'.

Implicit speech acts are expressed via modal auxiliaries (for example may, shall). For Kurzon (1986:16), speech acts occur with 'may' or 'shall' or their negative forms. In this case the whole sentence has an illocutionary force of permission (may), ordering (shall), or prohibition (shall not). Modal auxiliaries are elaborated on below:

Modal auxiliaries

The concept of modality is one of the aspects investigated in the study of legal translation by a number of writers such as Goodrich (1987), Šarčević (1997), Foley (2002), Tiersma (1999), Bhatia, Candlin and Gotti (2003) and Tribel (2009) among others. For Goodrich (1987:181) modality is 'a key feature of the legal text and as has been recognized, the prevalent forms of modality within legal texts are imperative and axiomatic'.

Deontic modals (shall, must, should and may) are the most common modals in English legal discourse due to the performative nature of legal documents. Charrow, Crandall and Charrow, in Kittredge and Lehrebeger (1982:186) discuss the use of shall, may, must and will in legal discourse as follows:

> Courts have managed to totally confuse and twist the meanings of shall, may, must and will so that may has been interpreted to have the mandatory meaning must. Must or shall have been interpreted as may and shall has been interpreted as may, must or will.

(A) SHALL

Shall is a formulaic predominant modal in legal texts. It dates back to the English translations of Roman law texts. For example, *Magna Carta* was described as 'an exercise in shall' (Šarčević, 1997:138).

> As used in statutes, contracts, or the like, this word [shall] is generally imperative or mandatory. In common or ordinary parlance and its ordinary signification, the term shall is a word of command and one which has always or which must be given a compulsory meaning as denoting obligation.
>
> (*Black's Law Dictionary*, 2009:1002)

In general English, it denotes future whereas in legal English, it is used as a means of 'totem, to conjure up some flavour of the law' (Bowers, 1989:294). It functions differently in legal contexts as Triebel (2009:154) comments: 'in legal documents *shall* is not used to express future time but to express obligation'. Crystal and Davy (1969:99) identify the general meaning of 'shall as that of obligation'. Similarly, Garzone (in Bhatia, Candlin and Gotti, 2003:197) maintains that 'deontic *shall* is the standard deontic performative form in arbitration rules and it imposes a binding obligation on the arbitrators'. Coates, however, (1983:189) demonstrates that the obligatory sense of *shall* 'is restricted to formal legal contexts'. It (shall)[27] unambiguously indicates that something is intended to be legally binding' (Tiersma, 1999:106).

Shall is used 'in the imperative sense to impose a duty or obligation on the legal subject to whom it refers' (Bhatia, Candlin and Gotti, 2003:347). It expresses the idea of procedural right (ibid.:348). In fact, lawyers tend to use *shall* all the time without thinking, just in case the present imperative is not the appropriate one. However, the present tense and not *shall* is appropriate in definition clauses because a declaration is being made (Triebel, 2009:155). Although it is common in more formal styles, it does not occur in some English dialects, notably in Scotland and the USA (Palmer, 1990:137).

(B) MUST

Sometimes *must* is used in place of *shall* to express the same sense of necessity. Nevertheless, Tessuto (in Bhatia, Candlin and Gotti, 2003:198) argues that 'it is used in a directory sense to signify that it is necessary to take some steps if a right or option is to be exercised (i.e. in procedural rather than substantive provisions)'.

According to Triebel (2009:155), 'must denotes all required action, whether or not the subject of the clause performs the action of the verb. Hence, notice must be given within 14 days'. Foley (2002:369) distinguishes between the use of *shall* and *must* in legal texts:

> some authorities would distinguish shall for an obligation imposed on a human agent with legal consequences as in:
>
> > Upon your return, you shall report to the Agency your activities while abroad.
>
> and must for conditions precedent or subsequent as in:
>
> > The report must include details of your activities while abroad.

Although *must* is used to denote emphasized obligation, it is also used to refer to epistemic meaning which weakens its use in a legal context and the first preference goes to *shall* (Foley, 2002:365).

(C) MAY

May is used in legal discourse to indicate a permissive[28] discretionary act (a right, power or privilege being conferred' (Bhatia, Candlin and Gotti, 2003:348; and Tribel, 2009:156). Bhatia, Candlin and Gotti (ibid.:106) have found out that *may* is the second most frequent modal in the legal documents investigated. Its meaning is mainly deontic (permission). Sometimes (rarely), it expresses epistemic possibility which demands a high degree of caution in distinguishing what is possible and what is permissible. In this context, Foley is quoted: 'may expresses both epistemic possibility and deontic permission. The two meanings are related because you can only give permission to something possible' (2002:364). He (ibid.:365) adds: 'the high frequency of the use of may in legal texts shows that it is so "entrusted" in legal texts that no other modal is used in its place.'

In negative passive forms, it implies a prohibition (Bhatia, Candlin and Gotti, 2003:348). Triebel (2009:157) suggests the use of *must not* instead of *may not*: 'May not can express a prohibition, but is ambiguous: "May not transfer shares" may mean one of these: (i) may possibly not transfer, (ii) is authorized not to transfer or (iii) is not authorized to transfer. Thus, it is better to use must not.'

Comparing *must* to *shall* and *may*, Garazone comments:

> The use of must to express prescriptive deontic meaning in normative texts in English is relatively rare . . . This reflects the standard drafting practices in English law where the use of must in a sample corpus of 20 English statutes, there are only 20 occurrences of must against 3,030 occurrences of shall and 2,035 of may.
>
> (quoted in Bhatia, Candlin and Gotti, 2003:198)

Further to the above brief discussion of *shall*, *may* and *must*, it seems that the use of modal auxiliaries in legal drafting is surrounded by many obstacles and interpretations. In response to this, Foley (2002:373–4) suggests the following solution: 'abandoning the modals in favour of lexical equivalents such as "is obliged to" and "is entitled to", would overcome the problems stemming from the seemingly inherent ambiguity'. An example of this given in the UDHR: 'Everyone is entitled to all the rights and freedoms set forth in this Declaration'. This solution, I believe, is not sufficient since English lexical items expressing modality are limited.

3.2.2.7 The use of negation

Negative and double negative are used in legal English. They are expressed either in 'not', 'never', in negative prefixes such as 'un' or in words like 'unless' and 'except'. Here are some quoted examples:

> The tenant agrees with the landlord . . . not to do or allow, not *to assign* . . . without the consent of the Landlord, that consent not to be unreasonably withheld . . . not to do anything as a result of the notice unless required . . .
>
> (Tenancy Agreement, articles 2–3)

> He was not unduly nervous.
>
> (Report to the Court)

3.2.2.8 Binomial expressions/doublets and triplets

Gustafsson (1975:9) defines binomial expressions as 'sequences of two words belonging to the same class, which are syntactically coordinated and semantically related'. Danet (1985:283) considers them a type of syntactic parallelism. Triebel (2009:160) refers to what he calls 'doubling': the use of several terms to describe a single concept, where a single term would be adequate for that purpose . . . it is misleading as it has the appearance of added certainty or suggests some additional meaning which does not exist'. According to Tiersma (1999:13), a juxtaposition of two or may be three words is known as doublets or triplets. Sometimes, they are called word pairs such as 'true and correct'; 'false and untrue' or conjoined phrases: 'by and with the consent and advice of . . .'. Danet (1985:280) comments that these pairs are 'frozen expressions which are irreversible; they are formal syntactic features rather than lexical ones'. Following are two examples for doublets and triplets:

> I make, publish and declare this instrument to be my Last Will and Testament. By signing this document, I revoke any and all former Wills or Codicils, previously made by me, if such documents existed prior to the signing of this Last Will and Testament.
>
> (Last Will and Testament)

> No one shall be held in slavery or servitude; . . . shall be subjected to torture or to cruel, inhuman or degrading treatment . . .; no one shall be subjected to attacks on his honour or reputation.
>
> (UDHR: preamble and articles 5, 12 and 20 subsequently)

As shown from the above examples, doublets and triplets are considered synonymous or near-synonymous words that come to existence in English legal language as a result of common law courts shifting from French to English, 'there was some concern as to whether the words of the same referent had the same meaning. To avoid any problems drafters began to include both terms, just to be safe' (Beveridge, 2002:59).

Doublets and triplets and other parallel structures are considered good examples of the prosodic features of legal discourse (for example alliteration, as in slavery/servitude above).

The above underlined examples of doublets show more 'end weight' in the second part of the phrase: 'there are more beats, or phonetic material, in the second half of a two-part expression' (Danet, 1985:284).

3.2.3 Textual features

Textual features are concerned with the text as a macro unit. Cohesion is a major textual area that will be analysed below:

3.2.3.1 Elements of cohesion

According to Halliday and Hasan (1976) the major elements of cohesion are reference, conjunction, substitution, ellipsis and lexical repetition. In legal English some cohesive devices are commonly used in legal discourse such as lexical cohesion and conjunctions; some are used with caution (for example reference). That is, they should not be used at the expense of clarity; some others are rarely used (for example ellipsis). The main aim behind such variation in using cohesion is achieving accuracy and avoiding ambiguity. The following is a discussion of lexical repetition, conjunctions and reference.

(a) Lexical repetition

Lexical repetition is expressed by different means whether through words, phrases and sometimes clauses. It is called reiteration which means 'insertion of a lexical item identical to another one mentioned earlier in the same text or context. This could be a synonym, near synonym, superordinate or general word' (Halliday and Hasan, 1976:278).

In legal English, lexical repetition is used instead of pronouns in most of the cases where the antecedent of the pronouns cannot be figured out easily 'because pronouns can have ambiguous reference, the legal profession tends to shy away from them . . . lawyers use pronouns only where the antecedent is very evident and even then may decide to use the name or a noun instead' (Tiersma, 1999:72). He (ibid.) adds that 'avoiding pronouns makes sense in documents such as contracts where it is essential to carefully distinguish the rights and obligations of two or more parties'.

As noted above this phraseology is sometimes purposeful, in which case pronouns 'can be deleted without altering the meaning of the text' because 'it is often said that lawyers are noted for never using one word when ten will do' (Meredith, 1979:64). Below is an example of lexical repetition:

> To keep the interior of the property, the internal decorations and the fixtures, furniture and effects in good repair and condition . . . and to replace if necessary any items of the fixtures, furniture and effects.
>
> (Tenancy Agreement, article 3)

Lexical chains joined by commas, with and/or at the end of the chain are also a common characteristic of legal English:

> Everyone is entitled to all the rights and freedoms . . . without distinction of any kind, such as colour, sex, language, religion, political or other opinion, national or social origin, property, birth or other status.
>
> (UDHR, article 2)

> The contractor shall indemnify and keep indemnified the Council against all losses, costs, demands, charges, proceedings, damages, expenses and all other liabilities . . .
>
> (Partnership Contract, article 20)

(b) Conjunctions

Conjunctions signal the way the writer wants the reader to relate what is about to be said to what has been said before (Baker, 1992:190). They are classified into 'additive, adversative, causal, temporal and continuatives' (Halliday and Hasan, 1976). The most recurrent conjunctions in legal English are 'and' and 'or'. They sometimes lead to ambiguities and this has led to the rise of the hybrid conjunction 'and/or' (Triebel, 2009:156). This combination, according to Mellinkoff (1963:307), is 'traditional, habitual . . . and has caused uncertainty, litigation and courtroom failure'; since 'there is not always agreement as to what and/or means especially where it is used to link more than two nouns or adjectives' (Triebel, 2009:157). Below are some instances of the occurrence of such a conjunction combination:

> The authorized officer and/or instructing Officers; to secure such compliance and/or to comply with advice . . . ; The Contractor shall in circumstances be entitled to any additional payment for its encounter of and/or dealing with such physical conditions . . .'.
>
> (Partnership Contract: pp. 13, 21 and 27 subsequently)

(c) Reference

Generally, reference is only effective in legal discourse when the reference and its antecedent are clearly laid out and there is no possibility of ambiguity. Lexical repetition is to be used if any ambiguity could arise, even if repetition will result in redundancy.

Archaic terms are common means of reference in English legal documents. These include 'hereinunder', 'hereafter', 'herein', 'aforesaid', 'such', 'this' and 'that' to list just a few. They are indeterminate: they do not specify the element they refer to. For example, '"aforesaid", refers to something that has been said before but you cannot be sure what it refers to' (Mellinkoff, 1963:305).[29] The use of 'said' and 'such' is also distinguished in legal English. Kurzon (1986:49) comments: 'instead of the usual "this" and "that" as determiners in cases of noun repetition, the adjectives "said", "such" and "same" may occur as in the said property and such persons'. Tiersma (1999:88) criticizes the use of 'same', 'such', 'said' and its variant 'aforesaid' to substitute a pronoun, or an article. He gives the following example to explain the vagueness that 'same' may cause in a sentence:

> She made an offer in a letter to buy the machinery and I accepted same.
>
> (Tiersma, 1999:88)

For Tiersma, 'same' adds nothing to the sentence; it contributes to the vagueness that the pronoun 'it' may have caused and gives the sentence a more archaic nature. Meredith (1979:64) and Triebel (2009:160) suggest the replacement of some of these unspecific words by other more specific terms. For instance, 'such' can be replaced by 'the', 'that', 'those', 'this', 'them' depending on the context. 'Said' can be replaced by 'the', 'that', or 'those'. Similarly, 'same' can be replaced by 'it' or 'them'. Cataphoric reference is not cited in the legal documents investigated; but below is one example of anaphoric reference:[30]

X presented as a pleasant and cooperative 7 year old . . . His mental state was intact . . . He was not depressed . . . He was not tearful . . . He related well to his mother.

(Report to Court)

3.3 FEATURES OF ARABIC LEGAL DISCOURSE

Test your knowledge before studying the features of legal Arabic.

Exercise: With reference to the features of legal English, discuss in small groups the following questions:

1. How many of these features exist in legal Arabic? Name some of them on the lexical level, the syntactic level and the textual level.
2. What are the features that do not exist in legal Arabic?
3. Do archaic terms exist in legal Arabic? If so give some examples?

3.3.1 Introduction

Arabic, stated Basil Hatim, in March 2008, 'does not have its legal register'.[31] He also declared in December 2009[32] that 'there is no well-defined register of legal discourse in Arabic'. I will take Hatim's words as my point of departure in this section. I will try to investigate this hypothesis in order to argue for or against.

Due to the lack of reference books that have dealt with the language of legal Arabic, discussing its features will be challenging.[33] To overcome this hurdle, I have consulted many books on Arabic linguistics and Arabic stylistics as well as Arabic translation. My aim is to figure out the main features of Arabic in general and see how many of these features apply to the language of legal Arabic. Moreover, I have taken the features of legal English as guidelines, according to which I will analyse the corpus of Arabic legal documents. Such an analysis will help me come up with the common features of these different legal subtypes and at the same time compare them to legal English.

3.3.2 Lexical features

The borderlines between different Arabic legal subtypes are not clear-cut. This may justify Edzard's (1996) categorization of legal texts. In 1996, he discussed the language of diplomacy, although he has quoted all his examples from international legal documents, namely treaties which are considered one of the subcategories of the language of the law. In 1997, Edzard referred again to international law documents, such as the Vienna Convention on the Law of Treaties which he categorized as a legal document.

In the case of legislative documents whether international or local, the language of such legislations involves diplomatic jargon and political emotive expressions. These can be represented in different ways such as hyperboles, repetition and metaphors. The following example of the occurrences of diplomatic jargon is taken from the Constitution of the People's Democratic Republic of Algeria 1989 (amended 1996).

يجب على كل مواطن أن يحمي ويصون استقلال البلاد وسيادتها وسلامة ترابها الوطني . . .	The duty of every citizen is to protect and safeguard the independence of the country and the integrity of its national territory . . . (Article 61)

<http://www.joradp.dz/har/consti.htm>
<http://www.conseil-constitutionnel.dz/Const89–5.htm>

The above phrases also co-occur in media Arabic. To substantiate such a claim, the following table represents the collocation of the word فض (settlement) in the Al-Hayat News Corpus (LDC-AR):

Table 3.2 Collocation of the word فض (settlement) in Al-Hayat News Corpus

Collocation	*Joint*	*Freq*	*LL score*
فض النزاعات	28	952	114.80
فض المنازعات	18	252	81.69
فض الاشتباك	19	488	80.34
فض النزاع	6	3674	15.68

It is also worthwhile to note that Arabic legal discourse shares other features of literary Arabic such as figures of speech. In this context, Gu (2006:140) compares the roots of Arabic with English:

> Whereas legal English adopted a Romanic vocabulary to build its legal (as distinct from literary) language, legal Arabic grew out of literary language and became more sophisticated with the development of its literary counterpart. In fact, there was neither a clear separation between legal, religious, linguistic and literary Arabic nor an absolute division of labour between grammarians, theologians and jurists in early Islam.

An example of the metaphoric nature of texts is cited in the Preamble of the Iraqi Constitution, 2005:

نحن أبناء وادي الرافدين ، موطن الرسل و الأنبياء . . . و مكتوين بلظى شجن المقابر الجماعية . . . و تجفيف منابعها الفكرية . . .	We, the people of Mesopotamia, the homeland of apostles and prophets . . . and burnt by the flames of grief of the mass graves . . . and drying out of its cultural and intellectual wells . . .

<http://www.iraqja.iq/view.77/>
FredT: The Iraqi Constitution:
<http://www.abovetopsecret.com/forum/thread177654/pg1#pid1771495>

The above excerpt is just a small quote of a two-page long preamble which is considered a masterpiece of the Arabic prose style. It is rich with many prosodic features (for example alliteration, rhyme) and figurative features (including metaphors). Metaphors occur in specialized language for some reasons given by Matulewska (2007:130):

> metaphors are rather unusual in languages for special purposes because they introduce a certain lack of precision. Some of them enter into legal discourse because judges use them while performing their job . . . There are also metaphors which penetrate the language as literal translations from Latin metaphorical phrases e.g. *nudum pactum* resulted in a naked or nude contract.

Two metaphors are used in the above Arabic excerpt: the first of which is: (مكتوين بلظى شجن المقابر الجماعية – burnt by the flames of grief of the mass graves) which gives an image of the grief and sorrow of the Iraqi people. This expression is used in Arabic to express a very complicated status of sorrow. The second phrase (تجفيف منابعها الفكرية – drying out of its cultural and intellectual wells . . .) talks of cultural and intellectual properties as wells which were dried out because of conflicts. In the Cairo Declaration of Human Rights in Islam, a similar metaphor is used:

يحرم اللجوء إلي وسائل تفضي إلي إفناء الينبوع البشري.	It is forbidden to resort to such means as may result in the genocidal annihilation of mankind. (Article1:b) <http://www1.umn.edu/humanrts/arab/a004.html> <http://www1.umn.edu/humanrts/instree/cairodeclaration.html>

The word (الينبوع – spring) is metaphorical since it refers to humankind as a spring.[34]

Nevertheless, technical terms or 'terms of art' (Mellinkoff, 1963:16) exist in legal Arabic, for official Arabic documents are loaded with words with specific legal meaning; some of them include synonymous words such as the bracketed words below:

عقد	contract
قضية	case
محكمة	court
قاضي	judge
المَدعَى عليه	the defendant
الإيجار (الكراء)	lease
المالك (المكري)	the landlord
المستأجر(المكتري)	the tenant

This class of legal terms gives the text (for example a certificate and a contract) a specialized legal nature because of the 'lack of figurative or emotive expressions' and the 'pure informative nature' (Abdul-Raof, 2001:117).

Arabic legal texts also involve common words with legal meaning such as الطرف (party) as in الطرف الأول و الطرف الثاني (the first party and the second party) in contracts and agreements, الدفاع (the defence or more precisely the lawyer), as is always the case in court hearings. These words are also used in non-legal contexts, for instance, 'الدفاع' in:

من حق كل مواطن الدفاع عن حريته.	It is the right of each citizen to defend his freedom. (Author's translation)

3.3.2.1 Religious, culture-specific and system-based terms and expressions

Culture-specific and system-based terms and expressions are common in Arabic private documents such as marriage contracts. Some religious terms are underlined below in the excerpt quoted from A Template for A Customary Marriage Contract:

عقد زواج عرفي

. . . وبعد ان أقرَ الطرفان علي أهليتهما للتعاقد فقد اتفقا على الآتي :-

اولا :-

قبل كل من الطرفين على ان يعقد زواجه علي الآخر وارتضي بالآخر زوجا له علي كتاب الله و سنة رسوله وعلي مذهب أبي حنيفة واعتبر هذا العقد بمثابة عقد زواج دائم منتج لكافة الأثار القانونية والشرعية

ثانيا :-

تقر (الزوجة) الطرف الثاني في هذا بأنها خالية من كافة الموانع الشرعية والقانونية التي تحرم عليها الزواج من الطرف الأول

ثالثا :-

يقر الطرف الأول بخلوه من الموانع الشرعية التي تحرم عليه الزواج من الطرف الثاني في هذا العقد بأنه غير متزوج بأكثر من أربعة وان زوجته الطرف الثاني في هذا العقد هي زوجة حسب الشريعة الإسلامية وطبقا

لاحكام القانون

رابعا :-

يقر طرفي التعاقد بأن ما تثمره الحياة الزوجية من نسل بكافة الحقوق القانونية الشرعية المقررة للأبناء من نسب ونفقة وميراث وكافة الحقوق الاخري

خامسا :-

ينسب الأولاد الذين تثمرهم الحياة الزوجية إلي الطرف الأول وفي حالة حدوث أي خلاف لاقدر الله يلتزم بالإنفاق عليهم بالنفقة اللازمة شرعا وقانونا . . .

<http://www.justice-lawhome.com/vb//showthread.php?t=13135>

A translation of the underlined Shariʿah Law and religious expressions in the above document is given below:

Arabic	English
أهليتهما	Their legal capacity
علي كتاب الله و سنة رسوله	According to the Holy Book of Allah and the Sunnah of His Messenger
وعلي مذهب أبي حنيفة	According to the doctrine of Abu-Hanifa
الموانع الشرعية والقانونية	Legal and religious impediments
نسب	Kinship
غير متزوج بأكثر من أربعة	Not married to more than four wives
لاقدر الله	Allah forbids
نفقة	Alimony

Religious elements include reference to the Hijri calendar as in Saudi Marriage Contract Template (حرر في 1429/2/10هـ وصلى الله وسلم على نبينا محمد وآله وصحبه وسلم issued at 10/02/1429 AH, blessings and peace be upon our Prophet Muhammad and upon his family and companions). Other contracts refer to the Hijri calendar along with the Gregorian calendar such as (انه في يوم . . . هـ الموافق . . . م حصل الرضا و الاتفاق بين كل من . . . – It has been agreed, on the . . . AH, . . . AD between . . .) in a Customary Marriage Contract.

Some contracts start with a religious reference such as: (بعد حمد الله و الصلاة و السلام على رسول الله – (After praising God and prayer and peace be upon His Messenger) in a Contractor's Contract; الحمد لله وحده والصلاة والسلام على من لا نبي بعده (Praise be to God, Prayers and Peace be upon the last of all the Prophets) in a Goods Distribution Contract; and بعون الله تعالى (with the help of Almighty Allah) in a Customary Marriage Contract. Other statements occur at the end of some contracts such as و الله تعالى خير الشاهدين (Allah is the best witness); and والله الموفق (May Allah give success) in a Marriage Contract.

3.3.2.2 Formality

Although both English and Arabic legal discourse are formal, the way legal Arabic expresses such formality is widely different from English. In Arabic, formality is done through forms of address or honorary titles due to the diverse social and political backgrounds in different Arab countries. Modes of address which are expressions of courtesy are one of the distinctive features of Arabic legal texts. The following excerpt from The Pact of the League of Arab States – II introduces examples of the titles used in a legal context. It should be mentioned that these titles are also initiated by the word (حضرة – Excellency) which is redundant and is omitted in the English rendition as given below:

حضرة صاحب الفخامة رئيس الجمهورية السورية، و حضرة صاحب السمو الملكي أمير شرق الأردن، حضرة صاحب الجلالة ملك العراق . . . حضرة صاحب الدولة السيد فارس الخوري ، حضرة صاحب المعالي سعيد المفتي باشا . . . و صاحب العزة عبد الرحمن عزام بك . . . (Mansoor, 1965a:1)	His Excellency the President of the Syrian Republic, His Royal Highness the Emir of Transjordan, His Majesty the King of Iraq . . . His Excellency Faris Al Khury, His Excellency Said Al Mufti Pasha . . . His Excellency Abd Rahman Azzam Bey . . . Minister (Mansoor, 1965b:1)

Sometimes, introductory statements that portray high levels of decorative phrases are employed. Consider the following excerpt from one of the meetings of the Islamic Educational, Scientific and Cultural Organization (ISESCO) in Paris 1999:

Arabic	English
أغتنم هذه المناسبة لأعبر لكم عن تمنياتي المخلصة بالنجاح و التوفيق في المهمة الجسيمة و الصعبة التي أناطكم بها زملاؤكم الوزراء و رؤساء الوفود. و ما تقليدكم المسؤولية إلا عربون تقدير لخصالكم كرجل دولة محنك و دليل ثقة في كفاءاتكم كشخص ذي باع طويل في حقول التربية و التعليم.	I seize this opportunity to wish you every success in accomplishing the challenging and difficult task which has been entrusted to you by your colleague ministers and the heads of delegations. It is nothing but an appreciation of your qualities as a wise statesman and confidence in your skills and long experience in the field of teaching and learning. (Author's translation)

<http://www.isesco.org.ma/index.php?option=com_k2&view=item&layout=item&id=64&Itemid=94&lang=ar>

The underlined part in the above example shows an elaborate way of expressing appreciation as well as the use of the plural second person pronoun throughout the whole example, for example لكم (you); أناطكم بها زملاؤكم الوزراء – has been entrusted to you by your colleague ministers; ما تقليدكم المسؤلية الا عربون تقدير لخصالكم (it is nothing but an appreciation of your qualities). This type of highly decorative language distinguishes formality in Arabic from its counterpart in English which does not employ such highly decorative expressions.[35]

This honorific feature of legal Arabic also exists in formal letters such as a concluding remark of appreciation and respect: و تفضلوا بقبول وافر الإحترام – please (you, masculine plural pronoun) accept my utmost respect; و لكم جزيل الشكر – many thanks (to you, masculine plural pronoun). These expressions correspond to the English concluding expressions of 'my kind regards' and/or 'yours sincerely'. First person plural is a means of expressing this formality in Arabic as given in the following excerpt from The Preamble of Federal Law of Civil Service in the Federal Government (No.21:2001), King Zayed declared:

Arabic	English
نحن زايد بن سلطان آل نهيان رئيس دولة الإمارات العربية المتحدة . . . اصدرنا القانون التالي:	We, Zayed bin Sultan Al-Niahayyan, the President of the United Arab Emirates . . . (we) have issued the following Law: (author's translation)

<http://64.251.200.14/Default.aspx?action=ArabicLaw&ID=184>

Such formal expressions are also common in other types of Arabic discourse (for example media and diplomatic discourse). In the United Arab Emirates, for example, referring to one of the royal family takes the following form:

Arabic	English
محمد بن راشد آل مكتوم، نائب رئيس الدولة ، رئيس مجلس الوزراء، وحاكم دبي ، حفظه الله و رعاه.	Muhammad bin Rashid al Maktoom, the Vice-President, the Prime Minister and the ruler of Dubai, may Allah preserve and watch over him. (Author's translation)

Each country uses their own way of expressing modes of address. In pre-2011-revolution Libya, for example, they referred to their president as:

الأخ العقيد معمر القذافي قائد ثورة الفاتح العظيم و ملك ملوك أفريقيا.	Brother and leader, Colonel Muʿammar al-Qadhafy, guide of the great victorious revolution and king of kings of Africa. (Author's translation)

The following is an excerpt of the concordance lines of the Al-Hayat news corpus which explains further the similarity between media Arabic and legal Arabic in terms of formality.

الأمة العربية والأمة الإسلامية المغفور له بإذن الله تعالى **حضرة صاحب** السمو الشيخ عيسى بن سلمان آل خليفة أمير البلاد، الذي وافاه

وبعون من المولى عز وجل، ثم بدعم ومؤازرة كريمة سامية، من لدن **حضرة صاحب** السمو أمير البلاد المفدى، تمكنت اللجنة من انجاز المهمة

الرغبة الشعبية في تحقيق مستقبل مستقر ومزدهر للبلاد بقيادة **حضرة صاحب** السمو الشيخ حمد بن عيسى آل خليفة أمير البلاد المفدى حفظه

وجاء التأييد والتضامن الذي شهدته البحرين عندما تولى . **حضرة صاحب** السمو الشيخ حمد بن عيسى آل خليفة أمير البلاد المفدى دليلاً

تناقضات صارخة لدى السلطة بين الطرح السامي المتضمن في خطابات **حضرة صاحب** السمو الأمير (الشيخ جابر الأحمد الصباح) منذ 1978 (تاريخ

على العدل والمساواة بين المواطنين ومراعاة مصالحهم، وحيث ان **حضرة صاحب** السمو أمير البلاد حفظه الله يطمح إلى تحقيق نهج ديموقراطي

العامة لدعم جمهورية القمر الاتحادية الإسلامية وإعلان **حضرة صاحب** السمو الشيخ حمد بن خليفة آل ثاني امير دولة قطر التبرع لهذا

،اللجنة، مع آفاق الرؤية الشاملة التي طرحها الأمير القائد **حضرة صاحب** السمو الشيخ حمد بن عيسى آل خليفة حفظه الله، من خلال نهجه

منصور باشا فهمي. وبوجهها الى رئيسي تحرير المجلة. تلتها كلمة **حضرة صاحب** السعادة الدكتور سليمان عزمي باشا - عميد كلية الطب في جامعة

الايام الحزينة لنستمد عزاءنا في عيسى من خليفته الابن العزيز **حضرة صاحب** السمو الشيخ حمد بن عيسى آل خليفة أمير البلاد المفدى، وكلنا

«:(بن الحسين ووزعتها وكالة الأنباء الأردنية (بترا **حضرة صاحب** الجلالة الملك عبدالله بن الحسين ملك المملكة الأردنية

والتدبير «نشر مقال طبي للدكتور المصري محمد ولي» شقيق **حضرة صاحب** المعالي جعفر باشا وزير المعارف المصرية «. ولم تتوقف

الثاني (نوفمبر) 2000، وثقته الكاملة بأن دولة قطر بقيادة **حضرة صاحب** السمو الشيخ حمد بن خليفة آل ثاني أمير دولة قطر، ستنهض خلال

العربية. وتصدر العدد صورة للملك فاروق وتحتها التعليق الآتي **حضرة صاحب** الجلالة الملك فاروق الاول - راعي العلم - والامين على التراث

هذا الميثاق الوطني، وثيقة تجديد للعهد والبيعة، إلى مقام **حضرة صاحب** السمو الشيخ حمد بن عيسى آل خليفة أمير البلاد المفدى أمانة

As the extract shows, the highlighted words given in the middle of the concordance lines represent honorific titles that exist in different news items about Gulf figures. Examples of these titles are ... حضرة صاحب السمو الشيخ (His Highness Sheikh . . .); ...حضرة صاحب السمو الأمير (His Highness Prince . . .); ... حضرة صاحب الجلالة الملك (His Majesty King . . .); ... حضرة صاحب السعادة الدكتور (His Excellency Dr. . . .).

3.3.2.3 Gender-biased terms

Baker (1992:92) notes that in Arabic 'gender distinctions are reflected in nouns and pronouns but also in the concord between these and their accompanying verbs and adjectives'. Legal Arabic uses words that are marked for masculine. Many of these words exist in official local documents such as contracts. One can find terms like المالك ، المستأجر، المتعاقد ، الشاهد (the landlord, the tenant, the contracted party and the witness, respectively). Consider the following examples from an Employment Contract:

يباشر <u>المتعاقد</u> واجبات وظيفة سكرتير لغات أجنبية في مقر الوزارة أو فروعها.	<u>The contracted party</u> shall carry out the duties of Foreign Languages Assistant in the headquarters or the branches of the Ministry. (Hatim, Shunnaq and Buckley, 1995:174–175)

According to the above example, the contract refers to male parties only and excludes any potential landladies or female tenants or even witnesses. The term المتعاقد (the contracted party) refers to a male because the term سكرتير (secretary), which is masculine, refers back to it. At the same time, the term سكرتير (secretary) was translated as a gender-neutral word (Foreign Languages Assistant). In other documents one cannot figure out the gender of some words (for example the parties). For instance, in the following excerpt from a Tenancy Agreement, the Arabic text refers only to male lessee and lessor.

يجب على <u>المستأجر</u> في حالة انتهاء مدة العقد و عدم رغبته في تجديده اخبار <u>المؤجر</u> بذلك خطيا قبل إنتهاء مدة العقد بثلاثة أشهر علي الأقل و إلا <u>يعتبر مستأجرا للمأجور</u> لمدة سنة أخري إلا إذا أراد <u>المؤجر</u> ذلك.	In the event of the expiry of the period of the contract and with no desire to renew the contract, the <u>lessee</u> must similarly give written notification of this to the <u>lessor</u> at least three months prior to the expiry of the period of the contract, otherwise <u>he/she will be deemed to be the lessee of the rented property</u> for another year if the <u>lessor</u> so wishes. (Hatim, Shunnaq and Buckley, 1995:186–187)

In court, one can hear terms like المُدَعِي ، المَدعَى عليه، الدفاع ، القاضي ، الحاجب ، الكاتب (the claimant – the defendant, the defence (lawyer), the judge, the bailiff and the clerk respectively).[36]

In international documents, there is inconsistency in the representation of gender in the ST. Sometimes neutral words are used as in example 1 below whereas gender-marked masculine is used in example 2.

1. لكل <u>فرد</u> الحق في الحياة وفى الحرية وفى سلامة شخصه	1. Every <u>individual</u> has the right to life, liberty and security of person. (AChHR, Article 5).
2. <u>المتهم بريئ</u> إلى أن تثبت <u>إدانته</u> بمحاكمة قانونية تؤمن <u>له</u> . . . للدفاع <u>عنه</u>	2. <u>The accused</u> shall be presumed innocent until proved guilty at a lawful trial in which <u>he</u> has enjoyed . . . for <u>his</u> defense. (AChHR, Article 7)
	<http://www1.umn.edu/humanrts/instree/loas2005.html> <http://www1.umn.edu/humanrts/arab/a003.html>

Similarly, in organisations, for example in a university, there are gender distinctions in the names of different departments where the Personnel Department (شئون العاملين), or the Graduate Office (شئون الخريجين), refer only to masculine staff or graduates, excluding any reference to women staff or female graduates.

Another interesting example of gender-biased terms is given during the inauguration of the ministers taking oath of office for the new Egyptian interim government in July 2013. This oath is written in masculine as given below:

أقسم بالله العظيم أن أحافظ مخلصاً على النظام الجمهوري و أن أحترم الدستور و القانون و أن أرعى مصالح الشعب رعاية كاملة و أن أحافظ على استقلال الوطن و سلامة أراضيه.	I swear by Almighty God to loyally uphold the Republican system, to respect the Constitution and the law, and fully safeguard the interests of the people and to safeguard the independence of the nation and the territory unity and integrity.

(From The Egyptian Satellite Channel: 5 o'clock news, July 2013) <http://www.emannabih.com/english-translation-of-the-egyptian-constitution-2013-long-live-egypt/>

The oath is written in masculine. There are three female ministers, all of them have uttered it as it is, and they did not use the feminine form of the word مخلصاً (sincerely) to agree with the verb.

It is worth mentioning that Arabic preference for the masculine element in writing has a close relation to the cultural and social background of the Arabic mind as a whole. It is an 'inclusive' or 'preference' element as Al-tha'aliby (2000:404) comments in the following quotation:

فصل الخطاب الشامل للذكران و الاناث و ما يفرق بينهم:	On the topic of addressing males and females and what distinguishes between them in discourse.
قال الله عز و جل: "يا أيها الذين أمنوا اتقوا الله"	The Almighty Allah says: 'O mankind! Fear your Lord!' (Yusuf Ali, Sura 22:1) <http://www.islam101.com/quran/yusufAli/QURAN/22.htm>
و قال عز و جل: "فأقيموا الصلاة و آتوا الزكاة"	And the Almighty says: 'So establish regular Prayer, give regular Charity'[37] (Yusuf Ali, Sura 22:78) <http://www.islam101.com/quran/yusufAli/QURAN/22.htm>
فعم بهذا الخطاب الرجال و النساء و غلب الرجال و تغليبهم من سنن العرب.	In the above verses, the address includes both men and women, but only the masculine form is used because male preference in discourse is a convention of the Arabs.

(Author's translation except for the Qur'anic verses)

That is, if a choice is to be made in writing about both sexes it will be made in favour of the masculine not the feminine. This attitude, however, needs to be adapted in legal discourse as it may have its legal consequences.

3.3.2.4 Archaic terms

Archaic terms are also called 'the frozen patterns of language' (Baker, 1992:63), whereas Hatim and Mason (1997:190) refer to them as 'routines'. They are very frequent in English as they keep the reservoirs of register. Arabic legal discourse, on the other hand, uses fewer archaic terms because there is much greater fluidity between different Arabic registers. Similarly, Classical Arabic terms and morphology continue to exist in today's Modern Standard Arabic (MSA).

Compared to English archaic terms, they can rather be called template terms in Arabic legal discourse. Examples of them which continued to exist in MSA are: المذكور اعلاه (mentioned above), سالف الذكر (the aforementioned), المذكور (the said) and الوارد(ة) (mentioned). Example of template phrases are underlined below:

أنا المحضر سالف الذكر قد انتقلت في التاريخ المذكور أعلاه إلى حيث المعلن إليهم وسلمتهم صورة من هذه الصحيفة، وكلفتهم بالحضور أمام محكمة ... الابتدائية ...	I, the aforementioned bailiff, have moved on the above date to where the informed parties live, handed over a copy of this document and summoned them to appear before the primary court of . . . (a suit for the appointment of a liquidator of a company) (author's translation) <http://www.arlawfirm.com/ADVdetails.asp?id=882>

Not all the template terms, however, continued to exist in MSA. For instance, in a collection of legal documents published in the seventeenth century Ottoman period, there are template terms such as المسفور (the stated) and المزبور (the aforementioned) (Ebeid and Young, 1976:14 and 36 subsequently) which have disappeared from modern Arabic legal texts.

3.3.3 Syntactic features

Arabic has two major tenses: الماضي (perfect) and المضارع (imperfect); the exact tense and aspect is determined in Arabic through temporal elements such as لما (when) مازال (still) to denote perfect and س (will) / سوف (will) to denote future. The imperfect and the impersonal in legal Arabic are common, particularly in international documents and legislations which are addressing general topics and not specifying individuals. Below is a discussion of the syntactic features of legal Arabic in more detail.

3.3.3.1 Nominalization

The nominal form of the verb إسم الفعل (verbal noun) is common in Arabic and in legal documents. Holes (2004:320) points out that: 'nominalization like passivization, allows "un-attributable" claims to be made, for example at its simplest, hunaka "'tiqad 'nna . . ./ there is a belief that" as opposed to "I"/ "he" / "they" believe that . . .' Both syntactic structures obscure agents; hence the text appears more objective. Nominalization is more common in certain text types than in others, for example in constitutions, legislations and in international documents where there is a need for inclusiveness in writing. In contracts, however, it can be less common. To substantiate this claim, the following excerpt from the Egyptian Constitution 2012 presents a good number of nominal forms in one article:

يهدف الاقتصاد الوطنى إلى تحقيق التنمية المطردة الشاملة، ورفع مستوى المعيشة وتحقيق الرفاه، والقضاء على الفقر والبطالة، وزيادة فرص العمل . . .	The national economy aims at achieving comprehensive, constant development, raising the standard of living, achieving welfare, eliminating poverty and unemployment, increasing job opportunities . . . (Article 14) (author's translation)

<http://egelections-2011.appspot.com/Referendum2012/dostor_masr_final.pdf>

Nominalization is also common in other types of MSA (for example media discourse). Holes (2004:314–324) lists the common features of Arabic news discourse, among which is nominalization. I have found that nominalization in the Al-Hayat Arabic news corpus available online is highly frequent.

3.3.3.2 Passivization

Legal Arabic, like any legal language seeks accuracy and precision by avoiding obscurity of agents. That is why legal Arabic favours active to passive – a characteristic which is specific to MSA – as Rosenhouse (1988:92) argues: 'Arabic is known to avoid passive verb forms and not to favour much use of them in its sentences'. This attitude, however, has changed and a tendency to use passive has begun, albeit basic and inconsistent. The following examples are cited in two subtypes of legal Arabic:

يُفسخ هذا العقد فوراً و تلقائياً و بدون تنبيه أو إنذار في حالة . . .	This contract is revoked immediately and absolutely without any prior notice if . . . (Tenancy Agreement, article 12) (author's translation)
لا يفرض التشغيل الالزامي على أحد غير أنه يجوز بمقتضى القانون فرض شغل أو خدمة على أي شخص . . . . لا يُؤجر الشخص المحكوم عليه إلي اشخاص . . . أو يُوضع تحت تصرفها.	Compulsory labour may not be imposed on any person but any person may be required to do any work or to render any service in circumstances prescribed by law . . . no convicted person shall be hired to, or be placed at the disposal of, any persons . . .

(Constitution of the Hashemite Kingdom of Jordan 1952, Article 13)

<http://www.parliament.jo/node/137>
<http://www.kinghussein.gov.jo/constitution_jo.html>

As shown in the above examples, passive occurs in contracts, and constitutions. We can also argue that it exists in administrative and technical texts. However, to substantiate this claim, we need further studies using corpus-based tools and this can be done in a separate study.

3.3.3.3 Modals

Arabic does not have a well-defined set of modal auxiliaries. Suleiman (1999) calls them modal expressions rather than modal verbs. By 'expressions' is meant the phrasal modals such as the ones initiated by the preposition 'min' من اللازم (it is necessary). Based on the analysis of a collection of Arabic legal documents, the most frequent lexical modal verbs are يجوز (may), يجب (must); prepositions and particles are also frequent such as لِ . . . أن (for . . . to) which is a short version of: يجوز لِ . . . أن (it is allowed for (somebody(ies)) to) على . . . أن (on . . . to) which is an abbreviated version of يجب على . . . أن – (it is incumbent on (somebody (ies)) to). The particle قد (may) is also used. All these forms correspond to the English modal verbs: shall, must, may and these verbs, among some other less frequent forms take an imperfect clause initiated with أن (to) or as Abdul-Raof puts it 'a verb-first sentence' (2001:35). The following are examples of modal verbs which are quoted from the Egyptian Labour Law:

Arabic	English
يجب أن يتم الإخطار قبل الإنهاء بشهرين.	The notification shall be given two months before terminating the contract. (Article 111)
لا يجوز الاتفاق على الإعفاء من شرط الإخطار أو تخفيض مدته، ولكن يجوز الاتفاق على زيادة هذه المدة.	No agreement on exemption from the notification condition or reduction of its period shall be reached. However, agreement shall be reached on increasing that period. (Article 115)

<http://www.egypt.gov.eg/arabic/laws/labour/Law_work/F_worklaw_wrel.aspx>
<http://www.egypt.gov.eg/english/laws/pdf/Book2.pdf>

3.3.3.4 Complex sentence structure

Lack of well-defined sentence boundaries and inconsistent use of punctuation marks result in long complex sentences. Although it is a common feature of Arabic to favour coordination through the conjunction و (and), legal Arabic displays complexity by using both coordinated clauses and embedded and relative clauses initiated by one of the relative pronouns التي ، الذي (who, whom, which, that). The excerpt below from the Administrative Provisions in the Egyptian Civil Courts, exemplifies the complexity of legal Arabic: the long unpunctuated sentences, the number of embedded and complex conditional clauses.

Arabic	English
والقاعدة المقررة في الفقه الجنائي أن العقوبة التي ينص عليها المشرع هي التي تحدد نوع الجريمة المرتكبة والمعاقب عليها فإذا كانت الجريمة يعاقب عليها القانون بالإعدام أو الأشغال الشاقة أو السجن فهي جناية وإن كان معاقباً عليها بالحبس الذي لا يزيد أقصى مدته عن أسبوع أو بالغرامة التي لا يزيد أقصى مقدارها عن جنيه مصري فهي جنحة.	The rule established in criminal law is that the punishment which is prescribed by the legislator determines the type of crime committed and which is therefore punishable. If the crime is to be punished by death or hard labour or imprisonment, it is a felony. If the crime is to be punished by imprisonment the maximum duration of which does not exceed a week or a fine the maximum amount of which does not exceed one Egyptian pound, it is a misdemeanour. (Author's translation)

<http://www.arlawfirm.com/ADVdetails.asp?id=5578>

In the case of official documents such as marriage and divorce certificates, sentences are not long. That is because of the arbitrary nature of the template which takes different formats and the fragmentary nature of sentences. One can see a whole certificate tabulated format, or half of it in a table while the other half is in normal writing. At other times, one can find the whole certificate written in fragmented statements, with sub-headers separated by commas.

3.3.3.5 Doublets and triplets

Arabic legal texts involve two or three words of related meanings, sometimes synonymous or near-synonymous which are conjoined by و (and) or أو (or). These are called by Badawi, Carter and Gully (2004:138) 'binomials or polynomials'; 'hendiadys' by Al-Qinai (1999:244); 'synonym couplets' by Williams (1989:62) and 'dyadic couplets' (quoted in Williams, 1989:62). Synonymous pairs are considered a form of repetition which is a broadly used stylistic device in MSA. Consider the following examples of doublets and triplets:

واذا خالف المستاجر هذا الشرط يعتبر العقد مفسوخا فورا بدون تنبيه او انذار . . .	If the tenant violates this condition, this contract revokes immediately without any prior notice . . . (Tenancy Agreement, Article 11) (author's translation) <http://mohamionline.com/>
وهذا إقرار وتعهد مني بذلك أقر وألتزم بكل ما ورد به دون أي ضغط أو إكراه.	This is to certify that I recognise and commit to whatever is stated herewith, without any pressure or coercion. (Tender) (author's translation) <http://www.daralsunna.com/arabic/?action=print&id=301>
يقر الطرف الثانى المشترى ، أنه استلمها ووضع يده عليها وقبلها بحالتها الراهنة . . .	The second party, the buyer, acknowledges that he has received and placed his hand on it and accepted it as it is . . . (Contract of Sale of Agricultural Land) (author's translation) <http://www.arlawfirm.com/ADVdetails.asp?id=2187>
و هو مصدق في قوله من جهة وجود العيب و التلف و الخلل و بمقدار ما أنفق . . .	The Lessor is deemed to be trustworthy in his account of the fault, the harm or the damage and the cost . . . (Contract of Lease, Hatim, Shunnaq and Buckley, 1995:186–187)

As shown above, doublets occur in two-word forms as in the first two examples or the three-word forms in the third example and three near-synonymous verbs in the final example.

3.3.3.6 Participles

There are some other grammatical features in Arabic legal texts, such as إسم المفعول (the passive participle),[38] المفعول المطلق – the absolute object, or 'cognate accusative' as Ryding (2005:83) calls it. Wright (1967:109) calls the passive participle 'nomen patients', classifying them as adjectives, 'but they have come to be used as substantives' (ibid.). For Gadalla (2010:2), the passive participle syntactically performs a number of functions, it can be used as a noun, adjective or a tense (for example replacing verbs).[39] Consider the following example from the Constitution of the Hashemite Kingdom of Jordan, 1952:

Arabic	English
تحمي الدولة حرية القيام بشعائر الأديان والعقائد طبقا للعادات . . . ما لم تكن مخلة بالنظام العام او منافية للآداب.	The State shall safeguard the free exercise of all forms of worship and religious rites . . . unless such is inconsistent with public order or morality. (Article 14)

<http://www.parliament.jo/node/137>
Copyright © 1998, The Royal Hashemite Court
<http://www.kinghussein.gov.jo/constitution_jo.html>

In the following example from the Constitution of Morocco 2011, the underlined words are examples of the present participle in Arabic which are rendered in English into nouns: 'the protector' and 'the guarantor' subsequently.

Arabic	English
الملك، أمير المؤمنين وحامي حمى الملة والدين، والضامن لحرية ممارسة الشؤون الدينية.	The King, Amir al-Mu'minin (Commander of the Faithful), protector of the faith and religion and the guarantor of the free exercise of religious affairs. (Chapter 41) (author's translation)

<http://www.mcrp.gov.ma/constitution.aspx?Lg=Ar&Rub=37&IDMenu=6#الباب
I>

The absolute object is a grammatical structure that involves emphasizing the verb by means of using a verbal noun from that same verb. The following two instances exemplify the absolute object in Arabic legal discourse.

Arabic	English
يقر الطرف الثانى أنه عاين الشقة موضوع البيع المعاينة التامة النافية للجهالة.	The second party acknowledges that he/she has fully inspected the apartment for sale, without any uncertainty or ignorance on his/her part. (Contract for Sale for an Apartment) (author's translation).
تخارج الطرفان وتصالحا مصالحة قطعيّة لا رجوع فيها ولا نكول . . . قبض الطرف الأول من الطرف الثاني نصيبه من أموال التركة عند التوقيع على هذا العقد ، و أبرأت ذمّتهم من حصتها إبراءا شاملا مسقطا كل حقّ ودعوى وطلب.	The two parties have exited and reached definitive reconciliation without the possibility of retraction or withdrawal. The first party has received her share of the legacy from the second party on the signing of this contract and has completely absolved the second party, quashing any right, lawsuit or request. (A Contract of Quittance from a Legacy: Article 2) (author's translation)

<http://www.arlawfirm.com/ADVdetails.asp?id=2332>

3.3.4 Textual features

Arabic has its own textual devices which are used as linguistic resources to achieve cohesion in all Arabic text types (Abdul-Raof, 2001:59). Many Arabic authors have been concerned with investigating the different textual features of Arabic and their impact on translation, for example repetition and punctuation (Al-Khafaji 1999, 2001, 2006, 2007; Emery 1990; Johnstone 1991 and Fareh 2006). The following sections consider more closely the common textual features. It is noteworthy that the excerpts quoted as examples of the textual features of legal Arabic are mostly from legislative and international text types, because the textual features are better represented in these text types than in official documents. These were rarely cited because some of these features are not as common as in other text types, due to the formulaic specialized nature of them.

3.3.4.1 Lexical repetition

Lexical repetition, also 'semantic redundancy', 'verbosity' or 'wordiness' (Shunnaq, 1994:103–4; 2000:209) is inevitable for achieving cohesion. Recurrence is used, according to Jawad (2009:754, 763), to achieve two major cohesive functions: textual and rhetorical as explained below:

> lexical repetition assumes the role of organizing and rendering the text cohesive in much the same way connectives do. Rhetorically, lexical repetition has to do with the expressive meaning that a marked repetitive pattern evokes . . . by the recurrence of certain lexical items in a short piece of text, a foregrounded image is projected on the surface of the text signalling a semantic weight that goes beyond the mere senses of the repeated utterances. Thus rhetorical repetition can be considered an extra layer, or extra regularity aimed at triggering extra meanings as well as organizing the overall composition of discourse.

Lexical repetition is employed in different text types for various purposes. In argumentative texts (for example political speeches), it is used for persuasion, whereas in legal documents, its function is accuracy. Repetition occurs within one sentence or across sentence boundaries. Hassan (2005a:87) lists the following reasons for employing lexical repetition within a text:

> Give more information about something vague.
> Mention something specific about something general (hyponymy).
> Mention the general after the specific.
> Abridge gaps in information: to remind the recipient of something mentioned long before.

Emery (1990:130) comments on prolixity and brevity in Arabic as follows:

> The tension between prolixity and brevity continues to run through Arabic writing. On the one hand, Arabic discourse is often characterized as having abundance of synonymy e.g. in a string of postmodifying adjectives . . . on the other hand, Arabic may exhibit (in structures consisting of general words or function words) an austerity and economy unmatched in English; here the strategy is expansion and/or substitution of lexical words.

Emery (ibid.:130) discusses lexical repetition as 'a feature of written Arabic which manifests itself in many forms: lexical recurrence, root-echo or paronomasia, binomials, clausal structures'. Below is a discussion of the elements of lexical repetition in detail.

(a) Same word and root repetition

As clear from the title, this element means the occurrence of the same word more than one time in the text. The following extract is taken from the Immigration and Care Act of Egyptians Abroad 1983:

مع عدم الإخلال بحق المصريين في الهجرة يقيد راغبو الهجرة الدائمة بناء على طلبهم في **سجل** بالوزارة المختصة بشئون الهجرة، وتوزع فرص الهجرة التي قد تتوافر لدى الوزارة المذكورة على المقيدين بهذا **السجل** على أساس تخصصاتهم وإمكانياتهم و والاحتياجات المطلوبة في دول المهجر مع الالتزام بأسبقية القيد في **السجل**.

Without prejudice to the right of the Egyptians to emigration, names of those wishing permanent emigration are to be recorded, at their request, with the Ministry of Emigration. With a commitment to the primacy enrolment in a **register**, emigration opportunities that may be available to the said Ministry are to be distributed on those enrolled in the **register** on the basis of their specialization and their abilities and the requirements of the countries they will emigrate to.

(Article 6) (author's translation)
<http://www.arlawfirm.com/ADVdetails.asp?id=801>

As the example shows, there are two cases of same word and root repetition: the first is the underlined word الهجرة (immigration) which occurs five times in the Arabic example. The second example is the bold face word سجل (register) which occurs three times in the ST but only two times in the TT. The next example is quoted from *The Treaty of Friendship between the Union of Soviet Socialist Republics and the Mutawakkilite Kingdom of Yemen*:

يتعهد الطرفان المتعاقدان بتسهيل المبادلات التجارية بين الدولتين، ووفقاً لهذا **التعهد** يكون لكل من رعايا الدولتين في بلاد الدولة الأخرى بعد الحصول على الإذن منها الدخول والإقامة طبق نظمها . . . **ويتعهد** الطرفان المتعاقدان أن يساعدا بتطبيق كل تسهيل موافق للنظم المحلية في معاملات رعايا الدولتين في التجارة فما يختص بالضرائب والرسوم الجمركية.

The two Contracting Parties **undertake** to facilitate trade exchange between the two countries. According to **this pledge**, the nationals of each state reside in the territory of the other state after obtaining the permission of entry and residence according to its regulations . . . The two Contracting Parties **pledge** to help implement all facilities, subject to their local systems, in the treatment of the nationals of the two countries in trade, with regards to taxes and customs duties. (Article 2) (author's translation)
<http://www.yemen-nic.net/personal/site_use.php>

In the above example, the word الدولة (state) is repeated four times in the ST whereas the word تعهد (to pledge) occurs three times.

Arabic is well-known for a common root and pattern morphology. It employs three consonants or radicals and a vowel pattern such as كتب (to write); the repetition of the same root is very common in Arabic generally and in legal Arabic specifically. It is further divided into two types. The first type occurs when two words have the same root but occur in a different pattern as in كتب كتابا (he wrote a book) (Dickins, Hervey and Higgins, 2002: 104). The following instances are quoted in The Tunisian Code of Personal Status II:

تعتد زوجة المفقود عدة الوفاة بعد صدور الحكم بفقدانه. (Mansoor, 1965a: 300)	The wife of a missing person, following a court decision designating him as a missing person, shall observe the same period of iddat as that applicable in case of death. (Mansoor, 1965b:140)

The above excerpt shows instances of root repetition: تحتد عدة الوفاة (observe the period of *iddat* in case of death), المفقود ، فقدانه (missing person, designating him a missing person).

The second type of root repetition is the 'absolute object' as in رفض رفضا باتا (he definitely disagreed). Dickins, Hervey and Higgins (2002:105) list the following forms of root repetition in Arabic as follows:

Table 3.3 Examples of root repetition in Arabic

Category	*Example*	*English Translation*
Subject + verb	ثار ثائرة	to fly into a rage
Verb + object	طلب طلباً	to make a request
Verb + prepositional phrase	صبغ بصبغة أخرى	to transform
Conjoined nouns	عزة و اعتزاز	honour and self-esteem
Noun + adjective	الظل الظليل	shady shade
Genitive	أطماع الطامعين	the ambitions of the covetous
Conjoined adjectives	الضعفاء و المستضعفون	the weak and the oppressed

The list and the examples given above are illustrative of the point of root repetition in Arabic. Not all the categories occur in Arabic legal discourse such as 'noun + adjective', 'genitive' and 'conjoined adjectives'. It is also worth pointing out that the example given for the first element, however, is not the right example for the category of 'verb + subject'. That is, ثار ثائرة (he violently outraged) is a not a subject + verb relation. It is rather a verb + object (absolute object) relation. The 'absolute object' is employed in Arabic legal texts to add force to the verb.

(b) Phrase repetition

Phrase repetition is common in the Arabic legal texts analysed. The example quoted is from an Agreement between Libya and the USA.

يجوز لسلطات الولايات المتحدة أن تدفع لقوات الولايات المتحدة صكوكا مالية قيمتها مبينه بعملة الولايات المتحدة أو عملة عسكرية قيمتها مبينه بوحدات عملة الولايات المتحدة أو عملة ليبية أو عملة الولايات المتحدة علي شرط أن يتم الدفع بعملة الولايات المتحدة . . . و تتخذ سلطات الولايات المتحدة . . . بوحدات عملة الولايات المتحدة . . . . قوات الولايات المتحدة. (Mansoor, 1965a:284)	The United States authorities may pay the United States forces in checks expressed in United States currency, or military scrip denominated in units of United States currency, or in Libyan or in United States currency, provided the payment in United States currency shall take place . . . The United States authorities will take . . . in the units of the United States currency . . . the United States forces. (Mansoor, 1965b:125)

The above example shows the repetition of the underlined Arabic phrases (الولايات المتحدة – The United States) linked with different nouns (for example سلطات – authorities, قوات – forces, عملة – currency) forming an *idafa* construct and their counterparts in the English text. The main purpose of the translator is the quest for precision which is perceived in the above example as a dream or a 'myth' as Mellinkoff (1963:423) puts it. Another example of phrase repetition is cited in a Contract of a Lawyer's Fees:

إذا تأخر الطرف الثاني عن سداد أي من الدفعات في مواعيدها المنصوص عليها في هذا العقد لمدة أقصاها خمسة عشر يوماً من تاريخ استحقاقها ، فإن للطرف الأول الحق في التوقف عن مباشرة العمل المتفق عليه مع الطرف الثاني ، ويتحمل الطرف الثاني كافة النتائج التي قد تلحق به من جراء هذا التوقف.	If the second party delays any of the due payments set forth in this contract in a timely manner for a maximum period of fifteen days from the due date, the first party has the right to halt immediately the work agreed upon with the second party and the second party will be responsible for whatever ensues as a result of the halt. (author's translation)

<http://www.arlawfirm.com/ADVdetails.asp?id=1744>

(c) Lexical density and parallel structures

Lexical density (for example listing) is common in Arabic. Dickins, Hervey and Higgins (2002:59) classify it into two types (i) syndetic: و (and), أو (or) and (ii) asyndetic: no connector. Arabic legal discourse lists a long string of consecutive nouns separated from each other by means of أو (or) or و (and). The following example is quoted from the Amendment of the Penal Code to Combat Acts of Bullying:

يعاقب بالحبس مدة لا تقل عن سنة كل من قام بنفسه أو بواسطة الغير باستعراض القوة أو التلويح بالعنف أو التهديد بأيهما أو استخدامه ضد المجنى عليه أو مع زوجه أو أحد أصوله أو فروعه وذلك بقصد ترويعه أو التخويف بإلحاق أي أذى مادى أو معنوي أو الإضرار بممتلكاته أو سلب ماله أو الحصول على منفعه منه أو التأثير في إرادته لفرض السطو عليه .	Whosoever demonstrates the use of force or insinuates violence or threatens to use either of them himself or via another shall be punished by imprisonment for not less than one year for using them against the victim or against his spouse or one of his ascendants or descendants, with a view to terrify or intimidate them through any material or moral harm or damage to his possessions or stealing his money or getting a benefit from him or influence his will to impose robbery upon him. (article 1) (author's translation)

<http://www.arlawfirm.com/ADVdetails.asp?id=5570>

It is worth noting that lexical density also exists in old legal documents published in the seventeenth century such as the following lexical string:

بعناه المسفور بالثمن المذكور فاشتراه منا بيعا صحيحا شرعيا قاطعا ماضيا ممضيا خاليا من كلما يمنع صحته و نفوذه من الشرط و الغر و الغبن و التلجية و الاكراه و الاجبار غب النظر و الاختبار . . .	We have sold him the stated site for the aforementioned price and he has purchased it from us through a valid, lawful, definitive, effectual, ratified sale, free of any stipulation, deception, fraud, coercion, duress or compulsion, after viewing and verification . . . (Ebeid and Young, 1976: 14–46).

Parallelism, in Arabic, is a textual feature and it is employed for maintaining cohesion in the text. It occurs at various levels, whether, phonological, (for example sound repetition), morphological (for example suffix repetition), lexical (for example couplets), syntactical (for example phrase and clause repetition). Koch gives the following definition of parallelism:

> to say that two linguistic structures are parallel is to say that they share a common structural frame and that within this frame, some element or elements differ in form. What is on the face of it most curious is that the elements that differ always stand in a close relationship to one another. They can be phonological, morphological, register or dialect variants, synonyms or antonyms, metaphorical versions of one another, or any of a number of other things. Parallelism is the way paradigms are created.
>
> (quoted in Williams, 1989:62)

Williams (1989:63) considers repetition at word level (for example root and pattern repetition); repetition at clause level; and paraphrase (for example repetition of content) instances of parallel structures in the text. Abdul-Raof (2001:56) defines parallel structures as 'phrases which have the same structural rhythmical pattern employed for a stylistic effect'. The excerpt below from Preamble of the Iraqi Constitution, 2005 presents an example of rhythmical pattern, especially the underlined parts of it where three verbal sentences are used. Each has a verb and two subjects separated by و (w) and each sentence ends in the same sounds: long vowel plus a glottal stop اء (aa') resulting in a rhymed prose style.

نحنُ ابناء وادي الرافدين موطن الرسل والأنبياء وسثوى الأئمة الأطهار مهد الحضارة وصناع الكتابة ورواد الزراعة ووضاع الترقيم، على أرضنا سنَّ أولُ قانونٍ وضعه الإنسان، وفي وطننا خُطَّ أعرقُ عهدٍ عادلٍ لسياسة الأوطان، وفوقَ ترابنا صلى الصحابةُ والأولياء، ونظّرَ الفلاسفةُ والعلماء، وأبدعَ الأدباءُ والشعراءْ.	We are the people of the land between two rivers, the homeland of the apostles and prophets, abode of the virtuous imams, pioneers of civilization, crafters of writing and cradle of numeration. Upon our land the first law made by man was passed, the most ancient just pact for homelands policy was inscribed and upon our soil, companions of the Prophet and saints prayed, philosophers and scientists theorized and writers and poets excelled.

<http://www.iraqja.iq/view.77/>
FredT: The Iraqi Constitution:
<http://www.abovetopsecret.com/forum/thread177654/pg1#pid1771495>

For Shunnaq (2000:213) parallelism is considered a form of lexical repetition and 'involves similar phrases and clauses'. Below is an example of parallel structures cited in the Preamble of the AChHR:

Conscious of the fact that the entire Arab World has always worked together to preserve its faith, believing in its unity, struggling to protect its freedom, defending the right of nations to self-determination and to safeguard their resources . . .	وإذ بقى الوطن العربي يتنادى من أقصاه إلى أقصاه حفاظا على عقيدته، مؤمنا بوحدته، مناضلا دون حريته مدافعا عن حق الأمم في تقرير مصيرها والحفاظ على ثرواتها ، . . .

<http://www1.umn.edu/humanrts/arab/a003.html>

<http://www1.umn.edu/humanrts/instree/arabhrcharter.html>

In the above example, parallelism occurs all through the whole excerpt by using the same structure at phrase level. For instance, each phrase consists of a present participle + a prepositional phrase ending with a reference pronoun. It is worth mentioning that not all the parallel structures are translated into similar structures in English, such as the prepositional phrase من أقصاه إلى أقصاه (the entire Arab World . . . together).

3.3.4.2 Reference

Baker (1992:189) maintains that Arabic favours pronominal reference as a common device of tracing participants and establishing cohesive links in general. There are two types of reference: endophoric, within the text and exphoric, outside the text. Each can be recognized through the context of the situation. Endophoric reference consists of anaphora and cataphora; the former refers to reference that follows the word while the latter describes pronominal reference that precedes the word. An example of cataphoric reference is derived from news discourse as follows:

In his speech, the President said. و في حديثه، قال الرئيس.

As the example shows, the pronoun (his – ه) occurs first and then comes the antecedent (the president – الرئيس). Arabic here copies the English style which opts for a stylistic variation by means of fronting the prepositional phrase (in his speech – في حديثه), hence, achieving markedness. Another example of cataphoric reference is given by Emery (1989:5) in the translation of the following example:

الى أن يتم جلاء القوات البريطانية عن الأردن تظل هذه القوات متمتعه بِ . . .

Until their evacuation from Jordan is complete, the British forces shall continue to enjoy . . .

Anaphoric reference, for example pronominalization is common in Arabic legal discourse. A good example of such anaphoric reference is the logo of the Democratic Party's nominee, Barack Obama, in the 2008 presidential election campaign: 'change we need'.

This clause can be markedly rendered with an anaphora referring back to the noun 'change' (التغييرنحتاجه). The following excerpt is an example of anaphoric reference from the Charter of the ISESCO:

تتمتع الإيسيسكو في أشخاص المسؤولين عنها والعاملين بها وفي مبانيها ومكاتبها ووثائقها ورسائلها، بالحماية والحصانة القانونية والامتيازات التي تتمتع بها منظمة التعاون الإسلامي . . .	ISESCO, its officials, personnel, premises, offices, documents and mail shall enjoy the protection, immunities and privileges enjoyed by the Organization of the Islamic Conference . . . (article 8)

<http://www.isesco.org.ma/index.php?option=com_k2&view=item&layout=item&id=3&Itemid=58&lang=ar>
<http://www.isesco.org.ma/index.php?option=com_k2&view=item&layout=item&id=3&Itemid=58&lang=en>

This pronominal system and verb conjugation in Arabic prove true its economy. That is, a verb is inflected for case, number and gender and it also agrees with its subject in such elements, the matter that makes 'the link between the verb and its subject clear even if they are separated by a number of embedded clauses with their own subjects and verbs' (Baker, 1992:187).

3.3.4.3 Conjunctions and punctuation

Generally, there are no well-defined rules for the usage of punctuation in Arabic. It varies considerably across different Arabic registers. The style sometimes follows the author's subjective judgments as in literary writing. Although Classical Arabic grammarians took the initiative towards the grammaticalization of the Arabic language, they were not concerned about the setting up of finite rules for sentence endings and punctuation.[40] In fact, punctuation marks are said to have been introduced to the Arabic language in the early twentieth century by the Egyptian scholar Ahmed Zeki, who adopted punctuation marks used in the European languages and introduced them into Arabic texts (quoted in Al-Khafaji, 2001:7). Holes (2004:251) argues that 'until perhaps the latter part of the nineteenth century much Arabic writing contained no punctuation at all and no fully standardized system of punctuation exists even today'. Holes (ibid.) goes on, saying:

> This does not in fact matter: whether punctuation is used or not, it functions alongside the native system of textual chunking, which relies on coordinating and subordinating conjunctions that perform the dual role of signalling formally the beginnings and endings of sense groups and indicating the nature of the logical or functional relationships between them.

Holes also notes that 'Arab writers still "pile up" clauses loosely connected by و (and) and ف (so), despite the introduction of the full-stop and the comma into Arabic'. و (and) 'can mark temporal sequence, simultaneous action, semantic contrast and semantic equivalence amongst other things'. ف (so) 'can be a marker of temporal sequence, purpose, result, or concession' (Holes, 1984:234).

Al-Khafaji (2001:8) has conducted research on a small literary corpus written originally in Arabic to analyse the most common punctuation marks in such texts. He found that the comma and the period are the most common (85 percent), whereas other punctuations identified in the corpus are rarely used. Analysis of various Arabic legal texts such as the AChHR, the Charter of the ISESCO, the Egyptian Constitution, Convention on the Implementation of Provisions among the Arab League, 37 texts for the Egyptian Law, 21 texts from the Supreme Constitutional Court and 146 Provisions of the Egyptian Supreme Administrative Court, online contracts and certificates, among others. I have also considered other published documents such as those in Hatim, Shunnaq and Buckley (1995) and in Mansoor (1965a). These are some of the findings of that investigation:

1. The period and the comma are the most common punctuation marks used; the former is used at the end of sentences or paragraphs. Yet, this is not always the norm since some articles end with nothing. The comma is used to separate independent clauses within the whole complete sentence or a paragraph; it is also used with appositive phrases or clauses. Other punctuation marks are used but their frequency depends on the text type such as the colon used to introduce chapters, articles in legislative documents, quotation marks in court hearings, interviews and dashes as appositives in any text type.
2. By analysing these documents, I can offer no justification for such inconsistency, nor can I derive any rules from the punctuation patterns used in different documents. I also did not present excerpts for my above argument because of word limitations.[41] In spite of the existence of such punctuation marks, conjunctions such as و (and),[42] أو (or), ف (and), كما (also / in addition), هذا (this), إن (verily), قد (indeed / verily) and و ذلك (and that) still play a major role in the Arabic punctuation system 'to compensate for the lack of adherence to strict system of punctuation and sentence division' (Al-Qinai, 1999:248).

From the above analysis, it is noteworthy that MSA shares most of its features with other language varieties in Arabic. For example, Arabic is very rich with prosodic features (assonance, alliteration, rhyme, rhythm, meter) and this applies to legal discourse. Textual features of Arabic such as lexical repetition, suffix repetition, root repetition, parallel structures, etc. are also specific to legal Arabic. Some of them, however, are more common in legal discourse such as lexical repetition.

3.4 EXERCISES AND DISCUSSIONS: FEATURES OF LEGAL ENGLISH AND LEGAL ARABIC

Exercise 1: Define the following terms and give examples from English legal documents:

1. Terms of art
2. Abstract terms
3. Archaic terms
4. Doublets and triplets

Exercise 2: Explain passivization and nominalization in legal English and legal Arabic, and provide examples from different text types.

Exercise 3: What are the common textual features used in Legal English?

Exercise 4: 'Reference and ellipsis are scarce features in legal English.' Discuss this statement in pairs.

Exercise 5: List the most common lexical, syntactic and textual features in the following document:

LAST WILL AND TESTAMENT

OF [CLIENT'S NAME]

I, [Client's name] of [City], [County's name] County, __________ am over the age of eighteen (18) years of age.

At the time I signed this Last Will and Testament, I was of sound and disposing mind and memory. I was not acting under the undue influence of any person at the time that I signed this Last Will and Testament.

I make, publish and declare this instrument to be my Last Will and Testament. By signing this document, I revoke any and all former Wills or Codicils, previously made by me, if such documents existed prior to the signing of this Last Will and Testament.

1. IDENTITY OF TESTATOR OR TESTATRIX'S FAMILY

[If the client is married, then state the following:]

1.1 I declare that I am now married to [Client's spouse] and all references in this Will to 'my spouse' are to [him or her].

[Or if the client is not married, then state the following:]

1.1 I declare that I am not currently married. All references in this Will to 'my spouse' are to the person, if any, that I marry after the date this will is signed.

[If the client has living children, then state:]

1.2 I have [Number and names of the client's children]

(a) All references in this Will to 'my children' are to such children and to any children subsequently born to or adopted by me.

[If the client does not have any living children, then state the following:]

1.2 I currently have no living children. All references in this Will to 'my children' are to any children subsequently born to or adopted by me.

[If the client's spouse has children from previous marriages, then state the following:]

My spouse has [Number of client's spouse's children from previous marriages:]

[Next: should those children be included in the will or not: If so then state:]

My spouse's children from previous marriages as identified above shall be included in this will as my children for purposes of inheritance under this Last Will and Testament.

[If those children shall not be included in the gift, then state:]

My spouse's children from previous marriages as identified above shall not be included in this will as my children for purposes of inheritance under this Last Will and Testament.

[If the client has grandchildren, then state the following:]

1.3 I have [Number of client's grandchildren:]

(a) All references to grandchildren in this will are to such grandchildren and to any other grandchildren subsequently born to or adopted by my children after the date this will is signed prior to my death.

[If the client does not have any grandchildren, then state the following:]

1.3 I have no grandchildren. All references to grandchildren in this will are to any grandchildren subsequently born to or adopted by my children after the date this will is signed prior to my death.

[If the client has deceased children, then state the following:]

1.4 I have [Number of client's deceased children] deceased children.

[If the client does not have any deceased children, then state the following:

1.4 I have no deceased children.

2. PAYMENT OF FUNERAL EXPENSES AND TAXES

2.1 I direct that my funeral expenses shall be paid by my Executor as soon as practicable after my death.

2.2 All debts, funeral expenses, taxes and administration expenses including any interest and penalties, which may be payable by reason of my death or due at the time of my death shall be charged against and paid out of my residuary estate unless my spouse and children all agree to a different payment method. I do not intend specific gifts to be exempt from taxes and expenses.

2.3 Payment for the above expenses shall not be made from the proceeds of any life insurance policies payable to my beneficiaries unless the insurance policy is payable to my estate instead of a named beneficiary.

2.4 My Executor is specifically given the right to renew and extend, in any form that my Executor deems best, any debt or charge existing at the time of my death.

3. PROPERTY BEING DISPOSED

3.1 It is my intention to dispose of all of my property that I may own or control including but not limited to all real and personal property or other interests, community and separate, which I have the right to dispose of by this Last Will and Testament.

4. BEQUESTS AND DEVISES

[If the client desires to make any specific bequests, then state:

4.1 I make the following specific gifts: I give, bequeath and devise to [Recipient's name or names and list the property given:]

[Describe the specific bequest]

I give, bequeath and devise the rest and residue of my property, except for the specific gift made above, including but not limited to real, personal, separate and community property, wherever situated of which I may die seized or possessed or to which I may be entitled at the time of my death to my spouse, [Client's spouse].

[If the client does not want to make any specific gifts, then state the following:]

4.1 I give, bequeath and devise all of my property, real, personal, separate and community, wherever situated of which I may die seized or possessed or to which I may be entitled at the time of my death to my spouse, [Client's spouse].

4.2 In the event that my spouse predeceases me, then I give, devise and bequeath all of my property, real, personal, separate and community, of every kind and character and wheresoever situated to my children in equal shares per stirpes.

4.3 By use of the term 'per stirpes' I mean that if any of my children have predeceased me, then I direct my Executor to give that predeceased child's share to his or her issue in the inheritance that the deceased child would have received if the child had survived me.

4.4 If at the time of my death I leave surviving me any other child or children born to or adopted by me subsequent to the date of this Will, then it is my will and I direct that this Paragraph (4.4) shall inure to the benefit of and shall include as a beneficiary hereunder along with my children named above, any and all children born to or adopted by me so that all of my children shall take and receive such property under this provision of my Will in equal proportions.

4.5 If all of my children should predecease me and there are no other children born to or adopted by me, and there are no issue of such predeceased child or children, then I bequeath and devise all of the rest and residue of my property, real, personal, separate and community to [State the names of the alternate beneficiaries and the amount of property they shall inherit and whether it shall be an equal or unequal division such as to share and share alike in equal shares.]

4.6 Should the beneficiaries described above predecease me, then I bequeath and devise all my property of whatever character to my heirs at law, to share and share alike in equal shares.

4.7 In the event that any beneficiary or devisee under this will shall die within a period of ninety (90) days after my death, then such beneficiary or devisee shall be deemed to have predeceased me. In that event, I direct that all the provisions of this Will be construed upon that assumption.

<www.worldlawdirect.com/>

Exercise 6: List the most common lexical, syntactic and textual features of the following text:

قانون الاحوال الشخصية لعام 1959

الباب الثاني

الفصل الأول: المحرمات وزواج الكتابيات

المادة الثانية عشرة :

يشترط لصحة الزواج أن تكون المرأة غير محرمة شرعاً على من يريد التزوج بها.

المادة الثالثة عشرة :

أسباب التحريم قسمان مؤبدة ومؤقتة فالمؤبدة هي القرابة والمصاهرة والرضاع والمؤقتة الجمع بين زوجات يزدن على أربع وعدم الدين السماوي والتطليق ثلاثاً وتعلق حق الغير بنكاح أو عدة وزواج إحدى المحرمين مع قيام الزوجة بالأخرى.

المادة الرابعة عشرة :

يحرم على الرجل أن يتزوج من النسب أمه وجدته وإن علت وبنته وبنت إبنه وبنت بنته وإن نزلت. وأخته وبنت أخته وبنت أخيه وإن نزلت وعمته وعمة أصوله وخالته وخالة أصوله .
ويحرم على المرأة التزوج بنظير ذلك من الرجال.

المادة الخامسة عشرة :

يحرم على الرجل أن يتزوج بنت زوجته التي دخل بها وأم زوجته التي عقد عليها. وزوجة أصله وإن علا وزوجة فرعه وإن نزل.

المادة السادسة عشرة :

كل من تحرم بالقرابة والمصاهرة تحرم بالرضاع إلّا فيما أستثني شرعاً.

المادة السابعة عشرة :

يصح للمسلم أن يتزوج كتابية، ولا يصح زواج المسلمة من غير المسلم.

المادة الثامنة عشرة :

إسلام أحد الزوجين قبل الآخر تابع لأحكام الشريعة في بقاء الزوجية أو التفريق بين الزوجين .

<https://docs.google.com/file/d/OB81TLJi5y4TKcXF3MFJnUTFwUmc/edit?pli=1>

Exercise 7:

1. What are the system-based and culture-specific terms in the above document? Explain these terms in English.
2. Translate the document into English.
3. In small groups discuss the procedures you used to translate the above document (refer to chapter 4 for information on the procedures of translation and techniques of adaptation).

Exercise 8: Distinguish between formality in legal English and legal Arabic, and give examples to support your arguments.

Exercise 9: Read the parallel Arabic–English versions of the Arab Charter of Human Rights, discuss the use of gender terms and pronouns in the Arabic version, and compare them to the English version.

Exercise 10: Compare between archaic terms in English and their counterparts in Arabic.

Exercise 11:

1. What are the elements that make the following Arabic excerpt complex?
2. Give other examples of complex sentences from English and Arabic legal documents and list the major elements that make them complex.

في حال مخالفة المورد لكل أو بعض شروط التعاقد أو في حال امتناعه أو عرقلته للتوريد بما يمس بمصلحة وزارة الصحة أو يعرض مصالحها للضرر يحق لوزارة المالية مصادرة كفالة حسن التنفيذ والرجوع عليه بالتعويض عن كل عطل أو ضرر لحق بها كما أن لها الحق في الحصول على المواد التي يتخلف المورد عن توفيرها من المورد الذي يليه في السعر أو الشراء بالطرق التي تراها محققة لمصلحتها وإلغاء التعاقد معه ودفع فروق الأسعار مضافًا إليها 10 % مصاريف إدارية من ضمانته البنكية وليس للمورد الذي خالف أي شرط من شروط التعاقد أو تخلف عن أو عرقل عمليات التوريد الحق في المطالبة بأية تعويضات أو المطالبة باسترداد كفالة حسن التنفيذ أو المطالبة بفروق الأسعار إذا تمكنت الوزارة من توفير تلك المواد بسعر اقل من سعر المناقصة الذي تم التعاقد بموجبه وفى حال عدم كفاية الضمانة لتغطية فروق الأسعار لوزارة المالية الحق في خصم أي مبالغ تتبقى من مستحقاته لديها.

<www.mof.gov.ps>

Exercise 12: Discuss the parallel translation of the following doublets and triplets in Examples 1, 2 and 3:

1. Is the technique of translating them justified?
2. Suggest other translations if you disagree with these translations.

Example 1

وصيا شرعيا و متكلما مرعيا	legal guardian and competent spokesman
بطوعي و اختياري	voluntarily and of my own free will
و انا لست مدهوشا و متمتع بقواي العقلية	being fully aware and of sound mind
عصمتي و عقد نكاحي	my matrimonial authority and to my contract of marriage.

Example 2

زوجتك و أنكحتك	I have given you my daughter in marriage
قبلت و رضيت بزواجها و نكاحها	I accept your daughter in marriage
المفقود الغائب	the missing person

(Hatim, Shunnaq and Buckley, 1995: 86–87)

Example 3

THIS LEASE AGREEMENT made and entered into this _________ day of _______, 20____, (Lease Agreement)	حُرر عقد الإيجار هذا في يوم______من شهر___________سنة___________ 20______
Whereas Landlord desires to lease the Premises to Tenant upon the terms and conditions as herein contained; (Lease Agreement)	بما أن أن المستأجر يرغب في تأجير العقار من المؤجر بموجب الشروط الواردة في هذا العقد؛
The standing instructions shall become null and void if the Account does not have sufficient balance to cover the transaction. (Account Opening Form, article 2.5)	تعتبر التعليمات القائمة باطلة و لاغية اذا كان الرصيد الموجود في حساب صاحب الحساب كافية لتغطية قيمة العملية.

Exercise 13: From the discussion of the textual features of legal Arabic,

1. What are the textual features specific to legal Arabic?
2. What are the commonalities between the textual features of legal Arabic and other Arabic registers?
3. Analyse the textual features of the Preamble of the Iraqi Constitution.

Exercise 14: 'Boundaries between legal Arabic and other Arabic registers (for example Media Arabic) are fuzzy'. Do you agree or disagree with this statement? Prove your answers with examples and discuss them in small groups.

4 Framework for data analysis

4.1 INTRODUCTION

Chapter 3 discussed the features of English and Arabic legal discourse for the purpose of figuring out the similarities and differences between Arabic and English legal discourse. This chapter introduces the methodology for our analysis and the documents chosen for data analysis. It will be divided into three main parts, the first of which will discuss contrastive analysis as applied to translationally-parallel texts, mainly, Vinay and Darbelnet (1995). The techniques of adaptation, cited in Alcaraz Varó and Hughes (2002), will also be discussed because they are applicable in the translation of legal discourse for example (English–Spanish), hence will be used as guidelines according to which dissimilarities between English and Arabic are investigated. Baker's (1992/2011) model on levels of equivalence will be of value to the method and the analysis of data. It provides useful and relevant information and examples to our methodology and data analysis on the lexical and syntactic levels. The second part will introduce the two-stage framework for data analysis, namely, the quantitative frequency analysis of the translation techniques and the qualitative critical analysis. The third part introduces the list of documents for data analysis.

4.2 VINAY AND DARBELNET'S MODEL

In *Comparative Stylistics of French and English: A Methodology for Translation*, Vinay and Darbelnet (1995) propose their contrastive stylistic analysis of translation. They set up their model according to three basic microlinguistic aspects: vocabulary (lexicon), grammar (syntax) and composition (message) as they put it. The following table illustrates their three-dimensional planes of utterance (1995:30):

Table 4.1 Vinay and Darbelnet's planes of utterance

PLANES	I	II	III
metalinguistic information	units of thought (monemes)	phrases and molecules	tone, links, emphasis (context)
Borders of Stylistics	**Lexicon**	**Structure**	**Message**
microlinguistics	units of translation (vocabulary)	morphology and syntax (grammar)	sentences, paragraphs (composition)

Vinay and Darbelnet claim that 'certain stylistic effects cannot be transposed to the TL without upsetting the syntactic order or even the lexis' (1995:84). To tackle this stylistic problem, they suggest two general translation methods and seven translation procedures to be followed by the translator according to the above planes. The two main translation methods include direct and oblique translation.

4.2.1 Direct translation

Direct translation is further divided into the following subcategories:

4.2.1.1 Borrowing

The SL word form is transferred to the TL to fill a lexical gap or to create a certain effect. For instance, hijab, kebab and intifadah are taken from Arabic to English; كمبيوتر ، انترنت ، فيس بوك ، تويتر (computer, internet, Facebook, Twitter), are transferred from English to Arabic.

4.2.1.2 Calque

A calque is 'special kind of borrowing' (Vinay and Darbelnet, 1995:32) by transferring the same expression and structure of the SL by means of literal translation. Calques are clear in the translation of common collocation, names of organisations, the components of compounds and perhaps phrases as in the famous English–Arabic pairs: skyscrapers – ناطحات السحاب, and Spiderman – الرجل العنكبوت, and the Arab Spring – الربيع العربي.

4.2.1.3 Literal translation

Whereas literal translation can occur between languages of the same families and cultures such as Indo-European languages (Vinay and Darbelnet, 1995:33–4), it is far-fetched between languages of different families such as English and Arabic. It can sometimes be applicable as in the English–Arabic pair: I get up early every day – أستيقظ مبكراً كل يوم,

I get up	early	every	day
أستيقظ	مبكراً	كل	يوم

or the Arabic–English pair وصلت إلى المطار ليلا (في الليل) (I arrived at the airport at night).

وصلت	إلى	المطار	في	الليل/ليلًا
I arrived	at	the airport	at	night

These examples show that the task of the translator is limited to observing 'the adherence to the linguistic servitudes of the TL' (ibid.). Literal translation is the 'author's prescription for good translation' (Munday, 2001:27; 2012:87) unless the technique is unacceptable because it:

- gives a different meaning
- has no meaning
- is impossible for structural reasons

- 'does not have a corresponding expression within the metalinguistic experience of the TL'
- corresponds to something at a different level of language. (Munday, 2001:57)

The above restrictions show that literal translation cannot lead to 'a good translation'. If we take legal translation as an example, one can see that there is a certain degree of adherence to the ST, but the translator still faces, at some points, some cases where literal translation is not enough and adaptation or transposition is applied.

4.2.2 Oblique translation

Oblique translation involves the following four sub-classes:

4.2.2.1 Transposition

Transposition 'involves replacing one word class with another without changing the meaning of the message' (Vinay and Darbelnet, 1995:36). For example, the English sentence: 'The economy did not stop growing' can be translated into Arabic in two ways:

1. لم يتوقف الاقتصاد عن النمو
2. ينمو الاقتصاد نمواً ثابتاً

The first translation is literal, where no change has occurred, while in the second translation a transposition has occurred on two levels: when the verb ينمو (is growing) replaced the noun (growing) نمو and when the absolute object plus the adjective نمواً ثابتاً (steadily growing) replaced the verb (did not stop) لم يتوقف. Transposition can be either obligatory or optional as in the following two examples:

1. إدارتها إدارة فعالة – Operating it effectively (obligatory)
2. He heard noise when he got up – سمع ضجة عند استيقاظه (optional)

In the first example, an obligatory transposition has occurred when the Arabic phrase إدارة فعالة (effective management) which is categorized as an absolute object in Arabic which has no direct equivalent in the TT, is translated as an adverb. It can also be translated as a prepositional phrase: 'in an effective way'. More precisely, the noun (إدارة) and its adjective (فعالة) are translated into English as an adverb (effectively). In the second example, an optional transposition has occurred with the translation of the phrasal verb (got up) as a verbal noun (استيقاظه). Thus, a transposition has not occurred if the whole sentence is translated as:

2a. سمع ضجة حينما استيقظ

4.2.2.2 Modulation

Modulation entails a change of the message due to change of the point of view. A negative SL expression is changed to a positive TL expression such as 'it is not a strong argument' which can be translated as حجة واهيه. Like transposition, it can be obligatory or optional. It is optional if منبع العلم (the fountain of knowledge) is translated as 'the root of knowledge', but obligatory if one translates حجة باردة (cold argument) as 'weak argument'.

4.2.2.3 Equivalence

Equivalence in Vinay and Darbelnet (1995) is not the same term used by other theorists such as Nida (1964). A typical example is that of the proverbs and clichés that describe the same situation across languages by different stylistic means. This is exemplified by the English–Arabic proverb pair:

Birds of a feather flock together – الطيور على أشكالها تقع

4.2.2.4 Adaptation

Adaptation occurs in cases where the translator faces a situation in the SL culture which does not exist in the TL culture as in the case of translating story and film titles. This technique will be useful in translating culture-specific terms and expressions from and into Arabic.

4.3 ALCARAZ VARÓ AND HUGHES' TECHNIQUES OF ADAPTATION

In their book *Legal Translation Explained*, Alcaraz Varó and Hughes (2002) discuss legal translation between English and Spanish and the 'techniques of adaptation' which they suggest can deal with legal translation problems.

Alcaraz Varó and Hughes argue that word-by-word translation does not exist between languages and it is 'a metaphor albeit a buried one' (2002:180). Saying so, they differ from Vinay and Darbelnet who claim that literal translation is the author's prescription for 'good translation' (1995:34). As Alcaraz Varó and Hughes believe that 'the idea of identity is illusory', they support the idea that there must be some adaptation while translating between two languages, or more specifically they speak of 'naturalness or dynamic equivalence' (2002:179–80). Nevertheless, they do not advocate for free translation since there is 'no place for such free-ranging adaptation in the translation of legal texts' (ibid.). They rather meant to deal with translation by adopting Hamlet's principle 'by indirections, find directions out' (ibid.). To achieve this, they were inspired by Vázquez-Ayora's book (1977) entitled: *Introducción a la Traductología* and present the following techniques for producing a natural version of the original:

(a) transposition
(b) expansion
(c) modulation
(d) modifiers
(e) double conjunctions
(f) thematization
(g) textual coherence

(Alcaraz Varó and Hughes, 2002:181–90)

In the following section, we will only be concerned with the discussion of transposition, expansion and modulation. Other elements are not dealt with as they are beyond the scope of this book.

4.3.1 Transposition

According to Alcaraz Varó and Hughes (2002:181), transposition describes 'the substitution of one category for another, on the basis that they may be fairly said to possess the same semantic weight or equivalent semic density'. For example, 'for late delivery' (ibid.) can be translated into Arabic as لتأخر التسليم (due to delay in the delivery) where the SL adjective 'late' was rendered in the TL as a noun تأخر (delay). Categories of transposition include (i) verb for noun; (ii) pronoun for noun; (iii) noun for adjective; (iv) noun for verb; (v) active or impersonal form for passive; (vi) relative or noun phrase for gerund or prepositional phrase with 'with'; and (vii) noun phrase for adverbial phrase (ibid.:181–3).

4.3.2 Expansion

For Alcaraz Varó and Hughes (2002:184), expansion, periphrasis, or explicitation, as they put it, is 'one of the techniques that may be called for in translating virtually any part of speech, often in conjunction with transposition'. They maintain that this technique is helpful in translating prepositions and/or adverbials. An example of expansion is 'irrevocable divorce' (طلاق بائن لا رجعة فيه). In this example, the term 'irrevocable' is rendered into Arabic as بائن then the translator opted for an expansion of بائن with لا رجعة فيه to distinguish it from another type of divorce (revocable divorce) in which one can return his divorcee to his custody.

4.3.3 Modulation

Modulation involves changes to semantic categories or even alteration of the processes by which thoughts are expressed (Alcaraz Varó and Hughes, 2002:185). For them, it is more common in both general and literary translation than in specialized and technical translation as it involves a spill of the translator's own point of view and change of style through rhetorical figures.[43]

Discussion of the above techniques is not totally different from that given by Vinay and Darbelnet (1995).

4.4 BAKER'S LEVELS OF EQUIVALENCE

In her book *In Other Words*, Baker (1992/2011) divided the text into its hierarchy of constituent parts, starting from the word level, up to text level. The following review is a brief outline of Baker's multidimensional levels.

4.4.1 Equivalence at word level and above word level

Baker (1992:19, 2011:16–17) discusses the process of achieving equivalence at word level, referring to the importance of semantic fields (superordinates, hyponyms) to the translator in:

appreciating the value that a word has in a given system; and
developing strategies for dealing with non-equivalence.

The second point above is effective in understanding the non-correspondence between Arabic–English pairs of words due to them being culturally-dependent; they need a special strategy for translating them. That is, semantic fields help us determine the similarities and the differences between English and Arabic. Baker (2011:18–23) explains with examples from different languages the common problems of non-equivalence at word-level. These problems are listed below:

1. culture-specific concepts
2. the source-language concept is not lexicalized in the target language
3. the source-language word is semantically complex
4. the source and target languages make different distinctions in meaning
5. the target language lacks a superordinate
6. the target language lacks a specific term (hyponym)
7. differences in physical or interpersonal perspective
8. differences in expressive meaning
9. differences in form
10. differences in frequency and purpose of using specific words
11. the use of loan words in the source text.

Baker (2011:23–43) presents the strategies that professional translators use to deal with these problems. These strategies are given below:

1. translation by a more general word (superordinate)
2. translation by a more neutral/less expressive word
3. translation by cultural substitution
4. translation by using a loan word or a loan word plus explanation
5. translation by paraphrase using a related word
6. translation by paraphrase using unrelated words
7. translation by omission
8. translation by illustration.

For equivalence above word level, Baker discusses the lexical patterning between two languages and lists some problems of and strategies for translating collocations and idioms. She exemplifies this by referring to collocations and idioms in English and Arabic (1992:69–73; 2011:58–64). These examples are worth noting below:

> The engrossing effect of source text patterning (for example break the law – يخالف القانون).
>
> Misinterpreting the meaning of the source-language collocation. (A man of modest means – رجل مظهره متواضع و بسيط.)
>
> The tension between accuracy and naturalness (good / bad law) in English will be قانون عادل / غير عادل (just / unjust law) in Arabic.
>
> Culture-specific collocations and idioms: the problem with these is that they may not have an equivalent in the TL. In formal letters, Baker gives the Arabic concluding fixed expression و تفضلوا بقبول فائق الاحترام – 'and be kind enough to accept [our] highest respects' which corresponds to the English expressions 'yours faithfully or yours sincerely' though 'it bears no direct relationship to them' as Baker puts it.

Baker (ibid.:73–77; 2011:75–85) has suggested six strategies for rendering fixed expressions, these strategies are:

1. using an idiom of similar meaning and form
2. using an idiom of similar meaning but dissimilar form
3. borrowing the source language idiom
4. translation by paraphrase
5. translation by omission of a play on idiom
6. translation by omission of entire idiom.

These strategies will be of importance in data analysis because they will be applied in the analysis of archaic and template terms and expressions.

4.4.2 Grammatical equivalence

Baker (1992:83, 2011:93) views grammar as 'a straitjacket, forcing the translator along a certain course which may or may not follow that of the source text as closely as the translator would like to'. She (ibid.:90–102) discusses the constraints of grammatical equivalence across languages with particular reference to English and Arabic. This comparison was done with regard to number, gender, person, tense, aspect and voice.

4.4.3 Textual equivalence

Baker (1992:119–179, 2011:133–176) discusses the textual equivalence in relation to the thematic and information structures (theme–rheme). She also discusses the meaning, choice and markedness (fronting). She concludes her discussion of the thematic structure of sentences by highlighting the strategies for resolving the tension between syntactic and communicative functions in translation through 'voice change, change of verb, nominalization and extraposition' (1992:167–171).

Baker discusses cohesion as the second element of textual equivalence. She (1992:180; 2011:190) defines cohesion as 'the network of lexical, grammatical and other relations which provide links between various parts of the text. It is a surface relation; it connects together the actual words and expressions that we can see or hear'. She compared between English and Arabic cohesion. For English, she refers to Halliday and Hasan's (1976) five main cohesive categories: reference, substitution, ellipsis, conjunction and lexical repetition. She also contrasted these elements with Arabic whenever necessary.

The above discussion shows that transposition and literal translation presuppose a solid knowledge of the linguistic structures of the SL and the TL whereas modulation, equivalence and adaptation require additional experience on part of the translator to be able to locate texts in their social contexts. It is also clear that both transposition and adaptation apply in the process of translating from English into Arabic and vice-versa. Thus, they will be useful as tools of analysing translationally-parallel legal texts.

4.5 METHODOLOGY

The above models pave the way to the method we will adopt in the analysis of the data (translationally-parallel authentic legal texts). The method will be applied to comparing and contrasting the ST and the TT with respect to some of the areas of difference discussed in the previous chapter. The analysis will involve some elements of the lexical and syntactic levels only.[44] Reference will also be eventually made to elements of omissions and additions besides the procedures of translation referred to earlier. The aim of the comparison is two-fold: (i) to describe how these areas are rendered; and (ii) what procedures (for example adaptations) are followed to overcome such hurdles. Thus, the method of analysis will be divided into a quantitative and a qualitative critical analysis. The following section introduces the elements that will be analysed on both the lexical and the syntactic levels.

4.5.1 The lexical level

Discussion of lexis means dealing with the text under sentence level, more specifically, at word level or phrase level. Lexis describes the semantic fields, synonymy relations, collocations, etc. Among the elements that will be under investigation at this level are archaic and template terms (English–Arabic–English), religious, culture-specific and system-based terms (Arabic–English–Arabic).

4.5.2 The syntactic level

In this section, we will discuss two syntactic areas of difference between English and Arabic which are commonly used in legal discourse, namely, modal auxiliaries and passivization. At this stage, a brief discussion of both elements is given below.

4.5.2.1 Modal auxiliaries in English and Arabic

Modal auxiliaries are important in the case of legal translation since they define aspects of obligation, possibilities, etc. Because the modal system in both English and Arabic is different, the task of the translator is challenging; if modals are not rendered accurately, they will leave the TT subject to many interpretations.

4.5.2.2 Modal auxiliaries in English

In chapter 3 (3.2.2.6), we discussed the most common modal auxiliaries in legal discourse. In this section, we will discuss auxiliaries in English in a bit more detail. They are divided into primary auxiliaries and modal auxiliaries. With the former, there is a variation in the present tense form of the verb for achieving agreement with the subject. But this is not true about the latter. A modal auxiliary occurs once and always at the beginning of a verbal phrase as in 'will have been writing'. The following is a list of the modal auxiliaries:

1. will, shall, may, can, must and ought to
2. dare and need (more marginal) but more modal than others
3. used to, have to, be able to, be willing to, be to and be going to (closely related semantically with some differences)
4. is to: problematic. (Palmer, 1990:3; Morley, 2000:35; and Coates, 1983:4)

Characteristics of English modal auxiliaries

Modal auxiliaries are generally characterized by what Palmer (1990:3–4) and Coates (1983:4) call 'NICE' criteria:

- negative form with n't (can't, mustn't)
- inversion with the subject (can I? must I?)
- code (he will come and so will she)
- emphasis or emphatic affirmation (Ann could solve the problem).

There are also some other elements that distinguish the modal from the primary auxiliaries, as well as from all other verbs:

- no 's' form of the 3rd person singular (cans)
- no non-finite forms (to can, musting)
- no co-occurrence (he may will come).

Nevertheless, these characteristics do not apply to all modals:

- May has no-(n't).
- Must does not have past form.
- Ought to is the only one that requires 'to'.
- Dare and need are both modals and non-modals. When they occur as modals, the first two NICE criteria are applicable: he daren't go, dare he go?
- Is to conforms to the NICE standards but Palmer (1987:158–61) argues that this is also true of the verb to be when it is not an auxiliary.
- Had better has no 's' form, no finite forms, no occurrence with other modals. It can be followed by an infinitive without to.
- Would rather can be explained in terms of would as a form of will.

Types of English modals

Linguists differ among them in classifying modals, but we can argue that there are three basic subcategories of modality, namely: epistemic,[45] deontic[46] (discussed below), and dynamic[47] (Nuyts, 2006:2). Hoffman (1976), Jenkins (1972), Perkins (1982), Coates (1983), Sweetser (1982), Huddleston (1988) and Palmer (1990) agree that modals can be classified into epistemic and deontic. Yet other linguists, von Wright (1951), Quirk et al. (1985) give different classifications. In his book on modality and logic (1951:1–2), von Wright distinguishes between four types of modals: 'epistemic, deontic, alethic and existential'. The following table offers a brief account of the four types:

Table 4.2 Types of modals according to von Wright

Epistemic modals	They are concerned with a subjective judgment of the proposition. They convey the meaning of verified, undecided, falsified through may (undecided) and must (inference of the speaker).
Deontic modals	They are concerned with influencing actions, states, or events. They express what is obligatory, permitted, or forbidden. Thus, they are subjective as it is the person who permits or forbids and they are also performative.
Alethic modals	They are the main concern of logicians. For example, 'John is a bachelor, so he must be unmarried.' Must is confusing as alethic or epistemic.
Existential modals	They express quantificational logic through the use of some, any, all, etc. For instance, 'Lions can be dangerous.'

Leech and Svartvik (1975:140–2) classify modality into 'volition,[48] permission and obligation'. Quirk et al. (1985) present their classification of modals into the following two types:

1. intrinsic[49] (permission, obligation, volition)
2. extrinsic[50] (possibility/ability, necessity, prediction).

Leech and Svartvik's three-dimensional classification corresponds to von Wright's (1951) types of modality, 'epistemic, deontic and alethic'.[51] The following diagram presents Palmer's (1990:37) classification of modals:

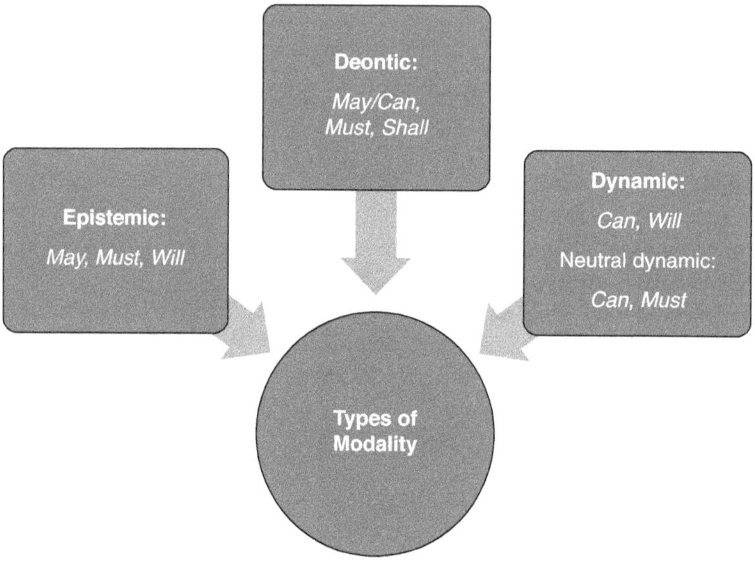

Figure 4.1 Palmer's types of modals.

Because deontic modals are common in the language of legal discourse, we will only be concerned with discussing them in this book.

DEONTIC MODALITY

Palmer (1990:69) argues that 'deontic modals are essentially performative', or as he puts it, 'the language as action' (1986:121). By using a deontic modal, a speaker may actually 'give permission (may, can); lay an obligation (must); or make a promise or threat (shall)' (Palmer, 1990: 69). There are two main types of deontic modality: possibility and necessity. Possibility is further divided into permission and command. Following is a brief account of each of these types:

Possibility: permission Permission is represented by may and can. May is used in a more formal context as given in the following examples:

> If you want to recall the doctor, you may do so.
>
> Can I pinch a ciggie? Course you can.

(Ibid, 1990:70)

Possibility: command Can is used to convey a command, often an impolite kind:

> Oh, you can leave me out.
>
> (ibid.:71)

Can and may are used interchangeably to issue a command as in:

> You can say that again.
>
> You may take it from me.
>
> (ibid.)

Necessity Necessity expresses the speaker's or writer's authority when he/she speaks or writes. Shall and must are used to express necessity. Consider the following instance:

> I have been telling Peter, you know, 'you must get into permanent jobs'.
>
> (Palmer, 1990:73)

Shall is stronger than must. It not only issues an obligation, it also guarantees that this obligation will happen. Sometimes the future meaning of shall overlaps with its deontic meaning. That is why deontic modals do not normally occur with *I* and *We* as their subject. With can and may, it would be odd to give oneself permission.

Negation of deontic modals

Quirk et al. (1985:794–9) and Palmer (1990:39) summarize the main aspects of negating deontic modality in the following table:

Table 4.3 Negation of English deontic modals

Type of modality	*Positive*	*Negative modality*	*Negative proposition*
Deontic possibility	may/can	may not/can't	____/(needn't)
Deontic necessity	must	needn't	mustn't

4.5.2.3 Modal Auxiliaries in Arabic

The richness of literature on the English modals lies in sharp contrast with the scarcity of studies on the Arabic modals. Being aware of the fact that modality is considered a universal aspect of human languages, some writers, however, have managed to discuss them within their writings on Arabic grammar and linguistics, namely, Wright (1967), Al-Karooni (1996), Suleiman (1999), Badawi, Carter and Gully (2004), Abdel-Fattah (2005) and Ryding (2005).

> Modality in Arabic can be described as 'a pragmatico-semantic category, a product of a culturally acquired attitude expressed by the speaker with the help of a qualifying expression (i.e. a formula, a verbal form, or a particle) towards a statement or a proposition embodied in his/her utterance.
>
> (Al-Karooni, 1996:76)

Anghelescu (in Suleiman, 1999:130) defined modals in Arabic as 'expressions which introduce further qualifications to a given sentence, the whole then becomes a different sentence'. Not all modals in Arabic are verbs; they may be nominal expressions that initiate the sentence and are preceded by the partitive 'min' and beginning with nominaliser (al-). They occur in three grammatical forms: passive (المتفق – agreed), participle (المعقول – reasonable), or an adjective (الواضح – clear). أنْ (to) and أنَّ (that) are sentence connectors and are considered part of the modal expression. According to Anghelescu (in Suleiman, 1999:138), *an* 'refers to a non-present fact' whereas *anna* 'situates a fact in the present or past'. There are also some adverbs in Arabic that act as modal expressions such as قلما ، طالما ، نادرا ما ، قليلا ما ، غالبا ما ، كثيرا ما (rarely, as long as, seldom, seldom, often, often). Moreover, there are some negative forms that are considered modals in Arabic such as لابد ، لاشك ، مازال (still, no doubt, must).

Types of Arabic modals

Suleiman (1999), Abdel-Fattah (2005) and Badawi, Carter and Gully (2004) categorized Arabic modal expressions and phrases into six main categories: epistemic, alethic, deontic[52], evaluative, boulomaic[53] and temporal.[54] We are concerned with the discussion of deontic modals as they are the most relevant to the purpose of this book.

DEONTIC MODALS

This type of modal expresses obligation, permission, or prohibition (Abdel-Fattah, 2005:41–2).

Obligation is represented by the following modal expressions:

> لابد أن ، من الواجب أن ، يجب أن ، ينبغي أن ، من المطلوب ، عليك \عليه أن
> It is a must that; it is a must that; must; should; it is demanded that; it is incumbent on you / him that (author's translation)

Permission is expressed through the following:

> يمكن(ك) ، ممكن ، من الجائز ، يجوز(لك) أن
> You may; may; it is possible; you may + infinitive (author's translation)

Prohibition involves the following expression: ممنوع

Badawi, Carter and Gully (2004:394–421) summarize the main Arabic deontic modal auxiliaries and their English counterparts as given below:

1. Must, ought, should: ينبغي ينبغي أن نيسرها لها	We ought to make it easier for it. يجب (أن) أو (على)
2. It is compulsory, incumbent on : يجب أن نتوقف عندهم قليلاً.	We must pause with them a little.
3. Must not, should not : لا يجب لا يجب أن تشكك فيه.	You should not doubt it. or It is not obligatory that you doubt.

With must not, the subordinated verb is negated in Arabic translation: . . .لابد ألا. . .بـجيـ ألا.

يجب ألا □ نفهم منها ما يفهمه أدباء ومفكرو أوروبا.	We must not understand from it what the scholars and intellectuals of Europe. or, It is necessary that we do not understand from it what intellectuals of Europe understand.

Abdel-Fattah (2005:42–45) offers some techniques for translating modals from English into Arabic and vice versa:

1. Classification of modals: to understand the real category of the modal involved (i.e. epistemic or root (deontic or dynamic)).
2. Modal rephrasing: paraphrasing the modal to its periphrastic counterpart.
3. Modal retranslation: retranslation after the first draft is finished helps in making sure that this is the 'original' rendering of the modal.
4. Utilizing ambiguity: sometimes ambiguity is utilized in translation only if there is another ambiguous counterpart in the target language.

4.5.2.4 Passivization in English and Arabic

Discussion of the passive is important for our analysis as it explains what it is and how it is composed in both languages, hence it will be useful to see how this structure is rendered from English into Arabic and vice versa.

Passive in English

Voice, in English, is a grammatical element that distinguishes between the active and the passive status of a verb phrase. It is further defined by Quirk et al. (1985:159) as 'the grammatical category which makes it possible to view the action of a sentence in either of two ways, without change in the facts reported'. This definition is exemplified below:

1. The judge made a decision.
1a. A decision was made by the judge.

The passive, in English, is formed by adding a form of the auxiliaries 'be' or 'get' in the same tense of the verb phrase plus the past participle of the verb, for example:

2. <u>The assembly issued the report</u>. (Active)
   (Subject) + (Verb) + (Object)
2a. <u>The report was issued by the assembly</u>. (Passive)
   (Object) + (auxiliary, be (past)) + (ed-form of issue) + by + (subject)

Other auxiliaries such as get can be used to form the passive but this is more likely to happen in informal contexts. They also can occur as a 'resulting copula' in sentences like 'my mother is getting old'; 'in sentences which could not be expanded by an agent: we are getting bogged down in all sorts of problems' (Quirk et al. 1985:160). English passive is used to obscure the agent; to avoid the heaviness in sentence initial position; to focus on some elements in the clause rather than others; if it is not important to mention the agent; or if the agent can be inferred from the context. Based on the classification of the English verbs into intransitive and transitive, only transitive verbs happen to be passivized. Consider the following examples:

3. The judge issued the verdict. (mono-transitive, active)
3a. The verdict was issued by the judge. (passive)
4. The teacher gave the student a certificate. (di-transitive)
4a. The student was given a certificate by the teacher. (passive)
4b. A certificate was given to the student by the teacher. (passive)

Nevertheless, some transitive verbs cannot be passivized, others occur in passive only.[55] Passive constructions are categorized according to Quirk et al. (ibid.:167–171) into the following subclasses:

(A) CENTRAL PASSIVES

'True' passive (ibid.:167) or 'agentive passives', as Svartvik (1966:141) puts it, is the main type of passive where formal correspondence of content occurs as in examples 3 and 4 above. This type can be 'agentive or agentless' (Quirk et al., 1985:168) as in:

5. The commander-in-chief has made the decision.
5a. A decision has been made by the commander-in-chief.
5b. A decision has been made.

(B) SEMI-PASSIVES

This class of passives is also known as 'quasi-agentive passives' (Svartvik, 1966:147). It involves either verbal or adjectival passives; each of which have their own characteristics. Verbal passives allow for 'an active analogue' as in the following examples cited in Quirk et al. (1985:168):

6. We are encouraged to go on with the project.
6a. (The results) encourage us to go on with the project.

Semi-passives are like an adjective in that they 'coordinate the participle with an adjective; modify the participle with quite, rather, more, etc.' as in 'we feel rather encouraged and content . . .'; 'replace be by a lexical copular verb such as feel or seem' as in 'Leonard seemed very interested in and keen on linguistics' (ibid.).

(C) PSEUDO-PASSIVES

This third category includes a formal, passive-like structure for which reason it is classified under passive. However, it neither requires addition of an agent nor does it accept a change to the active voice. The following examples from Quirk et al. (1985:170) explain the above notions:

7. The building is already demolished.
8. The modern world is getting more highly industrialized and mechanized.

This category is known as the 'statal passive' in which the verb 'to be' is not acting as an auxiliary, but it is rather a copula (ibid.).

Passive in Arabic

Passive, in Arabic, has been the subject of study by grammarians, namely, Wright (1967), Cantarino (1974) and Holes (2004). It has also been studied contrastively to English passive in the works of Khalil (1993), Al-Khafaji (1996), among some others.

It was stated earlier that English passive is composed of an auxiliary plus the past participle of the verb plus the agentive 'by-phrase'. Arabic, on the contrary, does not have an equivalent to the 'by-phrase' and the way passive is composed differs. Verbs in Arabic are passivized by means of changing the vocalic pattern through morphology such as كَتَبَ (to write) which in passive is changed into كُتِبَ (was written). In this, transitivity is not the determinant of passivization in Arabic as it is in English. Like English, the rules of forming passive have some exceptions. Forms having the meaning of to contract a disease, to be stricken with a disease occur only in the passive:

زُكم الطفل.	The child caught cold.
سُلت المرأة.	The woman developed tuberculosis.
حُم الولد.	The boy caught fever.
جُن الرجل.	The man went mad.

Nevertheless, the above examples can occur in the active voice in which case the passivized verbs will change to verbal nouns as follows:

أصاب الطفل الزكام.	The child caught cold.
أصاب المرأة السل.	The woman developed tuberculosis.
أصاب الولد الحمى.	The boy caught fever.
أصاب الرجل الجنون.	The man went mad.

Wright (1967:49) argues that 'both the verbal forms both primitive and derivative, have two voices, the active and the passive'. He adds a third type which he calls 'middle voice' such as انكسر (it was broken). It is worth mentioning that Wright's idea of 'middle voice' is further explained by Al-Khafaji (1996:23) by identifying two types of passive: formal and notional passive. The former is the normal type of passive while the latter is quite abnormal as the verb occurs in its active form but still gives the meaning of the passive. He states that Arabic flexible word order and the richness of its morphology lead to introducing the second type of Arabic passive known as the 'notional passive'. This is done by means of driving from the basic primary verb a number of verb forms through apophonic changes and prefixation. He (ibid.) gives the following example for clarification:

1. *kasara nabiil-un al-kaas-a* (active) Nabil broke the glass.
2. *kusira al-kaas-u* (formal passive with the verb in passive form) The glass was broken.
3. *inkasara al-kaas-u* (notional passive, with the verb in the active).

Wright (ibid.:50) and Cantarino (1974:52) give the following reasons for using passive in Arabic:

1. When God or some higher being is indicated as the author of the act.
2. When the author is unknown or at least not known for certain.
3. When the speaker or writer does not wish to name him.
4. When the attention of the hearer or reader is directed more to the person affected by the act (patients, the patient), than to the doer of it.

For Cantarino (ibid.), passive is mainly used for the above reasons in Classical Arabic, whereas he points out that Modern Standard Arabic 'makes extensive use of the passive' the purpose of which is 'to place a greater emphasis upon the action and its object'. Modern Arabic, for example media Arabic, is copying the syntax of European languages, English being one of them. One of these attempts to copy the English syntax in translation is the use of agentive passive represented by a prepositional phrase which will be discussed further by Badawi, Carter and Gully (2004:385–389) below:

(A) PERIPHRASTIC[56] AGENTS OF PASSIVE VERBS

Although the norm in Arabic passive is to eliminate the agent, it is nowadays added to the passive phrase by adding من قبل (on the part of) and other lexical items such as من جانب (by; lit.: from the side of), بواسطة (by means of), على أيدي (by; lit. at the hands of). The following examples from Badawi, Carter and Gully (2004:385–389) illustrate these elements in their order:

أُطلقت عليه النار من قبل عصابات المافيا.	He was fired on by Mafia gangs.
تُقدم الإرشادات من جانب إدارة خدمة الزراع.	Instructions are offered by the Directorate of Services to Farmers.
أُدين بواسطة المحاكم العسكرية.	He was sentenced by the military courts.
قد عولج على أيدي أطباء مهرة.	He was treated by skilled doctors.

(B) INSTRUMENT OF THE PASSIVE VERB

According to Badawi, Carter and Gully (ibid.:386), the true instrument of a passive verb is بِـ / bi – by as in:

جهوده لم تُكلل بالنجاح.	His efforts have not been crowned by/with success.

(C) PASSIVE VERBS WITH PREPOSITIONS

In this element, the verb takes its preposition in the passivized phrase as in:

لم يكن نظام الانتساب قد أُعترف به بعد.	The membership system had not yet been acknowledged. (Lit., recognition granted to it) (ibid.)

(D) IMPERSONAL AND IDIOMATIC PASSIVE

Arabic passive is also used impersonally and idiomatically as in the following examples:

و خُيل لغادة.	And Gada imagined. (Lit. it was made to appear to Gada)
لم يحقق مبيعات تُذكر	He achieved no sales worth mentioning. (Lit.: which are mentioned)
تُرج قبل الاستعمال.	To be shaken before use. (Lit. is shaken) (ibid.)

4.5.3 Addition and omission

Additions and omissions, 'over-translating', 'under-translating', or 'gain' and 'loss' (Dodds: 1985:284) are subject to some linguistic and non-linguistic elements. These are given by Al-Bainy (2002:9): 'culture, context, connotation, presupposition, intertextuality, grammatical structure, style, methods of expression, ambiguity (both lexical and grammatical), clarification, emphasis, kind of readership, linguistic background, expectations, semantic range, depth of intention, allusions, among others.'

Additions and omissions can be further divided into 'justified' and 'unjustified'. The latter may be motivated by the translator's stylistic preferences, adaptation, or paraphrasing. The justified additions and omissions referred to are the changes that occur as a result of different linguistic systems and/or cultural differences as well as legally remote disciplines (for example the case of Shariʿah Law and Common Law). To dissolve this problem in legal translation, Smith (1995:188–189) provides the following example:

> In general, the absence of equivalents for terms such as 'punitive damages' can be handled in three different ways. First one can provide additional information and explain that punitive damages are in excess of actual damages. They serve to punish the wrong-doer and to enhance the injured in excess . . . Under certain circumstances a more detailed explanation might be appropriate. Another option would be to find a short, yet sufficiently explanatory phrase . . . A third option, increasingly popular with German is 'non-translation' . . . The solution, in my opinion, lies in short, explanatory interlingual translation.

Additions and omissions will be included in the method of analysis because they reflect the translator's own view point and the way he/she decides to render a unit of translation. Addition is risky since it violates the rules of adequacy and accuracy, especially in legal translation where adherence to the ST is crucial. Yet, this rule may be violated as a means of clarification and/or compensating for the incongruent cultural backgrounds of both languages. Omission is also possible in translation between different languages. Yet, it must be accounted for and should not be done at the expense of ST content. To be more precise, the analysis of these two elements will be related to culture-specific and system-based terms from Arabic into English.

4.6 LIST OF DOCUMENTS FOR DATA ANALYSIS

The corpus of analysis consists of three legal subtypes: international, legislative and official. They contain plenty of examples for the lexical and syntactic areas under investigation, hence help identify the procedures of translating such areas, and arrive at some reliable results and conclusions that will be of help to legal translators and researchers.

Thus, the method of choosing these documents is based on convenience and availability, because finding parallel documents that deal with culture-specific and system-based terms was not easy especially in the case of English–Arabic. On the syntactic level, obtaining Arabic–English texts that include elements of passivization was also challenging. This may justify the arbitrary nature of the number of documents used to analyze each element. Below is a full list of the texts used from English into Arabic and vice versa.

4.6.1 English–Arabic documents

UN documents

- The Charter of the United Nations (ChUN)
- The Universal Declaration of Human Rights (UDHR)

A list of parallel documents from the UN Official Document Supply (ODS) regarding the topic of civil partnership and same-sex marriage as well as some other English system-based words are given below:

- Implementation of the International Covenant on Economic, Social and Cultural Rights (United Kingdom of Great Britain and Northern Ireland)
- Summary Prepared by the Office of the High Commissioner for Human Rights, in Accordance with Paragraph 15 (c) of the Annex to Human Rights Council Resolution 5/1 (Brazil)
- Summary Prepared by the Office of the High Commissioner for Human Rights, in Accordance with Paragraph 15 (c) of the Annex to Human Rights Council Resolution 5/1 (Slovenia)
- Summary Prepared by the Office of the High Commissioner for Human Rights, in Accordance with Paragraph 15 (c) of the Annex to Human Rights Council Resolution 5/1 (Germany)
- Committee on the Elimination of Discrimination against Women: Consideration of Reports Submitted by States Parties under article 18 of the Convention on the Elimination of all Forms of Discrimination against Women. Sixth Periodic Report of States Parties (United Kingdom of Great Britain and Northern Ireland: Civil Partnership Act 2004)
- Divorce and dissolution of civil partnership petitions
- Bank account opening form.

4.6.2 Arabic–English documents

International and legislative documents

- The Arab Charter of Human Rights (AChHR)
- The Universal Islamic Declaration of Human Rights (UIDHR)
- The Decree of the Establishment of the National Council of Women

Templates of official documents cited in Hatim, Shunnaq and Buckley (1995)

- Exchange of Religious Court marriage document for a marriage certificate
- Certificate of Legacy
- Certificate of Custody
- Certificate of Guardianship
- Marriage Contract
- Certificate of Conversion to Islam
- Certificate of Non-Liability
- Certificate of Stewardship
- Certificate of Maintenance of Legal Minors

- Certificate of Remarriage to a Divorced Wife
- Certificate of Conditional Divorce
- Certificate of Confirmation of Parentage
- Certificate of Irrevocable Divorce before the Consummation of Marriage
- Religious Court Power Special Attorney
- Authorization of Irrevocable Divorce in Return for Non-liability. After Consummation of Marriage.

Extracts from legislative texts cited in Mansoor (1965a and b)

- The Tunisian Code of Personal Status II
- The Pact of the League of Arab States II
- Agreement between Libya and the USA.

5 Analysis of Arabic–English–Arabic texts: the lexical level

5.1 INTRODUCTION

The analysis of data will be divided into two chapters, each of which will involve one linguistic level; Chapter 5 discusses the lexical level and Chapter 6 deals with the syntactic level. This chapter will be concerned with the translation of some lexical elements between English and Arabic and vice versa with reference to three legal subtypes, namely, international, legislative and official. From Arabic into English, these elements include religious, culture-specific and system-based terms and archaic terms. The documents analyzed include excerpts from Hatim, Shunnaq and Buckley (1995), Mansoor (1965a and b), the Universal Islamic Declaration of Human Rights (UIDHR) and the Arab Charter of Human Rights (AChHR). From English into Arabic, culture-specific and system-based terms and archaic terms will be analyzed. The documents investigated will discuss the issue of civil partnership as given in several UN documents obtained from the UN (ODS) as well as other documents such as the Charter of the United Nations (ChUN) and the Universal Declaration of Human Rights (UDHR) and other official documents obtained from law professionals such as an *Account Opening Form* and a *Lease Agreement*.

As mentioned in chapter 4, the analysis will be in two phases, the first of which is a tabulated quantitative frequency analysis of the procedures used in translating the element under investigation. The second phase is a qualitative critical analysis, the aim of which is to critically reflect on and criticize some of the examples given and attempt to provide some solutions wherever possible.

5.2 ANALYSIS OF RELIGIOUS, CULTURE-SPECIFIC AND SYSTEM-BASED TERMS AND PHRASES IN ARABIC–ENGLISH OFFICIAL AND LEGISLATIVE DOCUMENTS

This section aims to ascertain certain religious, culture-specific and system-based elements and which procedure is used in translating them as discussed by Vinay and Darbelnet (1995) and Alcaraz Varó and Hughes (2002).

5.2.1 Quantitative analysis of religious, culture-specific and system-based terms and phrases

The following table provides a frequency analysis of the procedures used in translating the above elements:

Table 5.1 Frequency analysis of the techniques of translating culture-specific and system-based terms and phrases in Arabic–English official and legislative documents

Technique of translation	No. of occurrences	Proportion of techniques found (%)
adaptation	6	30
expansion	5	25
literal	5	25
transposition	3	15
borrowing	1	5
Total	**20**	**100**

The above information can be presented in the following chart:

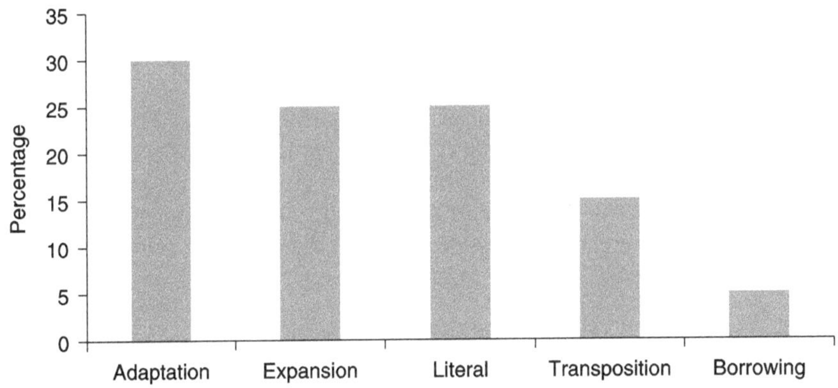

Figure 5.1 Frequency analysis of the techniques of translating culture-specific and system-based terms and phrases in Arabic–English official and legislative documents.

As shown in the above table and chart, 'adaptation' comes in first place with a percentage of 30 percent. In second place come both 'expansion' and 'literal translation', achieving the same degree of frequency of the total number of procedures 25 percent. 'Transposition' comes in third place with a frequency of 15 percent, whereas 'borrowing' has registered only 5 percent.

5.2.2 Qualitative analysis of religious, culture-specific and system-based terms and phrases

This section critically discusses the above elements in terms of the procedures presented in the table above. It is worthwhile dividing them into some subcategories as given below:

5.2.2.1 Reference to God

In matters of religious culture the problems of translation are often the most perplexing. The names of the deity are a continual difficulty. The native word may have a heavy connotative significance which makes it awkward to use. On the other hand a foreign word often implies an 'alien' God. Whether the translator is aware of it or not, the

> natives usually equate such a foreign term with one of their better known and understood deities.
>
> (Nida, 1964:94)

Reference to God includes elements such as the *basmalla* (بسم الله الرحمن الرحيم – in the name of God, the Merciful, the Compassionate). In this phrase, الله (Allah/the only creator) is rendered as 'God' following Venuti's (1995) 'domestication'. That is 'the translator . . . moves the reader towards the writer' (1995:20) and this makes the phrase more accepted in the TL. Translation of this term has been used as it is for a long time. It has been given a static form and has become an accepted translation. Mayoral Asensio (2003:21) suggests the possibility of omitting religious elements as follows:

> . . . formulas of salutation referring to God are intertextual references, fully meaningful in the Arabic text, but this intertextuality is lost in non-Islamic cultures . . . These ritual formulas do not have any relevance for the legal validity of the document; consequently, the possibility of omitting their translation remains open.

Aixela (1996:64) justifies the omission of culture-specific elements in cases where they are either unacceptable in the target culture or irrelevant to the target reader (TR) or when the item in question is ambiguous. However, the translator should not claim the liberty of omitting certain elements on the grounds of ambiguity. Rather, ambiguous terms and/or structures should be represented as they are in the TT. Alcaraz Varó and Hughes (2002:43) comment on structure ambiguity in the following lines:

> Although structure ambiguity is a problem, the translator must stick to the structure at hand. Then, he produces a similar ambiguous translation. He has no choice to choose from other alternatives. The best thing a translator can do is understand the context if he faces a linguistic ambiguity, if not he must stick to the literal sense of the source text and leave the interpretation to the court.

They (ibid.:153) added: 'also the translators might seek to use the most frequent structures that are specifically used in dealing with problems of legal discourse'. Although Alcaraz Varó and Hughes discuss the structural ambiguity, I believe, this can also be applied to lexical ambiguity. For example, the phrase بتقوى الله (to be God-fearing) in example 1 below does not make clear to the TR what the relationship between 'fearing God' and the importance of keeping an eye on the minor's money is. Although part of this meaning is given in the next clause: 'and to perform all tasks related to the guardian', one cannot decide to omit it because of this ambiguity.

Example 1: From A Certificate of Guardianship

و قد اوصيته <u>بتقوى الله</u> و القيام بشؤن هذه الوصاية بما فيه الحظ و النفع لجهة . . . فقبل ذلك مني و تعهد بالتزامه <u>حسبه الله تعالى</u>.	I have informed the guardian <u>to be God fearing</u> and to perform all tasks related to guardianship in the interest and in the benefit of . . . He has accepted this from me and undertaken to fulfill his obligation, <u>may God be his sufficiency</u>.

(Hatim, Shunnaq and Buckley, 1995: 84–85)

In the above example, the Arabic reader can easily understand the connotative or the implicit meaning of the first underlined phrase. That is, if somebody is a guardian of any person's money or any other interests, he/she needs to be careful not to steal them. The translator has given, in the TT, the denotative meaning of the phrase 'to be God fearing'. Because of this, the English reader does not get the same connotation given in the original and he/she needs to know the relationship between fearing God and the importance of keeping an eye on the minor's money.

The translator has followed the technique of 'adaptation' in translating حسبه الله تعالى (may God be his sufficiency). It means 'God' will be the only witness, whether the guardian will fulfil his commitments or not. This statement is one of the religious formulas added to the ST and it adds nothing to the TT and omitting it will not affect the legal validity of the document. This omission can be justified by the existence of the previous statement فقبل ذلك مني و تعهد بالتزامه (He has accepted this from me and undertaken to fulfil his obligation) which conveys that intended meaning.

5.2.2.2 Religious terms and concepts

Culture-specific terms pose difficulties when translating between two different languages. Because of this, the TR is confronted with a whole range of Islamic concepts that are very specific and require a strong legal background. The solution we may suggest is that the translator can provide an explanation in the form of a footnote. Alcaraz Varó and Hughes (2002) propose the technique of adaptation can be an effective means of overcoming the differences between two incongruent cultures. The following are some examples of the documents cited in Hatim, Shunnaq and Buckley (1995).

Translation of the term الشرعي *– legal or religious*

The ST term الشرعي is rendered in two ways, either as 'religious' or as 'legal'. Consider the example below:

Example 2: From A Certificate of Confirmation of Parentage

في المجلس الشرعي المعقود لدي أنا ... قاضي... الشرعي حضر لدي المكلف شرعا... من... و سكان... وبعد التعريف الشرعي عليه من قبل... قرر بحضورهما و هو في الحالة المعتبرة شرعا قائلا انه قد تولد لي من زوجتي الشرعية... على فراش الزوجية الأولاد أو الولد...	In the Legal Council convened in my presence, I . . . the religious judge of . . . received the legally capable . . . from . . . and resident in . . . and after the identification by . . . he deemed to be legally competent, resolved in their presence, stating: The children or child . . . was born to me from my legal wife within the state of matrimony. (Hatim, Shunnaq and Buckley 1995:102–103)

As the above excerpt shows, the term الشرعي / *al-shar'i* is used to denote two senses, the first of which is rendered as 'legal' and the other as 'religious' as it specifies the judge that deals with these matters as a religious judge not as a normal judge that deals with other cases. This religious judge's role is similar to the role of كاتب العدل (notary).

There is a problem in the translation of وبعد التعريف الشرعي as 'and after identification' which does not represent the same sense given in the ST. The translator has unjustifiably omitted the equivalent of the term الشرعي (legal), hence omitting an important piece of information for the validity of the TT as a document that can stand alone.

In the same excerpt given above, there is a shift of tenses in قد تولد لي with the modal particle (قد) denoting probability in the future. This clause is rendered inaccurately as 'was born to me': a passive in the past. It should be 'My wedded wife may give birth to . . .' by employing a 'voice shift' from passive in the ST to an active in the TT. The ST also refers to the baby(ies) that will be born to him from his legal wife as الأولاد أو الولد (the boys or the boy). The ST restricts the gender of the babies to boys only. In fact, Arabic still refers to both sexes in the form of an inclusive masculine element. The evidence of this argument is that the translator, being aware of this element, translates both words as 'children' or 'child' to include gender-neutral terms in the TT and make the TT more binding.

Terms related to marriage in Shariʿah Law: the term 'mahr'

Example 3

المهر و نوعه	Amount and type of dowry
المعجل	Down-payment
المؤجل	Deferred payment
توابع المهر	Extras

(Hatim, Shunnaq and Buckley, 1995:86–87)

Example 3 presents the translation of the term المهر/ *mahr* (dowry). *Faruqi's Law Dictionary Arabic–English* (1983:40) translates the word مهر as 'dower'.

'Dowery' is an archaic term defined by *Webster's Online Dictionary* as: Dower (1) the money, goods, or estate that a woman brings to her husband in marriage (2) a gift of money or property by a man to or for his bride. It is also defined in *Osborne's Concise Law Dictionary* (2001:142) as follows:

(1) The property which the bride brings to her groom in marriage. Also known as dowry or dowery.
(2) A widow's life interest in a portion of her deceased husband's property: that portion of lands or tenements which the wife has for a term of her life of the lands and tenements of her husband after his decease, for the sustenance of herself and the nurture and the education of her children . . .

The translator has used the technique of 'cultural adaptation' by giving the nearest equivalent in the English culture. However, if the document is legally binding, the exact concept of the word should be included in the TT (*mahr*) and then explained in a footnote. In this context Mayoral Asensio, 2003:62 argues:

> The Arabic *sadaq* is regularly translated as dowry. But the dowry (in fact, *shiwar*) is offered to the bride by her father as a custom whereas the *sadaq* is offered by the bridegroom as an element necessary for the legal validity of the marriage. This is usually law-risk information but could become critical. For instance, it could lead to the annulment of the marriage by a Spanish judge applying Moroccan law.

What Mayoral Asensio suggests is that there is a difference in meaning beween 'dowry' and '*mahr*' or '*sadaq*' as he puts it. He also suggests the translation of *sadaq* into Spanish as it is in Arabic, through glossing.

Translation of the term إبراء*/ ibra' (absolution)*

Example 4: From a Certificate of Non-liability

قررت قائلة و هي في الحالة المعشرعاً أنني أبرأت انني <u>ابرأت ذمة زوجي</u> . . .	She, being legally competent, resolved, saying: <u>I absolve my husband</u> . . . from responsibility over . . . (Hatim, Shunnaq and Buckley, 1995:92–93)

'Absolve' according to *Webster's Online Dictionary* is defined as follows:

(1) To set free from an obligation or the consequences of guilt.
(2) To remit (a sin) by <u>absolution</u>.

'Absolve' is translated into Arabic by *Faruqi's Law Dictionary (English–Arabic)* (2008:6) as: (من دين او التزام) يحل ,(ذمة), يبرئ ,(من التزام) يخلي. (الإبراء) is defined in the *Dictionary of Islamic Terms* (Al-Khudrawi, 1995:277) as:
'Acquittal, absolution, release, release of a debtor from his liabilities, remission of debt.'
إبراء is translated by *Faruqi Law Dictionary* (Arabic-English, 1983:2) as

acquittal, absolution	إبراء
release, discharge	إبراء (إخلاء ذمة)
quittance or acquittance	إبراء (كتابي)

According to the definitions given above, the Arabic term الابراء corresponds to both 'absolve' and 'acquit' in English, the former having a religious sense whereas the latter has a legal one. So we hear of 'absolving sins' and 'acquittance of debts'. Arabic, however, does not have such a distinction. The translator has 'added' the words 'responsibility over . . .' in the TT to make the absolution more specific and denoting what is exactly meant in this particular context (paying a fixed sum of money each month).

Translating the term طلاق *(divorce) and related terms*

It is very important to look at the translation of the term طلاق (divorce) and how its synonyms are rendered into English. But before we do this, it is beneficial to introduce the meaning of the term in Arabic culture. Talaq refers to the termination of marriage by the husband either verbally by declaring 'I divorce you' up to three times or through an authorized written form. In Arabic culture, if a marriage contract exists, its dissolution is called طلاق (divorce). It can also be called انفصال (separation).

Mayoral Asensio (2003:62) commented on the translation of the term طلاق from Arabic into Spanish as follows:

> Many official translators render the Arabic *talaq* as divorce, although it means repudiation. 'Divorce' benefits the Western local authority, which thus avoids the dilemma of validating a legal act, repudiation, that may be unconstitutional and against the local law.

Mayoral Asensio, in the above quotation, argues that '*talaq*' means 'repudiate/فسخ': 'to divorce or separate formally from (a woman)' (*Webster's Online Dictionary*), and highlights the existence of a difference between the concept of '*talaq*' and 'divorce'.[57] If the translator uses the term 'divorce' in the TT, he/she uses the strategy of approximation (choosing the nearest equivalent in the TT) which may 'benefit the Western local authority' (ibid.). Another way of keeping the spirit of the ST culture in the TT is to borrow the Arabic term (طلاق – *talaq*) and include the meaning of the concept in a footnote or in a bracketed paraphrase. Below are examples of the translation of the term (*talaq*) and other related terms:

Example 5: From حجة رجعة (Certificate of Remarriage to a Divorced Wife)

قرر قائلا إنني كنت قد طلقت زوجتي و مدخولتي الشرعية طلقة رجعية	He resolved stating: I revocably divorced my wife with whom I had consummated the marriage . . . (Hatim, Shunnaq and Buckley, 1995:98–99)

In the excerpt above, the Arabic text includes a doublet (زوجتي و مدخولتي – my wedded wife) in which the terms are near-synonymous but they are indeed different. In Shari'ah Law a man and a woman can be married with a legal marriage contract but they may not have consummated marriage. Thus, the translator employs the technique of 'expansion' according to Alcaraz Varó and Hughes (2002:184), by explaining the word مدخولتي: 'with whom I have consummated the marriage' to the word 'wife' giving the exact meaning of the Arabic term.

In the same example, the term طلقة رجعية is a Shari'ah Law term which is also referred to, according to Al-Khudrawi (1995:263–4), as طلاق رجعي (revocable divorce).

In the title of the document, the translator opted for 'explanation' of the term رجعة (return) in this case, of a wife to the husband's matrimonial authority and contract of marriage. This is common in translating titles which depend mainly on the main body and content of the document.

Example 6: From وثيقة طلاق بائن قبل الدخول (Certificate of Irrevocable Divorce before Consummation of Marriage)

... فأقول زوجتي المذكورة التي لم أدخل ولم أختل بها طالقاً من عصمتي و عقد نكاحي طلقة واحدة بائنة اطلب تسجيله و تبليغها. و حيث تحقق إلينا سبق الزوجية بينهما و عدم الدخول و الخلوة الصحيحة بإقراره وإفادة المعرفين المذكورين فقد أفهمته أنه وقع منه طلاق بائن بينونة صغرى على زوجته المذكورة.

... and I state that my aforementioned wife with whom I have not consummated the marriage and have not been alone is irrevocably divorced from my matrimonial authority and my contract of marriage once and for all and I request that be recorded and that she be notified. Whereas a state of matrimony previously existing between them, non-consummation of the marriage and not being together have been ascertained to us by his avowal and the testimony of the aforementioned identifiers, I have informed him he has concluded an irrevocable divorce of his aforementioned wife.

(Hatim, Shunnaq and Buckley, 1995:104–105)

The above excerpt gives the translation of the phrase طلاق بائن قبل الدخول which is one type of irrevocable divorce. It happens if the husband divorced his wife before the consummation of marriage; this counts as one divorce statement and is known as طلاق بائن بينونة صغرى (minor irrevocable divorce). In this type, if the husband needs to remarry his divorcee, this must happen through a new marriage contract with a new dowry. The above type is different from the one we introduced in example 5 above and is distinguished from الطلاق البائن بينونة كبرى (major irrevocable divorce) which is defined by Al-Khudrawi (1995:264): 'if the husband gives sentence of divorce to his wife a third time, it is not lawful for him to take her again, until she shall have married another husband'.

The clause لم ادخل ولم اختل بها is rendered as 'with whom I have not consummated the marriage and have not been alone'. The first part accurately renders the meaning of the ST; the underlined clause adds nothing to the meaning but confirms it, and it is a bit vague in the TT. For the TR, it does not represent the meaning included in the source culture. Menacere (1997:85) argues that '*lam akhtal biha* is a culture specific term with no equivalent in English. The literal translation "have not been alone" is thus meaningless in English, the Arabic concept requiring a lengthy footnote'.

Later in the text, the clause is repeated with a different wording: الخلوة الصحيحة (the right *khalwah*/privacy with a wife) and was vaguely rendered: 'not being together'. Although it is always advisable that the translator should keep the vagueness represented in the ST, for attaining the same sense given in the ST (Alcaraz Varó and Hughes, 2002:43,153), another suggestion is that the translator may add an explanatory footnote by providing the TR with the conditions of the right '*khalwah*' such as being separately in one room, with the door closed or curtains drawn.

Example 7: From the Tunisian Code of Personal Status II

الهدايا التي يعطيها الزوج للزوجة بعد العقد يسترد ما بقي منها قائما و لو تغير إذا وقع الفسخ قبل البناء بسبب منها و لا يسترجع منها شيئا بعد الدخول.(Article 28)	The husband in case of dissolution of marriage, recovers from his wife whatever remains of gifts he gave her after the conclusion of marriage contract if the dissolution occurs after the consummation of the marriage.

(Mansoor, 1965b:141)

<http://wrcati.cawtar.org/assets/documents/pdf/CodeduStatutPersonnel.pdf>

In the above example, wording of the Arabic ST is vague and requires reconsideration. The ST introduces an article in the Tunisian Code of Personal Status that explains two cases in relation to the husband's eligibility to recover any presents that he has given to his wife. In the first case, if the couples are officially married, but have not consummated marriage and their marriage contract comes to an end, from the side of the wife, the husband is eligible to receive all the remaining presents back even if they are used. In the second case, if the couples have already consummated marriage, then if divorce happens, the husband is not eligible to receive any of his presents back.[58]

The condition for recovering the husband's presents is exemplified in the conditional clause (اذا وقع الفسخ قبل البناء). What is meant by الفسخ (dissolution) is 'divorce' or 'dissolution' and what is meant by البناء (lit. building) is consummation of marriage. This term is omitted, leaving the meaning of the TT clause incomplete. Another unjustified omission is the phrase بسبب منها (because of her) which means that 'the reason of divorce emerged because of the wife'. This phrase, I suppose, is important in this context as it gives one of the cases for returning the husband's gifts, thus cannot be omitted. The conditional clause (و لو تغير lit. if they changed), which refers to the change of the status of these gifts was also unjustifiably omitted from the TT. A suggested translation for this excerpt is given below:

> The husband shall in case of the dissolution of marriage recover from his wife, if the dissolution occurs before the consummation of marriage because of her, whatever remains of gifts he gave her – even if the status of these gifts has changed. The husband shall not recover any gifts if the dissolution occurs after the consummation of marriage.
>
> (author's translation)

Example 8: From حجة رجعة (Certificate of Remarriage to a Divorced Wife)

و حيث إنها مازالت في العدة الشرعية فأنني أرجعها إلى عصمتي و عقد نكاحي . . .	And whereas she is still within the legally prescribed waiting period before remarrying, I return her to my matrimonial authority and to my contract of marriage.

(Hatim, Shunnaq and Buckley, 1995: 98–99)

The above excerpt represents another instance of the Shari'ah Law terms (العِدة الشرعية) which is rendered as 'the legally prescribed waiting period before remarrying'.[59] The translator has used the technique of 'explicitation' or 'expansion' (Alcaraz Varó and Hughes, 2002:184) by explaining the meaning of the term rather than, perhaps, transliterating it followed by this explanation. 'Explicitation' is viewed as one of the translation universals between many language pairs (Baker, 1992). Al-Khafaji (2007) has undertaken a study to validate the hypothesis that 'explicitation' and avoiding lexical repetition is one of the translation universals between English and Arabic. He comes up with the conclusion that this hypothesis is valid, bearing in mind the small-scale corpus he has used. Al-Khafaji has investigated such hypotheses in literary Arabic, not considering other Arabic registers such as legal Arabic. Based on the analysis of a small-scale legal corpus, we can claim that 'explicitation' applies in the case of translating legal texts from and into Arabic whereas avoiding lexical repetition is not a valid hypothesis in translating these legal subtypes.

Mansoor (1965b:141) has given the following translation of the term عدة (iddat):

Example 9: From the Tunisian Code of Personal Status II

تعتد زوجة المفقود عدة الوفاة بعد صدور الحكم بفقدانه. (Article 36)	The wife of the missing person, following a court decision designating him a missing person, shall observe the same period of 'iddat as that applicable in case of death.

(Mansoor, 1965b:141)

<http://wrcati.cawtar.org/assets/documents/pdf/CodeduStatutPersonnel.pdf>

In this example, Mansoor has 'borrowed' then transliterated the Shari'ah Law term (عدة 'iddat) which has no equivalent in the English culture, followed by an explanation: 'as that applicable in case of death' because there are two cases for *'iddat* in Shari'ah Law: in case of death or if the wife has been divorced. Al-Khudrawi (1995:277) has defined and distinguished between these two types of عِدة (*'iddah*) below:

> The term of probation incumbent upon a woman in consequence of dissolution of marriage either by divorce or the death of her husband. After a divorce, the period is three months and after the death of her husband, four months and ten days, both periods being enjoined by the Qur'an.

5.3 RELIGIOUS, CULTURE-SPECIFIC AND SYSTEM-BASED TERMS AND PHRASES IN ARABIC–ENGLISH INTERNATIONAL DOCUMENTS

The Universal Islamic Declaration of Human Rights (UIDHR) is an important text to analyse in the body of this book. It is one of the documents which addresses human rights in Islam and the translation of which should adequately transfer the message given in the ST. It is also rich with religious elements from the Qur'an and the Sunnah (customary practice of Prophet Mohammed) as well as Shari'ah Law.

5.3.1 Quantitative analysis of religious, culture-specific and system-based terms and phrases in the UIDHR

The following table gives the techniques used in translating the religious and culture-specific terms in the UIDHR:

Table 5.2 Frequency analysis of the techniques of translating culture-specific and system-based terms and phrases in the UIDHR

Technique of translation	No of occurrences	Proportion of techniques found (%)
omission	77	60.16
adaptation	27	21.09
borrowing	12	9.38
addition	8	6.25
literal	2	1.26
explanation	2	1.26
Total	**128**	**100.00**

As is shown in the above table, 'omission' is the most frequent technique in translating religious elements (for example Qur'anic verses and prophetic Hadiths) (60.16 percent). At the same time, 'adaptation' achieved 21.09 percent of the overall techniques which puts it in second place. 'Borrowing' comes in third place achieving 9.38 percent, a technique that has not been noticed in the analysis of the official and legislative documents mentioned earlier in this chapter. 'Addition' achieves 6.25 percent, which is higher than its counterparts in the official and legislative documents. Other techniques such as 'literal translation' and 'explanation' are not so frequent, with a percentage of 1.26 percent. Below is a chart illustrating the above information followed by the qualitative analysis:

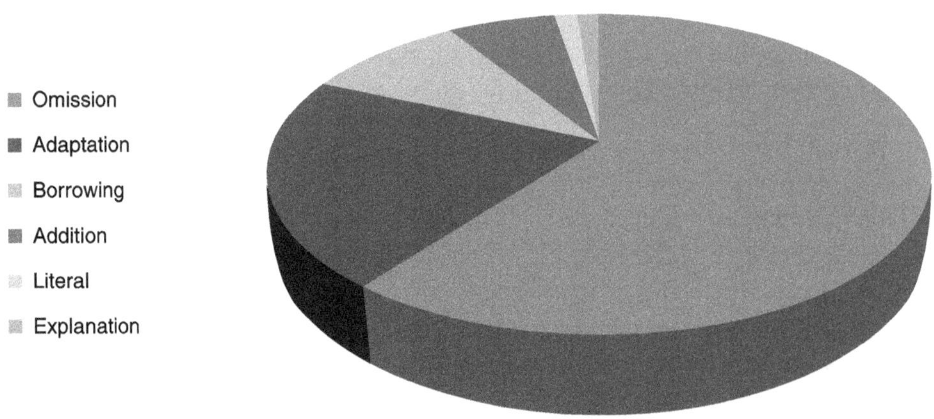

Figure 5.2 Frequency analysis of the techniques of translating culture-specific and system-based terms and phrases in the UIDHR.

5.3.2 Qualitative analysis of the frequency of techniques of translating culture-specific and system-based terms and phrases in the UIDHR

The discussion in this phase focuses on the techniques exemplified in the above chart. We will focus on 'omission', 'adaptation', 'borrowing' plus 'literal' 'translation' and 'addition'. It is worth noting that the method of analysis in this part has been slightly adapted from the way followed in analyzing the official and legislative documents before. In analyzing this document, I am referring to the technique of translation where 'omission' and 'adaptation' are the most dominant, a matter which poses a question about the validity of the TT, given that this is the only available translated text of this document and paves the way for a closer investigation of the techniques of translation used.

5.3.2.1 Translation by 'omission'

In the TT, the translator omitted every occurrence of Qur'anic verses and Hadiths, along with their citations.[60] At the end of the TT, he/she has given a separate 'Reference' section in which he/she has documented all the occurrences of the Qur'anic verses and the Prophet's Hadiths, according to the order of their occurrence in the text. This can justify why omission is the most frequent technique and leaves us with the questions of (i) whether or not the translator has the authority to omit almost all these examples, (ii) if he/she has done so, has he/she justified such omission? (iii) has he/she explained why he/she has referred to the citations of these examples at the end of the text? (iv) what is the value of including them so abruptly?

To answer the third and fourth questions, we can argue that adding these citations at the end of the TT does not change anything, nor does it add any information to the TR because they are used out of context. Even with them, the TR will not find them of much help as he/she requires the actual words to be able to accommodate them in the TT.

In answering question one and two, it is not the authority of translators to omit these big portions of the TT. He/she does not justify using such technique to the TR, leaving the TT one of the unreliable texts. One cannot claim that the TT is a parallel version of the ST. It can neither be viewed as an authentic nor as a binding legal document. One of the instances of the omissions, however, can be justified for as in the case of omitting the *basmalla* (بسم الله الرحمن الرحيم – In the name of God, the Merciful, the Compassionate).

It is worth mentioning that despite the 'omission' of almost all the occurrences of the Qur'an, the Hadith, sayings of the Prophet's companions and the adaptation of a few of such elements, the TT, surprisingly, includes one Qur'anic verse that has not been omitted as given below:

Example 1

ST	TT
الأوضاع الدينية للأقليات يحكمها المبدأ القرآني العام: 'لا إكراه في الدين' (البقرة: 256).	The Qur'anic principle "There is no compulsion in religion" shall govern the religious rights of non-Muslim minorities. (UIDHR, article 10:a)

<http://www1.umn.edu/humanrts/arab/UIDHR.html>

<http://www.barrypearson.co.uk/articles/gods/islam_universal.htm>

5.3.2.2 Translation by 'adaptation'

Examples of this translation technique are many in the body of the document; we will comment on some of them below:

Example 2

الزواج – بإطاره الإسلامي – حق لكل إنسان، وهو الطريق الشرعي لبناء الأسرة وإنجاب الذرية،؟ واعفاف النفس. . . لكل من الزوجين قبل الآخر – عليه وله – حقوق وواجبات متكافئة قررتها الشريعة (رواه الخمسة).	Every person is entitled to marry, to found a family and to bring up children in conformity with his religion, traditions and culture. Every spouse is entitled to such rights and privileges and carries such obligations as are stipulated by the Law. (article 19:a)

<http://www1.umn.edu/humanrts/arab/UIDHR.html>
<http://www.barrypearson.co.uk/articles/gods/islam_universal.htm>

The above excerpt exemplifies 'adaptation' of the term الشريعة (Shari'ah) which has been rendered as 'law' and it is repeated throughout the whole document. The translator mentioned this in the endnotes but offers no justification. The only justification one can provide is that the translator is after the 'domestication' of the TT. In fact, what the translator is trying to do is to give the TR the gist of the content of each article. This has happened at the expense of accuracy of the ST wording. For example, the two-part article is translated into one statement summarizing the message given in the ST. Consider the following statement:

وهو الطريق الشرعي لبناء الأسرة وإنجاب الذرية، واعفاف النفس	to found a family and to bring up children

The translator has omitted the phrases وهو الطريق الشرعي (which is the legitimate way) and واعفاف النفس (maintaining self-chastity). 'Adaptation' is also used in translating وإنجاب الذرية (and giving birth to offspring) into 'bring up children'. This adaptation, I believe, is inadequate as this results in a totally different piece of information that is not primarily given in the ST, as 'having children' is different from 'bringing up children'. A better translation could be: 'and this is the legitimate way to found a family, to have children and to preserve self-chastity' (author's translation).

Example 3

لكل إنسان أن يعمل وينتج، تحصيلا للرزق من وجوهه المشروعة.	All human beings are entitled to earn their living according to the Law. (article 15:b)

<http://www1.umn.edu/humanrts/arab/UIDHR.html>
<http://www.barrypearson.co.uk/articles/gods/islam_universal.htm>

'Adaptation' is also used in the above example in translating من وجوهه المشروعة (by its legitimate means) which is rendered as 'according to the law'. In this context, it has given the same sense as that of the original.

5.3.2.3 Translation by both 'literal' translation and 'borrowing'

Due to the religious nature of the document, it includes a considerable number of religious and jurisprudential concepts that are hard to render in the TT. For these elements, the translator has used two procedures of translating them, mainly, 'literal translation' and 'borrowing' as given by Vinay and Darbelnet (1995:84). We will refer to a few of these items below:

Example 4

مجتمع: تقرر فيه السياسات التي تنظم شئون الأمة، وتمارس السلطات التي تطبقها وتنفذها "بالشورى": "وأمرهم شورى بينهم" (الشورى 38).	Wherein all public affairs shall be determined and conducted and the authority to administer them shall be exercised after mutual consultation *(Shura)* between the believers qualified to contribute to a decision which would accord well with the Law and the public good; (Preamble: 8)
ii الشورى أساس العلاقة بين الحاكم والأمة.	Process of free consultation *(Shura)* is the basis of the administrative relationship between the government and the people. (Article 11:b)

<http://www1.umn.edu/humanrts/arab/UIDHR.html>
<http://www.barrypearson.co.uk/articles/gods/islam_universal.htm>

In the above example, the term الشورى (consultation) is rendered in two ways, by 'literal translation': 'mutual consultation' followed by 'borrowing' (*Shura*) as in (i) or 'process of free consultation' followed by *Shura* as in (ii). Newmark (1982:381) does not support the use of 'borrowing' in international documents:

> whether in translation or in original writing, a paper on a country's institutions transfers a higher proportion of legal than of any other type of institutional terms but an officially translated law or an international treaty must not use transferred or borrowed terms.

Newmark's argument above might not be applicable to the above document where there is a considerable number of religious and culture-specific terms the meaning of which will be distorted if not transferred to the TT through 'borrowing'. It is also advisable to start with the borrowed term then followed by the 'literal translation' as is given in the following example:

Example 5

بيت الله الحرام – بمكة المشرفة – هو مثابة وأمن للناس جميعا لا يصد عنه مسلم: "ومن دخله كان آمنا" (آل عمران: 97).	Al Masjid Al Haram (the sacred house of Allah) in Mecca is a sanctuary for all Muslims. (Article 9:b)

<http://www1.umn.edu/humanrts/arab/UIDHR.html>
<http://www.barrypearson.co.uk/articles/gods/islam_universal.htm>

In the above example, بيت الله الحرام (the Sacred House of Allah/Kaʿabah) is rendered in two ways: the first of which is through 'borrowing' and 'adaptation' (Al Masjid Al Haram – The Sacred Mosque) followed by bracketed 'literal translation' (The Sacred House of Allah – Kaʿabah). Although the borrowed phrase can be considered a justified adaptation as the meaning involved in the ST refers to the whole Mosque rather than the Kaʿabah, the translator should have stuck to the ST, or a footnote could have been included to explain this adaptation to the TR.

It is worthwhile that the translator combined the two phrases وأمن للناس جميعا (and security for all people) and لا يصد عنه مسلم (no Muslim should be deterred from it) as 'sanctuary for all Muslims'. By this, the translator limits visiting or resorting to the Mosque to Muslims only, a piece of information that does not exist in the ST. A suggested translation could be:

> 'The Sacred House of Allah – in Mecca – is sanctuary and security to all people and no Muslim should be deterred from visiting it.'
>
> (Author's translation)

Example 6

للزوجة: أن تطلب من زوجها: إنهاء عقد الزواج – وديا – عن طريق الخلع: "فإن خفتم ألا يقيما [الزوجان] حدود الله فلا جناح عليهما فيما افتدت به" (البقرة: 229). كما أن لها أن تطلب التطليق قضائياً في نطاق أحكام الشريعة.	Every married woman is entitled to seek and obtain dissolution of marriage (*Khul'a*) in accordance with the terms of the Law. This right is in addition to her right to seek divorce through the courts. (Article 20:d)

<http://www1.umn.edu/humanrts/arab/UIDHR.html>
<http://www.barrypearson.co.uk/articles/gods/islam_universal.htm>

In the above example, the ST phrase إنهاء عقد الزواج – وديا – عن طريق الخلع (entitled to seek and obtain dissolution of marriage (*Khul'a*)) uses a culture-specific term الخلع (al-Khulʿ). According to the ST, a wife can initiate divorce from her husband by means of الخلع

(*al-khul*ʿ).[61] This term does not have an equivalent, hence is rendered by 'borrowing'. However, a footnote could be included to explain this term to the TR:

> *Al-khul*ʿ: 'An agreement concluded for the purpose of dissolving marriage. The release from the marriage tie obtained by a wife upon payment of a compensation or consideration whenever enmity takes place between husband and wife and they both see reason to.'
>
> (Al-Khudrawi, 1995:124)

A suggested better translation of the above excerpt would be:

> A wife is entitled to demand from her husband – in an amicable manner – the dissolution of the marriage contract through 'al-khulʿ'
>
> (author's translation)

Sometimes there is a lack of consistency on the part of the translator in translating one term. For example, 'literal translation' plus ' borrowing' is used in rendering the word الأمة (the community) in one case: 'the community (*Ummah*)' and in another case it is rendered through 'literal translation' only as 'the community'.

5.3.2.4 Translation by 'addition'

There are several instances of addition in the body of the TT. Some of them are worth mentioning here:

Example 7

من حق كل فرد ومن واجبه: أن يعلن رفضه للظلم، وإنكاره له، وأن يقاومه، دون تهيب مواجهة سلطة متعسفة، أو حاكم جائر، أو نظام طاغ . . . وهذا أفضل أنواع الجهاد . . .	It is the right and duty of every Muslim to protest and strive (within the limits set out by the Law) against oppression even if it involves challenging the highest authority in the state. (article 12:c)

<http://www1.umn.edu/humanrts/arab/UIDHR.html>
<http://www.barrypearson.co.uk/articles/gods/islam_universal.htm>

An example of 'addition' (within the limits set by the law) can be seen where in the TT the translator was discussing the rights of every person to protest against oppression. The word فرد (individual/person) which is gender-neutral is rendered as 'every Muslim'. The translator has specified reference in the TT to Muslims only. There is no justification for that change in the footnotes. One can argue that the translator may have done so on the grounds that this document discusses human rights in Islam which should be addressed to all Muslims. Even so, the document does not restrict the rights and obligations to Muslims as other sects may still live under the umbrella of Islam and one should not exclude them.

There is also an 'adaptation' and 'omission' of the underlined phrase below (وهذا أفضل أنواع الجهاد – this is the best way of *jihad*) in the following excerpt:

دون تهيب مواجهة سلطة متعسفة، أو حاكم جائر، أو نظام طاغ . . . وهذا أفضل أنواع الجهاد . . .	against oppression even if it involves challenging the highest authority in the state

What the translator has provided us with in the above example is 'gist translation'. The complete translation of the ST statement could be:

> . . . without fearing the confrontation of an oppressive authority, unjust ruler, or tyrannical regime . . . and this is the best type of struggle . . .
>
> (author's translation)

Example 8

من حق الفرد أن ينال كفايته من ضروريات الحياة . . . من طعام، وشراب، وملبس، ومسكن . . . ومما يلزم لصحة بدنه من رعاية، وما يلزم لصحة روحه، وعقله، من علم، ومعرفة، وثقافة، في نطاق ما تسمح به موارد الأمة – ويمتد واجب الأمة في هذا ليشمل ما لا يستطيع الفرد أن يستقل بتوفيره لنفسه من ذلك.	Every person has the right to food, shelter, clothing, education and medical care consistent with the resources of the community. This obligation of the community extends in particular to all individuals who cannot take care of themselves due to some temporary or permanent disability. (article 18)

<http://www1.umn.edu/humanrts/arab/UIDHR.html>
<http://www.barrypearson.co.uk/articles/gods/islam_universal.htm>

As seen in the above example, the underlined phrase has been rendered differently in the TT. Translation has been done through both 'adaptation' and 'addition'. The article is discussing the duties of the community towards their people and in particular providing necessary resources, in particular for those who are not able to provide them themselves. The TT involves a mistranslation of this information and an addition of a piece of information that does not exist in the ST: 'due to some temporary or permanent disability'. A better translation should read as follows:

ويمتد واجب الأمة في هذا ليشمل ما لا يستطيع الفرد أن يستقل بتوفيره لنفسه من ذلك.	Duties of the community also involve providing what the individual cannot secure of these needs. (author's translation)

It is clear from the above discussion that the translation of this document is problematic; we have provided an overview of this and only commented on a few examples that deal with religious, culture-specific terms. The TT of this document, however, is not consistent and it is recommended that it should be retranslated.

5.4 ANALYSIS OF ENGLISH–ARABIC SYSTEM-BASED AND CULTURE-SPECIFIC TERMS

This section discusses the techniques of translating culture-specific and system-based terms from English into Arabic, with a certain focus on the concept of 'civil partnership' rendered in some UN documents introduced in Chapter 4 (section 4.6).

5.4.1 A note on the concept of civil partnership

The term 'partner' is defined by *Webster's Online Dictionary* as 'someone's husband or wife or the person someone has sexual relations with'. A civil partnership is 'a relationship between two people of the same sex ("civil partners")' (Civil Partnership Act 2004, article 1 available online from: <http://www.legislation.gov.uk/ukpga/2004/33/section/1>).

Civil partnership is distinguished from civil marriage in that the two male or female partners can go to a specified civil partnership registrar and utter certain vows[62]. In the UK, for example, the two partners perform official arrangements for living together legally and share the rights that married couples have such as the right for pension or property ownership if one of the partners dies.[63]

5.4.2 Quantitative analysis of English–Arabic culture-specific system-based terms and phrases

The table below gives the frequency of the techniques used in translating English–Arabic culture-specific and system-based terms:

Table 5.3 Quantitative analysis of the techniques of translating English–Arabic system-based and culture-specific terms

Technique	**No of occurrences**	**Proportion of techniques found (%)**
literal	18	46
expansion	9	23
adaptation	8	21
shift	2	5
explicitation	2	5
Total	**39**	**100**

The information given in this table is represented again in Figure 5.3.

As the two figures show, 'literal translation' is one of the most frequent techniques used in translating system-based and culture-specific terms from English into Arabic at 46 percent. Expansion achieves 23 percent whereas 'adaptation' comes in third place with a percentage of 21 percent. Both 'shift' and 'explicitation' come last with 5 percent for each technique.

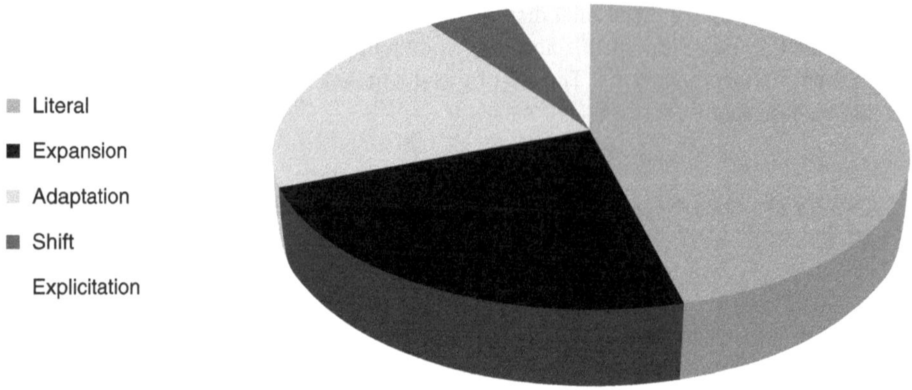

Figure 5.3 Frequency analysis of the techniques for translating English–Arabic system-based and culture-specific terms.

5.4.3 Qualitative analysis of English–Arabic system-based and culture-specific terms

This section critically analyzes the techniques used in translating the system-based and culture-specific terms in some selected UN documents.[64] These terms include spouse, couples, marriage, divorce, dissolution, civil partnership and related terms.

Example 1

The marriage must have broken down for one of these reasons:	يجب أن يعود انهيار الزواج لأحد الأسباب التالية:
Your spouse has committed adultery and you find it intolerable to live together.	ارتكاب الشريك للزنا و عدم المقدرة على تحمل العيش معا
Your spouse has behaved in such a way that you cannot reasonably be expected to live together.	تصرف الشريك بطريقة ما بحيث من غير المعقول إمكانية العيش معاً.
You have been separated for two years and your spouse agrees to divorce.	مضي سنتين على فترة الانفصال و موافقة الشريك على الانفصال.
You have been separated for five years.	مضي خمس سنوات على الانفصال.
Your spouse deserted you more than two years ago.	هجر الشريك لك لأكثر من خمس سنوات.
(Resolution first for family law, fact sheet)	

The above example lists the reasons for dissolution of civil partnership. The author, however, has presupposed that civil partnership is referred to as 'marriage' and the dissolution of it is called 'divorce': where the term 'divorce' is used in this fact sheet it should be taken to include dissolution of civil partnership. Thus, the term 'spouse' refers to 'partner' in the ST. The translator has opted for an 'adaptation' technique in the TT to give the same meaning intended in the ST by rendering 'spouse' as الشريك (the partner) rather than الزوج (husband).

'Verb–noun transposition' is used in the translation of 'have broken down', 'separate' 'desert' and 'deserted'. The former is rendered as انهيار (collapsing / breaking), 'have been separated' as الانفصال (separation) and 'deserted' as هجر (deserting). There is one 'mistranslation': 'Your spouse deserted you more than two years ago' has been rendered as خمس (five).

It is interesting to look at the translation of the term 'partner' as it has occurred in the media discourse.[65]

Since 2006, Parliamentary rules have banned MPs from 'leasing accommodation from <u>a partner</u>'.	ومنذ العام 2006، تحظر القواعد البرلمانية على النواب تأجير محل الإقامة <u>من زوج أو صديق حميم</u>

<http://news.bbc.co.uk/1/hi/uk/10192614.stm>
<http://www.bbc.co.uk/arabic/multimedia/2010/05/100530_hs_uk_laws_resign_cabinet.shtml>

As given above, 'partner' is rendered as زوج أو صديق حميم (husband or intimate friend). Both TT words do not represent the meaning of the term 'partner' given in the ST. It neither means 'husband', nor does it mean 'intimate friend'. The translator has used 'adaptation' as a means of euphemism for representing the approximate equivalents in the TT culture. 'Expansion' is also used here as the translator has added 'intimate friend' to the TT. The translator has taken the liberty of translating the ST, assuming that it is not a binding text and the TR will still get the intended meaning once it is read in context. One can better translate it as:

ومنذ العام 2006، تحظر القواعد البرلمانية على النواب تأجير محل الإقامة <u>من شريك</u> <u>أو شريك مدني</u>

In the same article, the term 'partner' is rendered differently as 'to his partner' (الجنس لشريكه مثلي) which specifies the meaning of the term 'partner' to refer to British Treasury Minister David Laws' secret lover. The media also speaks of 'gay couple' for 'civil partners' as given in a news headline: '<u>Gay couple</u> set to christen children'.[66] It can be rendered into Arabic as شريكان مثليا الجنس يعمدان أطفالهم (author's translation).

Below is another example:

Example 2

Where the term 'divorce' is used in this fact sheet it should be taken to include <u>dissolution of civil partnership</u>. The only exception is adultery which is a specific legal term relating to heterosexual sex and which cannot therefore be used as grounds for <u>dissolving a civil partnership</u>. If your partner is unfaithful the grounds for <u>dissolution</u> would instead be unreasonable behaviour. (Resolution first for family law, fact sheet)	فمصطلح "الطلاق" في ورقة الوقائع هذه يشمل <u>فسخ الشراكة المدنية</u>. والاستثناء الوحيد هو الزنا الذي هو مصطلح قانوني محدد يتعلق بممارسة الجنس بين الجنسين والتي لا يمكن بالتالي أن تستخدم كأساس <u>لإنهاء شراكة مدنية</u>. و إذا كان الشريك غير مخلص يصبح أساس <u>انحلال الشراكة</u> بدلًا من ذلك التصرف الغير عقلاني.

In the above excerpt, translation of the term 'dissolution' has varied; once it is فسخ in the first instance, إنهاء in the second; and انحلال in the third. In the first two instances 'literal translation' has been used. In the third, it is also 'literal' and 'addition' as the translator has opted for adding the term الشراكة (partnership) to make it explicit in the TT what 'dissolution' refers to. It is of value to note that the Arabic term الشراكة (partnership) has been newly introduced to Arabic as a verbal noun of the verb شارك (to take part) and it is now frequently used in business and in law. Below is another example given in a Bank Account Contract Opening Form below:

Example 3

Authorized Signatures: Notice of revocation; dissolution of partnership. (Article 2.9)	المفوضون بالتوقيع و اخطار الإلغاء و حل الشراكة.
Death of any partner of the Account Holder or of its dissolution. (Ibid.)	وفاة أي شريك لصاحب الحساب أو تصفية الشراكة معه.

In other examples, 'civil partnership' can be called 'same-gender partnership':

Example 4

Civil recognition of same-gender partnerships. (E/C.12/GBR/5: article 21)	الاعتراف المدني بشراكات الأقران من نفس الجنس

As seen above, 'literal translation' is used but the term الأقران (fellows) has been 'added' to the TT for semantic reasons as the term 'partnerships' needs to be put in a whole meaningful context. It gives a better meaning than if it is rendered as شراكات من نفس الجنس (same-gender partnerships). Here is another phrase:

Example 5

same-sex couples to make a formal, legal commitment to each other by forming a civil partnership. (E/C.12/GBR/5: article 21)	الأقران من نفس الجنس من الدخول في التزام قانوني، رسمي تجاه كل منهما الآخر بتكوين شراكة مدنية.

As seen above, 'same-sex couples' is rendered as الأقران من نفس الجنس (fellows of the same sex). There is 'adaptation' in rendering the term 'couples' into 'fellows'. The translator is motivated by addressing the target culture because 'couples' refer to 'two married persons from opposite sexes'. The term الأقران (fellows) is neutral here as it can refer to two persons from the same or different sexes. Another example of the occurrence of the term is given below:

Example 6

same-sex civil partnership (A/HRC/14/15/Add.1: article 5, 6, 7, 8, 9)	المعاشرة بين شريكين من جنس واحد

In this example, the translator has 'adapted' the translation with an 'addition' of thc term المعاشرة (cohabitation) and unjustifiably omitting the term 'civil'. To keep consistency of the translation of the term, one can render it as:

الشراكة المدنية بين شريكين من نفس الجنس

(author's translation)

The following example investigates the translation of 'homosexuals':

Example 7

. . . it is believed that such incidents are underreported because families are unwilling to admit that targeted members were homosexuals, for fear of further abuse. (GEN/G09/173/85: article 30)	. . . وإلى مزاعم تفيد أن عدم التبليغ عن هذه الحوادث يُعزى إلى عدم رغبة الأسر في التسليم بأن الأفراد المستهدفين هم مثليون جنسيًا خوفًا من تعرضهم لاعتداءات.

It is clear from the above example that the term 'homosexuals' is rendered 'literally' as مثليون جنسيًا. One can even argue that it is a 'calque' according to Vinay and Darbelnet (1995:84). This term has also been rendered in the media as مثلي جنسي.[67]

Example 8

Gender Recognition Act 2004 Civil recognition of transsexual people in their acquired gender. (E/C.12/GBR/5: article 21)	قانون الاعتراف بالجنس لعام ٢٠٠٤ الاعتراف المدني بالجنس المكتسب لمن يغيّرون جنسهم.

'Transsexual people' in the above example is rendered as لمن يغيّرون جنسهم (who change their sex (gender)). This phrase is rendered into a clause following 'phrase-clause transposition'. It is worth noting that both transsexual and transgender are used interchangeably although there is a slight distinction between both. 'Transsexualism' describes the wish to change one's sex or the change itself. This is known in Arabic as تغيير الجنس (gender change) or اشتهاء تغيير الجنس (the wish to change gender). The second is 'transgender' (التحول الجنسي) which shows that the process of gender change has already been done.

There are a few system-based items in the corpus of analysis, the first of which is given below:

Example 9

The Crown Dependencies The UK is responsible for the defence and international representation of the CDs. The CDs are: the Bailiwick of Jersey, the Bailiwick of Guernsey and the Isle of Man. (E/C.12/GBR/5: article 9)	الأقاليم التابعة للتاج المملكة المتحدة مسؤولة عن حماية الأقاليم التابعة للتاج وعن تمثيلها. والأقاليم التابعة للتاج هي جزيرة مان وإقليم جيرسي و إقليم غيرنسي.

The title of the article, 'The Crown Dependencies' is rendered 'literally' as: الأقاليم التابعة للتاج (lit. 'the regions which belong to the throne'). The ST has replaced the phrase by the abbreviated form (CDs) to avoid repetition. However, the TT has followed the technique of 'explicitation' by rendering the full words for the ST initials.

Example 10

The Crown exercises its responsibilities for the Islands through the Privy Council and also makes appointments to the judiciary in each Island. (E/C.12/GBR/5: article 9)	ويمارس التاج مسؤولياته عن الجزر من خلال مجلس الملكة الخاص كما يعيّن السلطة القضائية في كل جزيرة.

The 'privy council' generally refers to the advisers of a monarchic government. It was established in many countries, such as France, Japan, Russia, where it has now been abolished, but it is still functioning in countries such as Canada, Denmark and the UK. It is commonly known in the UK as 'Her Majesty's Most Honourable Privy Council'. It has been rendered as مجلس الملكة الخاص (the Queen's Private Council). The technique of 'adaptation' is used as the translator gives the corresponding equivalent in the TT. It can also be rendered as المجلس الاستشاري الخاص بالملكة (the Queen's Private Council of Advisers) following the technique of 'explicitation'.

5.5 ANALYSIS OF ARCHAIC TERMS IN ARABIC–ENGLISH DOCUMENTS

In Chapter 3, we pointed out that Arabic legal documents use template terms which have continued to exist in the legal tradition such as المذكور (the said or the abovementioned). We can argue that the use of such terms gives an Arabic legal document a specialized nature and that they are considered the equivalents of the English archaic terms.

5.5.1 Translation of archaic terms in Arabic–English official documents

Examples of the term المذكور (the said or the abovementioned) have occurred in the official documents cited in Hatim, Shunnaq and Buckley (1995) as given below:

Table 5.4 Archaic terms in Arabic–English official documents

Arabic	English	Citation
. . . لتركة المتوفى المذكور . . .	. . . the bequest of the aforementioned deceased Mr/Ms . . .	(80–81)
. . . لذلك فقد ثبت ولايته علي القاصرتين المذكورتين . . . و مراعاته مصلحة القاصر المذكور	I have accordingly confirmed his custody of the aforementioned legal minors. . . . and safeguard the interests of the aforementioned legal minors.	(82–83)
لا يحق للوصي المذكور بيع شئ . . .	The said guardian may not sell any . . .	(84–85)
و طلبت تسجيله و بناء عليه تقرر ذلك . . .	She requested that this be recorded and in accordance therewith has made this resolution . . .	(92–93)
. . . إنني وكلت . . . . ب . . . . وكالة خاصة بما ذكر مفوضة لقوله و فعله و رأيه،	I have appointed . . . as my representative concerning . . . by means of power of special attorney over the hereinbefore stated authorizing his statements, actions, and judgments,	(106–107)

The term المذكور and other forms of it as underlined in the above examples have been used as lexical substitutions for name(s) of person(s) rather than repeating this/these name(s). It has been translated into English as 'aforementioned', 'hereinbefore', 'therewith' and 'said'. The procedure used in translating this term is 'transposition' according to Vinay and Darbelnet (1995:36). Sometimes, the noun المذكور is rendered as an adjective (a noun functioning as an adjective) as in example 3 in Table 5.4. In example 5 in the table, the passive verb ذكر (mentioned) is rendered into the passive form 'stated' and an added archaic adverb 'hereinbefore'.

Example 2 in Table 5.4, however, is mistranslated and requires further consideration below:

- القاصرتين المذكورتين . . . / the aforementioned legal minors . . .
- القاصر المذكور / the aforementioned legal minors (a *Certificate of Custody* 82–83)

As shown above, there is inconsistency in referring to the two feminine minors. In 1, the same specification is used in the ST, but the translation shifts to the plural and is lacking a gender-specific term. In 2, reference is altered to the masculine singular in the ST with the translator following the same strategy as in 1. He/she should have added the numeral 'two' plus a gender specific term (female). In both cases, the translation should be: 'The aforementioned two female legal minors'.

It is beneficial to look at some of these Arabic template terms in another legal subtype (for example international documents) such as the Arab Charter of Human Rights (AChHR):

Example 1

تتعهد كل دولة طرف في هذا الميثاق بأن تكفل لكل إنسان موجود على أراضيها وخاضع لسلطتها حق التمتع بكافة الحقوق والحريات الواردة فيه.	Each State Party to the present Charter undertakes to ensure to all individuals within its territory and subject to its Jurisdiction the right to enjoy all the rights and freedoms recognized herein. (AChHR, part 2: article 2)

<http://www1.umn.edu/humanrts/instree/loas2005.html>
<http://www1.umn.edu/humanrts/arab/a003.html>

Example 1 presents other forms of template Arabic terms: الواردة فيه (mentioned in it) is rendered into English as 'recognized herein'. The technique of 'transposition' is used: a 'present participle' (الواردة – mentioned) is rendered as 'past participle' and the Arabic preposition فيه (in it) is 'transposed' as an archaic adverb 'herein'. Sometimes archaic terms are used in place of demonstrative pronouns or prepositional phrases as in the following instance:

Example 2

تحمى الدول الأطراف كل إنسان . . . وتتخذ التدابير الفعالة لمنع ذلك وتعتبر ممارسة هذه التصرفات أو الإسهام فيها جريمة يعاقب عنها،	The States parties shall protect every person . . . They shall take effective measures to prevent such acts and shall regard the practice thereof, or participation therein, as a punishable offence. (AChHR, part 2: article 13a)

<http://www1.umn.edu/humanrts/arab/a003.html>
<http://www1.umn.edu/humanrts/instree/arabcharter.html>

As shown in example 2, there is no template term in the ST. Rather; there is either the demonstrative pronoun هذه (these – referring to a feminine plural noun) which is rendered into the archaic term 'thereof', hence through a 'class shift' of a pronoun to an adverb. 'Therein' is also used in the TT as an equivalent to the prepositional phrase فيها (in them) thus a 'structure shift' (Catford, 1965:76) of an adverb in place of a phrase.[68]

5.6 ANALYSIS OF ARCHAIC TERMS IN ENGLISH–ARABIC DOCUMENTS

English archaic terms are considered part and parcel of English legal discourse. Rendition of these terms into Arabic varies; they are rendered into non-archaic Arabic terms or archaic template terms. To illustrate this point, some examples from the ChUN, an Account Opening Form and an English–Arabic Lease Agreement will be considered:

Example 1

THIS LEASE AGREEMENT is made and entered into on _____ (day) of _____ (month), _____ (year), by and between ___________________________ hereinafter referred to as 'Landlord' and ___________________________, hereinafter referred to as 'Tenant'.
(Lease Agreement Template)

حرر عقد الإيجار هذا في يوم_____من
شهر__________سنة__________
بين كل من________(المشار إليه فيما
بعد في هذا العقد ''المالك'')
وبين________(المشار إليه فيما بعد في
هذا العقد 'المستأجر')
(author's translation)

<http://www.totalrealestatesolutions.com/realestateforms/html/rentalcontract1.html>

As the parallel example shows, 'hereinafter' is rendered as فيما بعد (later in the document). 'Transposition' of an adverb to a prepositional phrase is used but the translator added في هذا العقد (in this contract). This addition can be justified as it helps in making the reference of the archaic term clearer in the TT. The translator added this phrase in most of the cases where there is a rendition of an archaic term as in the second example given below. 'Herein' is translated as الواردة (mentioned) with an addition of the phrase في هذا العقد (in this contract) and 'hereto' is rendered as بموجب (as in) with an addition of في هذا العقد (in this contract).

Example 2

NOW, THEREFORE, in consideration of the covenants and obligations herein contained and other good and valuable consideration, the receipt and sufficiency of which is hereby acknowledged, the parties hereto agree as follows: (Lease Agreement Template)

ونظرا للتعهدات والالتزامات الواردة
في هذا العقد وكذلك مقابل عوض
مادي معتبر وبموجب الإقرار على
الإيصال وكفايته. تم اتفاق الطرفين
بموجب هذا العقد على ما يلي:

<https://docs.google.com/document/d/1MTBRPxlYNGcqEheR2gLCknIr8-TPMKLWFQF0n1ehqz8/preview?pli=1>
<http://www.translationdirectory.com/articles/article1775.php>

Example 3

Nothing in this Declaration may be interpreted as implying for any State, group or person any right to engage in any activity or to perform any act aimed at the destruction of any of the rights and freedoms set forth herein. (UDHR: article 30)

ليس في هذا الإعلان نص يجوز
تأويله على أنه يخول لدولة أو جماعة
أو فرد أي حق في القيام بنشاط أو
تأدية عمل يهدف إلى هدم الحقوق
والحريات الواردة فيه.

<http://www.un.org/en/documents/udhr/index.shtml>
<http://www.un.org/ar/documents/udhr/index.shtml>

'Set forth' occurs in the above example in combination with 'herein'. These are rendered as الواردة فيه (mentioned in it). 'Set forth' is also rendered in a different way in other contexts: in the ChUN (article 83:2), it is rendered as المبينة (illustrated (mentioned)); in the UNHR (article 28), it is translated as المنصوص عليها (mentioned). Other phrases such as 'foregoing' are rendered into سالفة الذكر (pre-mentioned) in the ChUN, Article 77:2. Example 5 below gives the translation of 'thereof':

Example 5

So, in any one of such events, the Account will be debited for the value of the returned item, plus any charges thereof, whenever the same is returned, irrespective of the length of the time taken to return it. (Account Opening Form: article 3.5.1)	لذلك فانه في أي من تلك الحالات، سيخصم من الحالات قيمة البند المعاد، بالإضافة الى أية مصاريف تتعلق به، حيثما يعاد ذلك البند، بغض النظر عن طول المدة المستغرقة لإعادته.

As we see from example 5, the archaic term 'thereof' is rendered as the verbal phrase تتعلق به (related to it) by following a 'structure shift' (Catford, 1965:76) where an adverb is replaced by a verbal phrase.

5.7 EXERCISES AND DISCUSSIONS

Exercise 1: Do you agree with using 'omission' in the TT when rendering the ST terms and phrases referring to God?

Exercise 2: How can a translator deal with vague terms and/or structures? Discuss in small groups.

Exercise 3: Comment on the translation of the underlined terms in the following parallel examples:

Example 1

يدفع المبلغ المذكور لـ . . . لإنفاقه على القاصر . . . بالمعروف	He pays the said sum to . . . so that he may equitably provide for the legal minor. (Hatim, Shunnaq and Buckley, 1995:96–97)

Example 2

الزوج – الرجل – البالغ – العاقل – الأعزب – الزوجة – البنت – بكر / ثيب – البالغة العاقلة	The male spouse, a bachelor/married man of legal age and of sound mind: The female spouse, a virgin/non-virgin of legal age and of sound mind. (Hatim, Shunnaq and Buckley, 1995:86–87)

Example 3

يجب أن يكون كل من الزوجين بالغا خلواً من الموانع الشرعية و . . . و تزوج إحداهما دون السن المقررة يتوقف على إذن خاص من الحاكم و ذلك بعد ثبوت البلوغ الطبيعي. (Mansoor,1965a:299)	Both spouses shall have attained the age of puberty and should be free of all legal impediments . . . The marriage of either who is below the said ages shall be subject to a special authorization by the judge, and that will be given upon proof of attainment of physical maturity. (Mansoor, 1965b:140)

Exercise 4:

1. Translate the underlined culture-specific and Shariʿah Law terms and phrases into English.
2. What are the procedures you used in translating these terms? Justify your choice.
3. Translate the whole document. Discuss and compare your translations in pairs.

الباب الرابع: انحلال عقد الزواج
الفصل الأول:الطلاق
المادة الرابعة والثلاثون:
أولًا: الطلاق رفع قيد الزواج بإيقاع من الزوج أو من الزوجة وإن وكلت به أو فوضت أو من ولا يقع الطلاق إلا بالصيغة المخصصة له شرعاً.
ثانياً: لا يعتد بالوكالة في إجراءات البحث الإجتماعي والتحكيم وفي إيقاع الطلاق
المادة الخامسة والثلاثون: لا يقع طلاق الأشخاص الآتي بيانهم:
1. السكران والمجنون والمعتوه والمكره ومن كان فاقد التمييز من غضب أو مصيبة مفاجئة أو كبر أو مرض.
2. المريض في مرض الموت أو في حالة يغلب في مثلها الهلاك إذا مات في ذلك المرض أو تلك الحالة وترثه زوجته.
المادة السادسة والثلاثون:
لا يقع الطلاق غير المنجز أو المشروط أو المستعمل بصيغة اليمين.
المادة السابعة والثلاثون:
1. يملك الزوج على زوجته ثلاث طلقات.
2. الطلاق المقترن بعدد لفظاً أو إشارة لا يقع إلا واحدة.
3. المطلقة ثلاثاً متفرقات تبين من زوجها بينونة كبرى.
المادة الثامنة والثلاثون:
1. رجعي: وهو ما جاز للزوج مراجعة زوجته أثناء عدتها منه دون عقد وتثبت المرجعة بما يثبت به الطلاق.
2. بائن: وهو قسمان:
أ- بينونة صغرى - وهي ما جاز فيه للزوج التزوج بمطلقته بعقد جديد.
ب- بينونة كبرى - وهي ما حرم فيه على الزوج التزوج من مطلقته التي طلقها ثلاثاً متفرقات ومضت عدتها.

المادة التاسعة والثلاثون:

1. على من أراد الطلاق أن يقيم الدعوى في المحكمة الشرعية يطلب إيقاعه وإستحصال حكم به فإذا تعذر عليه مراجعة المحكمة وجب عليه تسجيل الطلاق في المحكمة خلال مدة العدة.
2. تبقى حجة الزواج معتبرة إلى حين إبطالها من المحكمة.
3. إذا طلق الزوج زوجته وتبين للمحكمة أن الزوج متعسف في طلاقها وإن الزوجة أصابها ضرر من جراء ذلك، تحكم المحكمة بطلب منها على مطلقها بتعويض يتناسب وحالته المادية ودرجة تعسفه، يقدر جملة، على أن لا يتجاوز نفقتها لمدة سنتين علاوة على حقوقها الثابتة الأخرى

<https://docs.geogle.com/file/d/0B8ITLJi5y4TKcXF3MFJnUTFwUmc/edit?pli=1>

Exercise 5:

1. Translate the English or Arabic terms, phrases and sentences as given in the table below, and mention the procedure of translation.
2. In pairs discuss your answers and the differences you may have.

English	Arabic
his honesty, uprightness, eligibility and competence	عقيدة راسخة
appointed and installed	و ايمان بالله سبحانه و تعالى
legal guardian and competent spokesman	المفقود الغائب
his eligibility and honesty	أمانته و أهليته
is below the legal age of maturity	زوجتي و مدخولتي
in the interests and in the benefit of . . .	عصمتي و عقد نكاحي
I have given you my daughter in marriage	بطوعي و اختياري
I accept your daughter in marriage	و أنا لست مدهوشاً و متمتع بقواي العقلية
funds and assets	يوكل أو ينيب غيره

Exercise 6:

1. Translate the following passage into English.
2. What are the procedures you used in translating the Shari‘ah Law and culture-specific terms?
3. Discuss your translations in small groups.

دعوى نشوز

بموجب وثيقة عقد زواج رسمية بتاريخ / / ولاتزال في عصمته وقد أعد لها مسكناً شرعياً ودعاها للدخول في طاعته بهذا المسكن فامتنعت بدون وجه حق شرعي فاستصدر ضدها بتاريخ / / حكما في الدعوى بدخولها في طاعته بالمسكن الموضح بصحيفة تلك الدعوى وقد طعنت على هذا الحكم بالاستئناف في الدعوى رقم وقضى فيها بتاريخ / / بتأييد الحكم المستأنف وقام الطالب بإعلانها بالصيغة التنفيذية للحكم ولكنها اصرت على الامتناع عن الدخول في طاعته بدون وجه حق شرعي الأمر الذى حدا به الى اقامة الدعوى للقضاء بطلباته.

<http://www.arlawfirm.com/ADVdetails.asp?id=635>

Exercise 7:

1. Compare the English Marriage Certificate in Text A below and the Arabic Marriage Contract in Text B in terms of layout.
2. List the main Shariʿah Law terms in Text A; compare the drafting of these terms to the drafting of similar terms in Text B.
3. Translate Text A into Arabic, and Text B into English.
4. What are the difficult areas you faced, and what are the procedures you used to render these areas? Discuss your translations in small groups.

Text A

In the name of Allah, the most Beneficent, the most Merciful 'The stipulations that deserve the highest priority that you fulfil are those through which you make marital relations lawful' (Bukhari)

Muslim Marriage Certificate

Serial No.:
Praise be to Allah, the Lord of the Worlds and salutations be upon His messenger Muhammad (peace and blessings be upon him), his family and his Companions.
With help and success granted by Allah, after confirming that neither contracting party has no legal or other impediments and with *ijab* (proposal) and *qabul* (acceptance):
The *nikah* (Muslim marriage) contract has been concluded between the bridegroom and bride, as per terms and conditions listed overleaf:
Bridegroom's full name: . . . .
Date of birth: . . . .
Nationality/ies: . . . .
Place of birth: . . . .
Address: . . . .
Status of Bridegroom: unmarried / divorced / widowed
Bride's full name: . . . .
Date of birth: . . . .
Nationality/ies: . . . .
Place of birth: . . . .
Address: . . . .
Status of Bride: unmarried / divorced / widowed
Amount of *mahr*: . . . .
The *mu'ajjal* (immediate/prompt) amount: . . . ./ The *mu'wajjal* (deferred) amount: . . . .

CIVIL MARRIAGE
Reg. No.: . . . .
Date: . . . .
District: . . . .

Whether any property was given in lieu of the whole or any portion of the *mahr* with specification of the same and its valuation agreed between the parties: ....

In the presence of two witnesses:

• First witness's name and address: ....

Date of birth: ....Nationality: ....

Relationship with bride/groom: ....

• Second witness's name and address: ....

Date of birth: ....Nationality: ....

Relationship with bride/groom: ....

The bride and bridegroom undertake to act properly toward each other in their marital life and in particular as per terms and conditions listed overleaf. Praise and thanks be to Allah.

The *nikah* (Muslim Marriage) ceremony was held at .... on the .... day of .... 14 ...... (Hijri). Coinciding with ....20.....

We, the undersigned, put our signature to this contract, being of sound mind and without compulsion or duress.

Bridegroom's signature Bride's signature

....

First witness Second witness

....

Signature of Imam/Qadi & stamp

Name of Imam/Qadi ....

Address of associated organisation ....

Note: For a Muslim marriage to be recognised in British law it must be held at a mosque registered as a place for the solemnisation of marriage, otherwise the civil ceremony must take place at a registry office first before the *nikah* (Muslim marriage) ceremony.

Terms and conditions of the Muslim marriage contract:

Definitions:

Nikah – The Muslim contract of marriage;

Mahr – prescribed amount (cash/kind, immediate or deferred) given by the bridegroom to the bride in consideration of the marriage;

Witness – two adult witnesses of good character;

Ijab/*qabul* – formal marriage proposal and acceptance;

Husband/wife – bridegroom/bride after marriage contract;

Talaq al-tafwid – delegation of the husband's power of *talaq* (divorce) to the wife.

<http://www.muslimparliament.org.uk/Documentation/Muslim%20Marriage%20Contract.pdf>

Text B

عقد نكاح للسعوديين

الحمد لله وحده والصلاة والسلام على من لا نبي بعده . .
أما بعد -:
فلدي أنا: .... (مأذون عقود الأنكحة) بـمكة المصرح لي بذلك من وزير العدل برقم422 وتاريخ 5241/5/01هـ حضر(اسم الولي الرباعي / الوكيل / الوصي): . . . .
بموجب بطاقة أحوال رقم: . . . .
رقم السجل المدني أو الإقامة للولي غير السعودي (عشرة أرقام): . . . .
تاريخ الهوية للولي الصادر من مكة بصفته ولي البكر/الثيب (تشطب على الثيب إن كانت بكرا والعكس لو كانت ثيبا): . . . .
اسم الزوجة: . . . . (سعودية الجنسية)
بموجب رقم السجل المدني الموجود بكرت العائلة المضافة فيها أو بطاقة الأحوال المدنية إن كانت لديها بطاقة مستقلة وطلب عقد النكاح عليها من الحاضر معه (اسم الزوج كما في بطاقته): .... (سعودي الجنسية)
بموجب بطاقة أحوال رقم: . . . . تاريخ الهوية: . . . . الصادر من مكة.
الصداق (وكم المسلم وكم المؤخر) : . . . .
الشروط كاملة من كلا الطرفين المتفق عليها إلأ شرطاً حرم حلالاً أو أحل حراماً: . . . .
وقد وافقت المرأة المذكورة على الزواج من (اسم الزوج): . . . . .وحضر للتعريف والشهادة كل من:
الشاهد الأول: . . . . ولا يكون من الأصول أو الفروع، (سعودي الجنسية)
بموجب بطاقة أحوال رقم: . . . . رقم الهوية و تاريخ الهوية: . . . . الصادر من مكة.
و اسم الشاهد الثاني: . . . . (سعودي ويمكن أن يكون غير سعودي) بموجب بطاقة أحوال رقم: . . . . رقم الهوية و تاريخ الهوية: . . . . الصادر من مكة.
ولتوفر أركان النكاح وشروطه وانتفاء موانعه أجريت عقد النكاح بين المذكورين بإيجاب من الولي وقبول من الزوج ، حرر في 10/2/1429هـ وصلى الله وسلم على نبينا محمد وآله وصحبة وسلم. .
اسم وتوقيع الولي: . . . .
اسم وتوقيع توقيع الزوج: . . . .
اسم وتوقيع الزوجة أو البصمة: . . . .
اسم وتوقيع الشاهد الأول: . . . .
اسم وتوقيع الشاهد الثاني: . . . .

<http://mathounn.com/showthread.php?t=2998>

Exercise 7:

1. Look at the table below. Write down the procedure used for translating the religious and culture-specific elements.
2. What are the problems of translating these elements (mistranslations, justified and unjustified omissions and additions)?
3. Retranslate the ST and list the procedures you used in rendering it.
4. In pairs, discuss the difficult elements in translating the ST.
5. Compare your translations and list the common procedures you used.

Arabic (ST)	English (TT)
(أ) الزواج – بإطاره الإسلامي – حق لكل إنسان، وهو الطريق الشرعي لبناء الأسرة وإنجاب الذرية، وإعفاف النفس: "يأيها الناس اتقوا ربكم الذي خلقكم من نفس واحدة وخلق منها زوجها وبث منهما رجالا كثيرا ونساء" (النساء: 1). لكل من الزوجين قبل الآخر – عليه وله – حقوق وواجبات متكافئة قررتها الشريعة" "ولهن مثل الذي عليهن بالمعروف وللرجال عليهن درجة" (البقرة: 228)، وللأب تربية أولاده: بدنياً، و خلقياً، و دينياً، وفقاً لعقيدته وشريعته، وهو مسئول عن اختياره الوجهة التي يوليهم إياها: "كلكم راع وكلكم مسئول عن رعيته" (رواه الخمسة).	a) Every person is entitled to marry, to found a family and to bring up children in conformity with his religion, traditions and culture. Every spouse is entitled to such rights and privileges and carries such obligations as are stipulated by the Law.
(ب) لكل من الزوجين – قبل الآخر – حق احترامه، وتقدير مشاعره، وظروفه، في إطار من التواد والتراحم: "ومن آياته أن خلق لكم من أنفسكم أزواجا لتسكنوا إليها وجعل بينكم مودة ورحمة" (الروم: 21).	b) Each of the partners in a marriage is entitled to respect and consideration from the other.
(ج) على الزوج أن ينفق على زوجته وأولاده دون تقتير عليهم: "لينفق ذو سعة من سعته ومن قدر عليه رزقه فلينفق مما آتاه الله" (الطلاق: 7).	c) Every husband is obligated to maintain his wife and children according to his means.
(د) لكل طفل على أبويه حق إحسان تربيته، وتعليمه، وتأديبه: "وقل رب ارحمهما كما ربياني صغيرا" (الإسراء: 24)، ولا يجوز تشغيل الأطفال في سن باكرة، ولا تحميلهم من الأعمال ما يرهقهم، أو يعوق نموهم أو يحول بينهم وبين حقهم في اللعب والتعلم.	d) Every child has the right to be maintained and properly brought up by its parents, it being forbidden that children are made to work at an early age or that any burden is put on them which would arrest or harm their natural development.
(هـ) إذا عجز والدا الطفل عن الوفاء بمسئوليتهما نحوه، انتقلت هذه المسئولية إلى المجتمع، وتكون نفقات الطفل في بيت مال المسلمين – الخزانة العامة للدولة : "أنا أولى بكل مؤمن من نفسه، فمن ترك دينا أو ضيعة [ضيعة: أي ذرية ضعافا يخشى عليهم الضياع] فعلي، ومن ترك مالا فلورثته" (رواه الشيخان وأبو داود والترمذي).	e) If parents are for some reason unable to discharge their obligations towards a child it becomes the responsibility of the community to fulfill these obligations at public expense.
(ز) للأمومة حق في رعاية خاصة من الأسرة: "يا رسول الله: من أحق الناس بحسن صحابتي؟ قال: أمك قال (السائل): ثم من؟ قال: أمك، قال: ثم من: قال: أمك: قال: ثم من؟ قال: أبوك" (رواه الشيخان).	g) Motherhood is entitled to special respect, care and assistance on the part of the family and the public organs of the community (Ummah).

<http://www1.umn.edu/humanrts/arab/UIDHR.html>
<http://www.barrypearson.co.uk/articles/gods/islam_universal.htm>

Exercise 8: Translate the following excerpts into Arabic:

Exchange of ring words

'I give you this ring as a sign of our partnership, and as a symbol of our friendship and loyalty. I promise to love, respect and care for you, through good times and bad, completely and forever.'

'I give you this ring as a token of my devotion and of my love for you . . . Accept this ring as a sign of our commitment, and my promise that I will care for and love you always.'

'I promise to love, honour and respect you and be true to you always. I will be loving, faithful and loyal to you in our life together.'

'I give you this ring as a symbol of my love and as evidence of the vows we have made together. May it forever signify the love we have for each other.'

<http://www.bracknell-forest.gov.uk/your-civil-partnership-ceremony-choices.pdf>

Exercise 9:

1. Translate the following excerpt into Arabic.
2. What are the procedures you used to translate culture-specific terms?
3. Do you agree with using the technique of adaptation in translating culture-specific and system-based terms into Arabic? Give reasons and examples to support your answers.

The Court establishes that the position of partners in registered same-sex partnerships is in its essential factual and legal aspects comparable with the position of spouses as regards the right to inheritance from a deceased partner. The differences in the regulation of inheritance between spouses and between partners in registered same-sex partnerships are therefore not based on any objective, non-personal circumstance, but on sexual orientation. Until the established inconsistency is remedied, the same rules apply for inheritance between partners in registered same-sex partnerships as apply for inheritance between spouses in accordance with the Inheritance Act.16. (A/HRC/WG.6/7/SVN/1: article 20)

Exercise 10:

1. Translate the underlined terms and phrases into Arabic.
2. Summarize the text into Arabic.

PRIORITIES:

UNESCO shall accord priority to Africa and to gender equality in all its fields of competence throughout the duration of the Medium-Term Strategy. Moreover, specific interventions will be envisaged for the following priority groups and groups of countries:

- youth, in particular addressing youth violence and other issues affecting the welfare of youth around the world, especially the needs of youth in rural areas and marginalized groups as well as of unemployed youth;
- the least developed countries (LDCs), in line with the results of the September 2006 High-Level Meeting on Review of the Brussels Programme of Action; and
- the small island developing states (SIDS) in line with the Mauritius Declaration and the Mauritius Strategy, developing a holistic and interdisciplinary approach and bearing in mind the latest report of the Intergovernmental Panel on Climate Change 'Climate Change 2007: Impacts, Adaptation and Vulnerability'

(13 April 2007)
<http://unesdoc.unesco.org/images/0014/001499/149999e.pdf>

Exercise 11:

1. Translate the following two texts into English.
2. What are the difficulties in translating them?
3. Discuss the procedures of translating the two texts (for example doublets, archaic terms, modal expressions, etc)

Text A

إقرار والتزام

أقر أنا الموقع أدناه:.....................هوية رقم:.........................
بصفتي ممثلا عن شركة:.....................:بالتالي
1. بأنني قرأت وتفهمت كافة ما ورد بوثائق العطاء المطروح رقم42 0102 من شروط عامة وخاصة ومواصفات وألتزم التزاماً قانونياً بتلك الشروط والمواصفات.
2. كما ألتزم بأن يبقى العرض المقدم مني ساري المفعول ولا يجوز لي الرجوع عنه لمدة ستون يوماً من تاريخ آخر موعد لتقديم العروض.
3. وكذلك ألتزم بتوريد الأصناف المحالة على بموجب العطاء المذكور أعلاه والتي يتم طلبها من قبل وزارة الصحة خلال شهر وذلك من تاريخ توقيع العقد واستلام أوامر التوريد على أن تكون تلك الأصناف الموردة من قبلي وفقًا للمواصفات والشروط المنصوص عليها في هذا العطاء.
وهذا إقرار وتعهد مني بذلك أقر وألتزم بكل ما ورد به دون أي ضغط أو إكراه.

<www.mof.gov.ps/>

Text B:

مقدمة الاتفاق: حيث أن الطرف الأول بصفته المذكورة أعلاه قام بطرح العطاء رقم ___ بشأن توريد غاز الهيليوم لصالح وزارة الصحة وحيث أن الطرف الثاني شركة مرخصة رسمياً ومختصة بهذا المجال ومؤهلة فنيا وُقامت بالاشتراك بالعطاء المطروح أعلاه وحيث أن الطرف الأول قام بإحالة العطاء
بالتجزئة وتم تسرية البند رقم الخاص بتوريد على الطرف الثاني كونه الأرخص
لذا فقد اتفق الطرفان بإرادة حرة وبإيجاب وقبول على ما يلي من الشروط:- . . . . .
لا يجوز لأي طرف من الأطراف النكول عما ذُكر أعلاه وفي حالة حدوث أي خلاف بينهما حول تفسير أي بند من البنود المذكورة أعلاه يتم حله بالطرق الودية وإلا يتم الفصل فيه وفقًا للقوانين والأنظمة المعمول بها في مناطق السلطة الوطنية الفلسطينية، وعلى هذا تم الاتفاق والتوقيع حسب الأصول من قبل طرف العقد وسلمت نسخة لكل منهما.

<www.mof.gov.ps/>

Exercise 12:

1. Translate the following passage into English.
2. What are the difficulties in translating it?
3. What are the procedures used in translating religious references and culture-specific terms and phrases?

دستور المملكة العربية السعودية

بعون الله تعالى: نحن فهد بن عبد العزيز آل سعود ملك المملكة العربية السعودية
بناء على ما تقتضيه المصلحة العامة ونظراً لتطور الدولة في مختلف المجالات ورغبة في تحقيق الأهداف التي نسعى إليها.
أمرنا بما هو آت:
أولًا – إصدار النظام الأساسي للحكم بالصيغة المرفقة.
ثانياً – يستمر العمل بكل الأنظمة والأوامر والقرارات المعمول بها عند نفاذ هذا النظام حتى تعدل بما يتفق معه.

الباب الأول

المبادئ العامة

المادة ١

المملكة العربية السعودية دولة عربية إسلامية ذات سيادة تامة ؛ دينها الإسلام ودستورها كتاب الله تعالى وسنة رسوله ولغتها هي اللغة العربية. وعاصمتها مدينة الرياض.

. . .

الباب الثاني

نظام الحكم

المادة ٥

أ– نظام الحكم في المملكة العربية السعودية . . . ملكي.
ب– يكون الحكم في أبناء الملك المؤسس عبد العزيز بن عبد الرحمن الفيصل آل سعود وأبناء الأبناء... ويبايع الأصلح منهم للحكم على كتاب الله تعالى وسنة ورسوله.
ج– يختار الملك ولي العهد. . ويعفيه بأمر ملكي.

(*continued*)

د– يتولى ولي العهد متفرغاً لولاية العهد. . وما يكلفه به الملك من أعمال.
ه – يتولى ولي العهد سلطات الملك عند وفاته حتى تتم البيعة.
المادة ٦
يبايع المواطنون الملك على كتاب الله تعالى وسنة رسوله وعلى السمع والطاعة في العسر واليسر والمنشط والمكره.
المادة ٧
يستمد الحكم في المملكة العربية السعودية سلطته من كتاب الله تعالى وسنة رسوله وهما الحاكمان على هذا النظام وجميع أنظمة الدولة.
المادة ٨
يقوم الحكم في المملكة العربية السعودية على أساس العدل والشورى والمساواة وفق الشريعة الإسلامية.
الباب الثالث
مقومات المجتمع السعودي
المادة ٩
الأسرة هي نواة المجتمع السعودي. ويربى أفرادها على أساس العقيدة الإسلامية وما تقتضيه من الولاء والطاعة لله ولرسوله ولأولي الأمر. . واحترام النظام وتنفيذه وحب الوطن والاعتزاز به وبتاريخه المجيد.
المادة ١٠
تحرص الدولة على توثيق أواصر الأسرة والحفاظ على قيمها العربية والإسلامية ورعاية جميع أفرادها وتوفير الظروف المناسبة لتنمية ملكاتهم وقدراتهم.
المادة ١١
يقوم المجتمع السعودي على أساس من اعتصام أفراده بحبل الله وتعاونهم على البر والتقوى والتكافل فيما بينهم وعدم تفرقهم.
المادة ١٢
تعزيز الوحدة الوطنية واجب وتمنع الدولة كل ما يؤدي للفرقة والفتنة والانقسام.

<http://www.constitutionnet.org/files/constitution_of_saudi_arabia-1992.pdf>

Exercise 13: Compare between the Arabic ST and its parallel English TT in Text A and Text B below:

1. Comment on the features and drafting of the ST.
2. What are the procedures used in translating religious elements and elaborate formal expressions?
3. Do you agree with these procedures? If not mention why and suggest others.

Text A

النمرة:ه ق ص/13/1/مجلد 16 — التاريخ:2012/11/19م

أخي الكريم الدكتور:. . . . . . .

السكرتير التنفيذي للجنة الإقتصادية و الأفريقية التابعة للأمم المتحدة

تحية من عند الله مباركة طيبة ، و دمتم في حفظ الله و رعايته

(continued)

(continued)

في البدء أنقل لسيادتك شكر و تقدير السيد/وزير شئون رئاسة الجمهورية . . . ، و كل العاملين بالهيئة و شكري الخاص على حسن لقائكم و حفاوتكم و اهتمامكم بزيارتنا و كريم تجاوبكم ليكون بين قاعة الصداقة و مؤسستكم العامرة، توأمة تعاون، ننقل من خلالها كم كبير من خبرتكم ممزوجة بتقنيات عملية لإدارة المؤتمرات بمختلف أجنحتها و فروعها.

سعادة الأخ الدكتور،

استثماراً لهذه العلاقة الطيبة ، أرجو كريم تفضلكم بالتصديق و السماح لتدريب الكوادر البشرية للهيئة العامة لقاعة الصداقة للشواغر وفق التخصصات الآتية:

أولاً: الإدارة العامة شاغرتان.

ثانياً: الإدارة المالية و التسويق و الترويج أربعة شواغر.

ثالثاً: الدائرة التلفزيونية شاغرتان.

رابعاً: الدائرة الثقافية شاغرتان.

خامساً: الفندقة و الضيافة أربعة شواغر.

أخي الكريم أرجو أن أسمع عنكم كل الخير، و أنا على يقين أن نجد الموافقة و نحسب أن كل المبعوثين للتدريب بطرفكم سينقلوا لنا و عبركم نقلة كبيرة، تدعم و تدفع بتطوير الأداء في بلادنا، و سيكونوا سفراء عنكم، يحفظون لكم حسن صنيعكم، و ينقلوا عنكم جميل خبرتكم لهذا الوطن العزيز.

جزاكم الله عنا خير الجزاء و دمتم ذخراً

و بالله التوفيق، ، ،

© from one of the correspondences to the UN Economic Commission for Africa

Text B

No. EOM/1/31/Vol. 16 Date: 19/11/2012

To: His Excellency Dr.
Deputy Executive Secretary,
United Nations Economic Commission for Africa

Dear Sir,

Allow me at the outset to convey to you the compliments of H.E. the Minister for Presidential Affairs, in charge of the general oversight of the Friendship Hall Corporation (FHC), my own compliments as well as those of the entire staff of the FHC, for the warm welcome we have received during our delegation's visit to the UNECA premises and Conference Centre facilities. We look forward to an exemplary and fruitful relationship between our two institutions, which would enable the FHC to benefit from the accumulated experience and technical expertise of UNECA in the various fields pertaining to conference management.

We would like to take this opportunity to express in concrete terms the training needs of the FHC and we are hopeful that UNECA, under your guidance and direction, would be in a position to facilitate the provision of training for the FHC staff in the following departments:

(*continued*)

(continued)

1. Department of Administration: two staff members.
2. Finance and Marketing Department: four staff members.
3. TV broadcasting: two staff members.
4. Cultural Department: two staff members.
5. Hotel and Hospitality Department: four staff members.

We would very much appreciate if the required training is provided as it would go a long way in improving the efficiency of the FHC service delivery and hence increase the overall capacity of our country in hosting and organizing conferences.

© from one of the correspondences to the UN Economic Commission for Africa

Exercise 14: Comment on the procedures of translating religious items in the table below. Then compare these strategies to those used in exercise 13 above.

ST	TT
بسم الله الرحمن الرحيم أيها الأخوة والأصدقاء الكرام: السلام عليكم ورحمة الله وبركاته ،،،	In the Name of God, Most Compassionate, Most Merciful. My Dear Brothers and Friends: May God's peace, mercy and blessings be upon you.
يسرني أن أشكركم على تلبية الدعوة لهذا اللقاء التاريخي ، وأن أرحّب بكم باسم أخي خادم الحرمين الشريفين – يحفظه الله – والشعب السعودي في المملكة العربية السعودية ، موطن الإسلام والسلام ، حيث انطلقت الدعوة إلى المساواة والصداقة بين البشر أجمعين في قوله تعالى : (يا أيها الناس إنّا خلقناكم من ذكر وأنثى وجعلناكم شعوبًا وقبائل لتعارفوا إن أكرمكم عند الله أتقاكم).	It is my pleasure to thank you for accepting the invitation to participate in this historic gathering, and to welcome you, on behalf of my brother, the Custodian of the Two Holy Mosques – may God protect him – and on behalf of the Saudi people, to the Kingdom of Saudi Arabia, the land of peace and Islam, from which an eternal message of equality and friendship between all people was launched. In the words of the Almighty: "O Mankind, we have created you from a male and female and made you into nations and tribes that you may know one another. Verily, the most honorable of you before God is the one who is most pious."
إن هذه الدعوة الربانية الخالدة هي التي تمثل روح الإسلام الحقيقي ، دين الحكمة والموعظة الحسنة . . .	This eternal call from Almighty God represents the true spirit of Islam, a religion of peace, wisdom and righteousness . . .
إنني أعرف أن خطر الإرهاب لا يمكن أن يزول بين يوم وليلة ، وأن حربنا ضد الإرهاب ستكون مريرة وطويلة ، وأن الإرهاب يزداد شراسة وعنفاً كلّما ضاق الخناق عليه.	I realize that the danger of terrorism cannot be eliminated overnight, and that our war against terrorism will be long and difficult and that terrorism is becoming increasingly violent and vicious as we tighten the noose around it. But
إلا أنني واثق بالله تماماً من النتيجة النهائية وهي انتصار قوى المحبة والتسامح والسلام على قوى الحقد والتطرف والإجرام، بعونه تعالى ، إنه نعم المولى ونعم النصير.	I am fully confident – God willing – that the final outcome will be a resounding victory for the forces of moderation, tolerance and peace against the forces of hatred, extremism, and crime – with the help of God Almighty, the ultimate supporter and protector.
وشكراً لكم . . . ،،، . . . والسلام عليكم ورحمة الله وبركاته.	Thank you, and may God's peace, mercy, and blessings be upon you.

<www.un.org/en/documents/ods/>
<www.un.org/ar/documents/ods/>

Exercise 15: Translate the contents of the following table into English.

1. What are the difficulties in translating it?
2. What are the procedures you used to deal with them?

أوجه الاختلاف وأوجه الشبه بين أنظمة التأمين الثلاثة :

الموضوع	**النظام التكافلي الاسلامي**	**النظام التعاوني التقليدي**	**نظام التأمين التجاري**
العقود المستخدمة	تبرع بقصد التعاون.	منفعة متبادلة.	تجاري يقصد منه الربح.
مسؤولية المؤمّن (الشركة)	دفع التعويضات والمصاريف من صندوق التكافل أو من القرض الحسن في حالة عجز الصندوق.	دفع المطالبات والمصاريف من صندوق الاشتراكات وفي حالة العجز يطلب اشتراكات اضافية من المشاركين.	دفع التعويضات والمصاريف من الصندوق المختلط (أقساط ورأس مال).
مسؤولية حملة الوثائق	دفع الاشتراكات.	دفع الاشتراكات الاساسية والاضافية عند اللزوم.	دفع الأقساط.
رأس المال المستخدم في دفع التعويضات	اشتراكات حملة وثائق التكافل.	اشتراكات المؤسسين.	رأس مال المساهمين والأقساط.
الاستـثـمـــار	مقيد بأحكام الشريعة الإسلامية.	لايوجد قيود شرعية.	لا يوجد قيود شرعية.
الحسابات الداخلية	يوجد حسابين(صندوقين) حساب حملة الوثائق. حساب المساهمين في الشركة.	يوجد حساب واحدفقط هو حساب المشاركين.	يوجد حساب واحد فقط مختلط لرأس المال والأقساط.
الفائض التأميني وعوائد استثمار الاشتراكات	من حق حملة الوثائق ويعاد توزيعه عليهم.	من حق المشاركين ويوزع عليهم.	يعتبر ربح للمساهمين.

<www.kantakji.com/media/1373/d223.doc>

6 Analysis of Arabic–English–Arabic texts: the syntactic level

6.1 INTRODUCTION

This chapter investigates the translation of modal auxiliaries and passivization. The first part is concerned with the analysis of English modal auxiliaries ('shall', 'may' and other less frequent modals) and Arabic modal expressions يجوز (may/it is allowed), لا يجوز (it is not permissible). The second part will investigate the translation of passive forms from English into Arabic and vice versa. The analysis will be in two phases, the first of which is a tabulated quantitative frequency analysis of the techniques used in translating the element under investigation. The second phase is a qualitative critical analysis, the aim of which is to critically reflect on and criticize some of the examples given and attempt to provide some solutions wherever possible.

6.2 ANALYSIS OF MODAL AUXILIARIES IN ENGLISH–ARABIC DOCUMENTS

This section analyzes the translation of modal auxiliaries in the ChUN. We will first give a frequency analysis of obligation and possibility modals based on a parallel alignment table. Section 6.2.2 deals with a critical analysis of some of the examples.

6.2.1 Quantitative analysis of modal auxiliaries in English–Arabic documents

Table 6.1 represents a frequency analysis of possibility and obligation modals in the ChUN followed by a figure clarifying these percentages.

As the table shows, deontic modals occur in combination with either the active or the passive. 'Shall' is the most frequent modal auxiliary representing 62.93%; 'may' is the second most frequent modal (29.96%). The remaining 7% is divided between 'might', 'will', 'should', 'must', 'is to' and 'is likely to'. The data can be illustrated in Figure 6.1.

It is of value to our analysis to look at the different types of Arabic modal expressions and/or particles that have been used as translations for the modals given in the previous table.

The number of the modal phrases and expressions used in the Arabic parallel version of the ChUN is less than half the number of modal auxiliaries used in the English version. Many English modal auxiliaries are rendered into Arabic as normal verbs in the imperfect tense, for example verbs used for the translation of 'shall'.

Table 6.1 Frequency analysis of English–Arabic modal auxiliaries in the ChUN

Modal type	**Number of occurrences**	**Proportion of modal type found (%)**	
Shall + Active	118	44.19	62.93
Shall + Passive	50	18.74	
May + Active	62	23.22	29.96
May + Passive	18	06.74	
Might + Active	3	01.13	1.13
Might + Passive	0	0	
Will + Active	5	01.87	3.00
Will + Passive	3	01.13	
Should + Active	2	0.74	1.11
Should + Passive	1	0.37	
Must + Active	0	0	0.37
Must + Passive	1	0.37	
Is to + Active	0	0	0.37
Is to + Passive	1	0.37	
Is likely to	3	01.13	1.13
Total	**267**	**100.00**	**100.00**

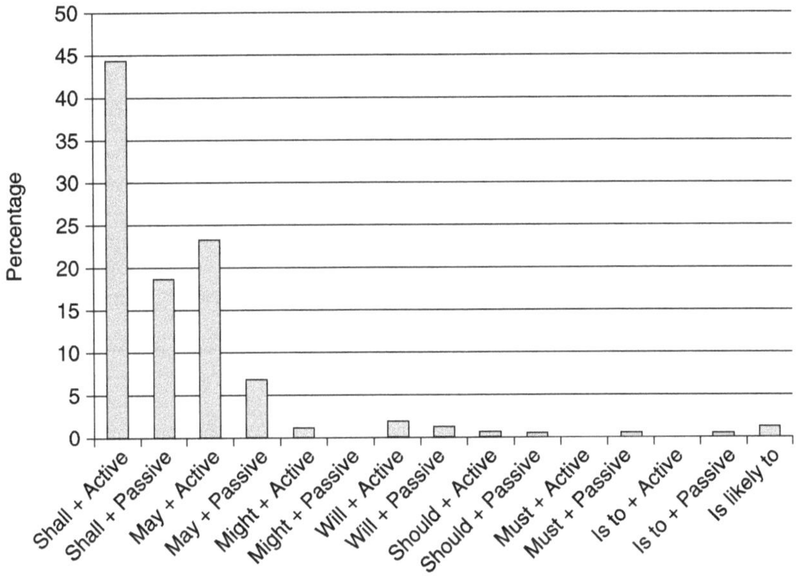

Figure 6.1 Frequency analysis of English–Arabic modal auxiliaries in the ChUN.

In Table 6.2, nearly half of the overall percentage (46.09%) of the modal expressions used in the document is for the preposition لِـ (for) plus the infinitive clause initiated by أن (that) in the positive and negative form. The positive verb of possibility (يجوز – it is allowed) and its negative form (لا يجوز – it is not allowed) come in second place (15.65%), yet the affirmative form is much more frequent than the negative form (11.30%). In third place comes قد (may), a particle of possibility (13.04%). The modal verb of necessity, يجب (it is compulsory (must)) comes in fourth place (12.17%) whereas its negative form does not

Table 6.2 Frequency analysis of modal expressions in the Arabic translation of English modals in the ChUN

Modal type	**Number of occurrences**	**Proportion of modal type found (%)**	
لِـ . . . أن	44	38.26	46.09
ليس لِـ . . . أن	9	07.83	
يجوز	13	11.30	15.65
لا يجوز	5	04.35	
يجب	14	12.17	12.17
لا يجب	0	0	
ينبغي	3	02.61	02.61
لا ينبغي	0	0	
قد	15	13.04	13.04
على . . . أن	5	04.35	04.35
بحسب ما / حسبما	3	02.61	02.61
من شأن	2	01.74	01.74
يمكن أن	1	0.87	0.87
من المهم أن	1	0.87	0.87
Total	**115**	**100**	**100**

register any occurrence at all. The rest of the modal expressions register low percentages with على . . . أن (it is incumbent on . . . that): 4.35%; ينبغي (should) and حسبما (as necessary): 2.61%; من شأن (is likely to): 1.74%; and finally يمكن أن (it is possible . . . that) and من المهم أن (it is important that): 0.87%. These percentages are represented in the following chart.

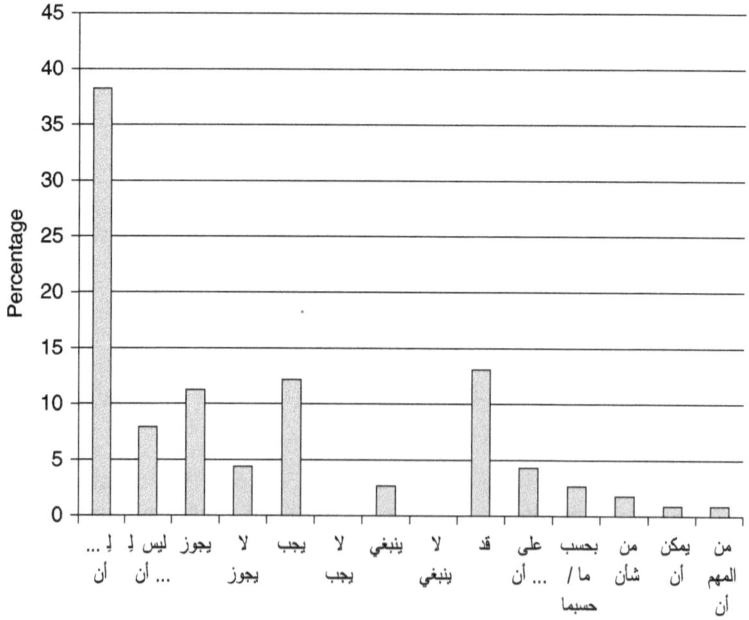

Figure 6.2 Frequency analysis of modal phrases and expressions in the Arabic translation of English modals in the ChUN.

6.2.2 Qualitative analysis of modal auxiliaries in English–Arabic documents

In this part I will discuss in more detail how the modal auxiliaries in the ChUN have been rendered into Arabic. This discussion will be divided into three subcategories:

6.2.2.1 Translation of shall

We have pointed out in Chapter 3 (section 3.2.2.6) that ‘shall’ is used in legal documents as a deontic modal of ‘obligation’ which guarantees that the act will happen and that ‘it is legally binding’ (Tiersma, 1999:106). In the following section, I investigate how ‘shall’ is rendered into Arabic.

Shall *plus infinitive (active) into imperfect*

All the patterns including ‘shall plus active’ are rendered into Arabic using the techniques of ‘linguistic adaptation’, according to Mayoral Asensio (2003:55) or ‘transposition’, according to Vinay and Darbelnet (1995:36). That is, ‘shall plus an infinitival active verb’ is translated into ‘imperfect’. Badawi, Carter and Gully (2004:30) define the ‘imperfect’ as ‘actions either not completed or regarded as such’. It is translated into English as ‘present’ as in the following examples:

Examples 1, 2 and 3

English	Arabic
1. The Organization and its Members shall act in accordance with the following principles. . . (ChUN, article 2)	1. تقوم الهيئة وأعضاؤها وفقاً للمبادئ الآتية . . .
2. All Members . . . shall fulfill the obligations . . . (ChUN, article 2:2)	2. أعضاء الهيئة . . . يقومون بالالتزامات . . .
3. All Members shall settle their international disputes . . . (ChUN, article 2:3)	3. يفض جميع أعضاء الهيئة منازعاتهم الدولية . . .

<http://www.un.org/en/documents/charter/index.shtml>
<http://www.un.org/ar/documents/charter/index.shtml>

In the above examples, ‘shall act’, ‘shall fulfil’ and ‘shall settle’ are rendered as تقوم ، يقومون ، يفض (acts, fulfil (plural), settles). Verbs in the TT occur in the ‘imperfect’ which is used in Arabic to express mood and it denotes that this action has already started and is yet to be finished. It is not known, however, when it will finish. If it finishes, it will be considered perfect which carries no mood itself. Thus, the ‘linguistic adaptation’ is considered one solution for the lack of correspondence between the English and the Arabic modal system. Yet, a better solution should have been using a lexical verb denoting necessity such as يجب (must or should).

Shall *plus infinitive (active) into lexical verbs of necessity*

The obligation modal ‘shall plus active’ is sometimes rendered into an equivalent lexical verb denoting obligation as in example 4 below:

Example 4

The parties to any dispute, the continuance of which is likely to endanger the maintenance of international peace and security <u>shall</u> first of all <u>seek</u> a solution . . . (ChUN, article 33:1)	<u>يجب</u> على أطراف أي نزاع من شأن استمراره أن يعرض حفظ السلم والأمن الدولي للخطر <u>أن يلتمسوا</u> حله بادئ ذي بدء. . .

<http://www.un.org/en/documents/charter/index.shtml>
<http://www.un.org/ar/documents/charter/index.shtml>

In this example, 'shall seek' is rendered as يجب على . . . أن يلتمسوا. . .. As shown يجب (it is compulsory) occurs in combination with على (on). It also takes as its agent a clause initiated with أن (that). It can sometimes take a verbal noun as its predicate as in يجب عليهم . . . التماس (it is incumbent on them seeking). In translating 'shall' as يجب, this is done through 'linguistic adaptation' of a modal as a lexical verb. The infinitive verb 'seek' is translated through 'literal translation' into an equivalent infinitive (أن يلتمسوا). The translator seeks the same equivalent that transfers the mood of obligation (for example the imperfect mood in Arabic) to guarantee that the action in question has already taken place.

Example 5

. . . they <u>shall refer</u> it to the Security Council. (ChUN, article 37:1)	. . . <u>وجب</u> عليها أن تعرضه على مجلس الأمن.

<http://www.un.org/en/documents/charter/index.shtml>
<http://www.un.org/ar/documents/charter/index.shtml>

In example 5, a lexical verb of necessity is used as an equivalent to the modal 'shall plus infinitive'. Yet, a shift of tense has occurred by using the verb وجب (must + perfect, it had been compulsory) in the perfect. It is known that in Arabic the perfect carries no mood and it expresses events that are 'either actually completed or regarded as such' (Badawi, Carter and Gully, 2004:62). Thus, the perfect tense is not the accurate equivalent of the English modal 'shall'. The solution for this is to use the imperfect (يجب – it is compulsory must . . .).

Example 6

The Security Council <u>shall duly take account of</u> failure to comply with such provisional measures. (ChUN, article 37:1)	و<u>على</u> مجلس الأمن <u>أن يحسب</u> لعدم أخذ المتنازعين بهذه التدابير المؤقتة حسابه . . .

<http://www.un.org/en/documents/charter/index.shtml>
<http://www.un.org/ar/documents/charter/index.shtml>

In this example, على (on) is used to denote obligation as an equivalent of 'shall'. In Arabic, the mood of necessity can be expressed through يجب على + أن or through على (on) alone as Badawi, Carter and Gully (2004:396) argue:

Note also that 'must' can be expressed by ʿala على alone:

علينا أن نعي هذا.	We must be aware of this.

على (on) described above by Badawi, Carter and Gully is different from what they call 'extended obligation' (ibid.:177), i.e. bearing a sense of burden such as that given below:

حيث نزلوا جميعا على نفقة الدولة.	Where they all stayed in a hotel <u>at</u> the expense of (the state).

There is no modal verb corresponding to this 'extended obligation' in the English translation as such since على (on) is rendered 'literally' into the preposition 'at' and there is no modality expressed either syntactically or semantically. It merits pointing out that no such type of obligation exists in the ChUN.

Example 7

When the Security Council has decided to use force it <u>shall</u>, . . . <u>invite</u> that Member, . . . (ChUN, article 44)	إذا قرر مجلس الأمن استخدام القوة، فإنه . . . <u>ينبغي له أن يدعو</u> هذا العضو . . .

<http://www.un.org/en/documents/charter/index.shtml>
<http://www.un.org/ar/documents/charter/index.shtml>

Another way of translating the English deontic verb 'shall plus infinitive (active)' is given in the above example. The TT uses the verb ينبغي (should) which means 'it is imperative', 'most desirable', 'ought' (Badawi, Carter and Gully, 2004:395). They give the following examples for clarification:

هذه الحقيقة التي ينبغي ان يعيها المؤمنون.	This is the fact of which believers ought to be aware.
الغضب علامة ينبغي الاصغاء لها.	Anger is the symptom which must be paid attention to.

According to the above examples, ينبغي (should) can also denote obligation, though not as strong as يجب (it is compulsory). It may imply that the action can be done or not.

Shall *plus the negative*

In this section, we will investigate different ways of translating 'shall plus the negative':

Examples 8, 9, 10 and 11

8. Each member <u>shall have not</u> more than five representatives in the General Assembly. (ChUN, article 9)	8. <u>لا يجوز</u> أن يكون للعضو الواحد أكثر من خمسة مندوبين في الجمعية العامة.

9. A retiring member shall not be eligible for immediate re-election . . . (ChUN, article 23:1)	9. والعضو الذي انتهت مدته لا يجوز إعادة انتخابه على الفور. . .
10. The trusteeship system shall not apply to territories which have become Members of the United Nations. . . (ChUN, article 78)	10. لا يطبق نظام الوصاية على الأقاليم التي أصبحت أعضاء في هيئة "الأمم المتحدة" . . .
11. In the performance of their duties the Secretary General and the staff shall not seek or receive instructions from any government or from any other authority external to the Organization. (ChUN, article 100:1)	11. ليس للأمين العام ولا للموظفين أن يطلبوا أو أن يتلقوا في تأدية واجبهم تعليمات من أية حكومة أو من أية سلطة خارجة عن الهيئة.

<http://www.un.org/en/documents/charter/index.shtml>
<http://www.un.org/ar/documents/charter/index.shtml>

Negation of modals may include either the modal or the verb (proposition). Difference in both depends on the type of the modal which results in a different meaning of the whole sentence. The following example cited in Palmer (1990:113) clarifies this idea:

John can't be in his office (it is possible that John is in his office).

John may not be in his office (it is possible that John is not in his office).

Quirk et al. (1985:794–799) and Palmer (1990:39) summarize the main aspects of negating deontic modality in the following table:

Table 6.3 Aspects of negating deontic modality

Type of modality	*Positive*	*Negative modality*	*Negative proposition*
Deontic possibility	may/can	may not/can't	____/needn't/
Deontic necessity	must	needn't	mustn't

Negation of 'shall' is not expressed in the above table although it is considered one of the 'necessity' modals according to Palmer (1990:73). As it is stronger than 'must', its negation expresses strong prohibition. In example 8, it is the proposition, not the modal, that is negated and in example 9, it is the modal, that is negated. In both cases, they are translated into Arabic as لا يجوز (it is not permissible, or not allowed). The Arabic equivalent to the modal 'shall' here is the deontic verb of possibility (يجوز – may) and its negative form shows lack of permissibility. Thus, a better translation can represent the prohibitive 'shall not' in Arabic as لا يجب (mustn't) or يجب ألا (must not) as given in Badawi, Carter and Gully (2004:398).

In examples 10 and 11, translation of the prohibition phrase 'shall not seek' is different since it is done through a lexical verb in the imperfect mood preceded by the negative particle لا (not) in 10 and through the particle لِ (for) preceded by ليس (not) in 11.[69] Negation in the two examples expresses lack of permissibility for the agent: الأمين العام والموظفين (the Secretary General and the Personnel).

Shall *plus the passive*

'Shall plus the passive' reaches nearly one-third of the total number of the occurrences of the modal 'shall'. To avoid redundancy, this section will be dealt with in greater detail in the analysis of passivization, Section 6.4.

6.2.2.2 Translation of **may**

As was stated before, 'may' is a deontic modal of possibility which denotes permissibility according to Palmer (1990:37). It occurs in the ST in combination with the infinitive either in the active or passive voice.

May *plus infinitive (active) into a lexical verb of 'possibility'*

The first case of translating 'may plus infinitive (active)' into Arabic is through the lexical verb denoting possibility (يجوز – it is allowed) as given below:

Examples 12 and 13

12. These may include complete or partial interruption of economic relations . . . (ChUN, article 41)	12. ويجوز أن يكون من بينها وقف الصلات الاقتصادية وقفا جزئياً أو كلياً . . .
13. Should the Security Council consider that measures provided for in Article 41 would be inadequate or have proved to be inadequate, it may take such action by air, sea, or land forces as may be necessary to maintain or restore international peace and security. (ChUN, article 41)	13. إذا رأى مجلس الأمن أن التدابير المنصوص عليها في المادة 41 لا تفي بالغرض أو ثبت أنها لم تف به، جاز له أن يتخذ بطريق القوات الجوية والبحرية والبرية من الأعمال ما يلزم لحفظ السلم والأمن الدولي أو لإعادته إلى نصابه.

<http://www.un.org/en/documents/charter/index.shtml>
<http://www.un.org/ar/documents/charter/index.shtml>

'May include' is translated 'literally' into a lexical verb denoting possibility plus a clause initiated with '*and*': ويجوز أن يكون (and may be) in example 12. In 13, translation of the modal may 'it may take' is changed from 'imperfect' to 'past': جاز له أن يتخذ (it was allowed for him to take). This shift is used in Arabic legal documents but unjustified; it can be used as a means of a stylistic variation but for the sake of consistency it is recommended to stick to the imperfect (يجوز – it is allowed). There is another occurrence of 'may' in example 13:

> as may be necessary to maintain or restore international peace and security.
> ما يلزم لحفظ السلم والأمن الدولي أو لإعادته إلى نصابه

The TT lacks a direct equivalent of the modal 'may'. The possibility particle قد (may) can be used in this context to fill in such a semantic gap. A 'class shift' (Catford, 1965:78) is used to render an adjective ‘necessary’ into a verb (يلزم – is needed/is required). A suggested translation of the above statement into Arabic can be:

ما قد يلزم لحفظ أو استعادة السلم والأمن الدوليين. (author’s translation)

The same ST pattern ‘may be necessary’ is translated into a different lexical verb in the TT as given in example 14 below:

Example 14

The Organization shall enjoy in the territory of each of its Members such legal capacity as may be necessary for the exercise of its functions and the fulfilment of its purposes. (ChUN, article 104)	تتمتع الهيئة في بلاد كل عضو من أعضائها بالأهلية القانونية التي يتطلبها قيامها بأعباء وظائفها وتحقيق مقاصدها.

<http://www.un.org/en/documents/charter/index.shtml>
<http://www.un.org/ar/documents/charter/index.shtml>

As underlined in example 14, ‘may be necessary’ is rendered as يتطلبه (needs/requires). The verb is used in the imperfect mood with no modal verb of possibility. A better translation for this can be achieved by including the particle قد (may) before the verb يتطلبه (needs or requires).

May *plus infinitive (active) into a preposition*

The same pattern: ‘may plus infinitive in the active voice’ presented above is translated into Arabic not by a lexical verb, but into a preposition plus a clause initiated by أن (that). Totter (2000:342) comments on the use of prepositions as modal:

> Modality is evidenced in contrasting use of prepositions in Arabic and auxiliary verbs or verb phrases in English. The Arabic particle لِ (lit. belonging to) is in contrast to the English expression *has the right to*. The construction على أن (lit. upon. . .to) contrasts with *must*.

Below are given some examples for consideration:

Examples 15 and 16

15. The General Assembly may discuss – may make recommendations. . . (ChUN, article 10)	15. للجمعية العامة أن تناقش – كما أن لها . . . أن توصي . . .
16. The General Assembly may make recommendations or may propose conventions to the Members of the United Nations for this purpose. (ChUN, article 105:3)	16. للجمعية العامة أن تقدم التوصيات . . . ولها أن تقترح على أعضاء الهيئة عقد اتفاقات لهذا الغرض.

<http://www.un.org/en/documents/charter/index.shtml>
<http://www.un.org/ar/documents/charter/index.shtml>

In Arabic, the verb يجوز (لك) أن ((you) are allowed to . . .) is one of the verbs used to denote permission. It corresponds to 'may' in English. In the two examples given above, the 'may' structure is rendered into the preposition لِ (for) plus the clause initiated by أن (that). This is done by a technique of 'omission' because the lexical verb denoting permissibility is deleted and the preposition لِ (for) is left. This 'omission' is justifiable as it does not affect the accuracy of the translation; rather, it is used for simplification. This pattern proves useful as is mentioned by Badawi, Carter and Gully (2004:394), in their explanation of the modal auxiliaries in Arabic:

> there are various verbal collocations, corresponding approximately to impersonal, modal and auxiliary verbs in English, though the categories are only loosely comparable. It is important to note also that many meanings which are conveyed in English by adverbs are expressed by verbs in Arabic.

May *plus passive*

Translation of this pattern is important but will be dealt with under the analysis of passive translation, in Section 6.4, to avoid redundancy.

6.2.2.3 Translation of other less frequent modals

Other less frequent deontic modal auxiliaries such as 'should', 'must', 'is to' for obligation and 'might' and 'is likely' for possibility have been cited in the ChUN. Following is an example for each of them.

Should

Modals of necessity (for example must, shall) can be translated into Arabic as ينبغي أن or على يجب or على. Consider the following example:

Example 17

17. the Security Council should also take into consideration that legal disputes should as a general rule be referred by the parties to the International Court of Justice . . . (ChUN, article 36:3)	على مجلس الأمن وهو يقدم توصياته وفقا لهذه المادة أن يراعي أيضاً أن المنازعات القانونية يجب على أطراف النزاع- بصفة عامة - أن يعرضوها على محكمة العدل الدولية . . .

<http://www.un.org/en/documents/charter/index.shtml>
<http://www.un.org/ar/documents/charter/index.shtml>

The above example presents translation of the modal 'should', which is rarely used in drafting legal documents. With deontic modals, neither the modality nor the proposition occurs in the past since it is a performative act, the proposition expresses the present (Palmer, 1990:91). Semantically, 'should' indicates more than one meaning, according to *Oxford Dictionaries*, 'obligation, duty, or correctness, typically when criticizing someone's actions; a desirable or expected state; what is probable . . .'

Although meaning of ‘should’ in the ST is not decisive, judging by the context, the TT rendition of it into على (on) to denote obligation makes the meaning of ‘should’ clearer. Thus, ‘should take into consideration’ is rendered as على مجلس الأمن أن يراعي (it is incumbent on the Security Council to consider).

‘Should be referred to’ is rendered as يجب على أطراف النزاع أن يعرضوها على (the dispute parties should (must) refer them (the legal disputes) to . . .). ‘Should’ is rendered into Arabic as a lexical verb of necessity in the imperfect active mood. Thus, a voice shift is used in this example by translating a passive structure in the ST to an active structure in the TT. If the passive is adhered to in the TT, the translation will be:

> على مجلس الأمن وهو يقدم توصياته وفقا لهذه المادة أن يراعي أيضاً أن المنازعات القانونية يجب ـ بصفة عامة ـ أن تُعرض على محكمة العدل الدولية من قبل أطراف النزاع . . . (author’s translation)

Must *and* is to

Both forms are used once in the whole text and the technique used in translating both is the same as given below:

Examples 18 and 19

18. The Security Council may decide what measures . . . are to be employed . . . (ChUN, article 41)	18. لمجلس الأمن أن يقرر ما يجب اتخاذه من التدابير . . .
19. Members of the United Nations also agree that their policy in respect of the territories to which this Chapter applies . . . must be based on the general principle of good-neighbourliness, (ChUN, article 74)	19. يوافق أعضاء الأمم المتحدة أيضاً على أن سياستهم إزاء الأقاليم التي ينطبق عليها هذا الفصل . . . يجب أن تقوم على مبدأ حسن الجوار،

<http://www.un.org/en/documents/charter/index.shtml>
<http://www.un.org/ar/documents/charter/index.shtml>

In the above table, there are two instances of deontic modals of necessity: ‘must’ as given in 18 and ‘are to’ in 19; both occur in the passive voice. Both are rendered into the TT by a voice shift from passive to active and using a corresponding lexical verb of necessity. In the first example, a verbal noun is used instead of the infinitival clause: اتخاذه (its taking), instead of أن يؤخذ (to be taken).

Might *and* is likely to

These two modals are not frequent in the ChUN. Each of them occurred a few times, some of which are given below:

Examples 20 and 21

20. They shall refrain from any action which <u>might reflect on</u> their position as international officials responsible only to the Organization. (ChUN, article 100:1)	20. وعليهم أن يمتنعوا عن القيام بأي عمل <u>قد يسيئ</u> إلى مراكزهم بوصفهم موظفين دوليين مسؤولين أمام الهيئة وحدها.
21. The parties to any dispute, the continuance of which <u>is likely to</u> endanger the maintenance of international peace and security <u>shall . . . seek</u> a solution . . . (ChUN, article 33:1)	21. <u>يجب</u> على أطراف أي نزاع <u>من شأن</u> استمراره <u>أن يعرض</u> حفظ السلم والأمن الدولي للخطر أن يلتمسوا حله . . .

<http://www.un.org/en/documents/charter/index.shtml>
<http://www.un.org/ar/documents/charter/index.shtml>

Example 20 above represents the possibility modal 'might'. Syntactically and morphologically, 'might' is the past form of 'may' and it is rarely used semantically. Most importantly, with deontic modals, neither the modality nor the proposition occurs in the past since it is a performative act, the proposition expresses the present (Palmer, 1990:91). This modal is translated into Arabic through the technique of 'adaptation'. This means that the translator looks for the most acceptable translation of 'might plus infinitive' in Arabic to give the meaning intended in the ST. This is done by using the particle قد (may) plus the imperfect form of the verb يسيئ (harms). This verb is used as an equivalent of the English verb 'reflect on'. A semantic 'adaptation' is used as the translator gives the meaning of the verb in context rather than the literal meaning ينعكس على (reflects on). If the translator adheres to the same verb, he/she may need to add a word specifying what sort of reflection, which is in this case a negative reflection: ينعكس سلبيا على (negatively reflects on).

Example 21 gives another possible phrase: 'it is likely'. This construction is classified in the English modal system according to Johannesson's (1976) stratificational approach for analyzing modals as commentative sentences. He divides modal auxiliaries into three types, namely, volition, attitude to the truth of the proposition (commentative) and the speaker evaluation of the event (fictive). By commentatives is meant that 'the speaker makes a comment on the proposition and the choice between different modal auxiliaries and other forms is primarily determined by the kind of attitude the speaker has towards the basic proposition' (Johannesson, 1976:49). The speaker's attitude towards a proposition can be either emotional (surprise, anger, etc.) or non-emotional (possibility, probability). The author realizes this through either a modal auxiliary or an adverb: *maybe*, *perhaps*, *possibly*, *presumably*, *probably*, an adjective as in the construction '*it is possible*, *likely*, *unlikely that* . . .' in an adjective or participle: '*I am sure*, *convinced that* . . .', or in an attitudinal verb as in '*I assume*, *guess*, *believe that* . . .' (ibid.).

'Is likely' is translated as من شأن (may) plus a clause initiated by أن (that). Therefore, a 'structural shift' (Catford, 1965:76) is seen when a clause in the ST is rendered as a 'prepositional phrase' in the TT. 'Is likely' can also be rendered as the expression من المحتمل (it is probable) plus an infinitival clause initiated by أن (that) or the particle قد (may) plus the imperfect form of the verb.

6.3 ANALYSIS OF MODAL EXPRESSIONS IN ARABIC–ENGLISH DOCUMENTS

In this section, we will discuss the translation of modal expressions from Arabic into English with reference to the AChHR. We will start with a frequency analysis followed by a critical analysis.

6.3.1 Quantitative analysis of modal expressions in Arabic–English documents

The following table presents the frequency of modal phrases and expressions in the AChHR.

Table 6.4 Frequency analysis of modal expressions in the AChHR

Modal type	Number of occurrences	Proportion of modal type found (%)
لِ . . . أن	2	07.41
يجوز	2	07.41
لا يجوز	21	77.78
يجب	1	03.70
من الواجب	1	03.70
Total	**27**	**100.00**

As is clear from the above table, the most frequent modal is the negative verb لا يجوز (it is not permissible, or it is not allowed) at 77.78 percent, and the active form of the verb is the second most frequent (7.41 percent) along with the prepositional phrase لِ . . . أن (for . . . to plus infinitive). The above information can be illustrated by the following figure:

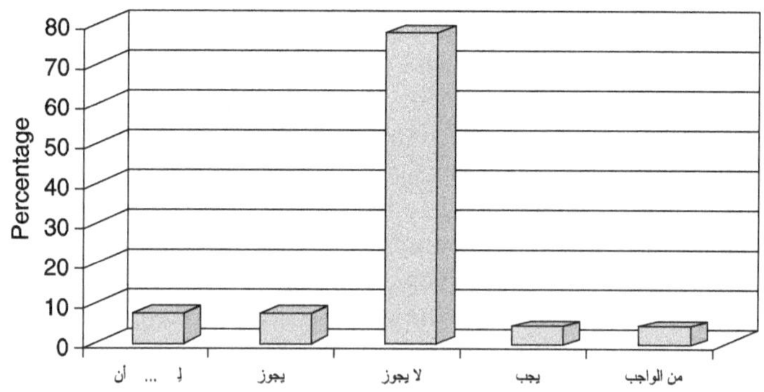

Figure 6.3 Frequency analysis of modal expressions in the AChHR.

6.3.2 Qualitative analysis of modal expressions in the AChHR

In this phase, we will look at how لا يجوز (it is not permissible) is rendered in the AChHR. Reference will also be made to some of the other less frequent modals.

6.3.2.1 Translation of لا يجوز *(it is not permissible/it is not allowed)*

This verb in the negative form: لا يجوز (it is not permissible or not allowed) is commonly used in Arabic legal documents to convey prohibition and it corresponds to 'shall not' in English. It takes either a clause initiated with (أن – that) or a verbal noun as in the following two examples:

You are not permitted <u>to breach</u> the law.	1. لا يجوز أن تخالف القانون
<u>Breaching</u> the law is not permissible.	2. لا يجوز مخالفة القانون

Translation of this structure into English varies. It is translated into the English deontic verb of prohibition 'shall not' as in the following example:

Example 1

<u>لا يجوز</u> بأي حال <u>أن تمس</u> تلك القيود أو <u>أن يشمل</u> هذا التحلل الحقوق والضمانات الخاصة . . . (AChHR, article 4:c)	Such measures or derogations <u>shall</u> under <u>no</u> circumstances <u>affect or apply to</u> the rights and special guarantees . . .

<http://www1.umn.edu/humanrts/instree/arabhrcharter.html>
<http://www1.umn.edu/humanrts/arab/a003-2.html>

The literal equivalent for لا يجوز (it is not allowed) is 'may not'. Thus, translation of it into 'shall under no circumstances' (for example 'shall not') conveys the binding nature of prohibition. If 'may not' is used, it opens the door for possibilities. The ST wording should have been more binding by using a modal of prohibition (لا يجب – shall not, must not) or a lexical term of prohibition such as ممنوع (prohibited). The TT translation rephrases, according to Abdel-Fattah (2005:42–45), this modal to convey the meaning in the ST. Translation of the ST modal (لا يجوز – it is not permissible) can occur in the passive voice as in the example below:

Example 2

<u>لا يجوز حرمان</u> الأقليات من حقها في التمتع بثقافتها أو اتباع تعاليم دياناتها (AChHR, article 37).	Minorities <u>shall not be deprived of</u> their right to enjoy their culture or to follow the teachings of their religions.

<http://www1.umn.edu/humanrts/instree/arabhrcharter.html>
<http://www1.umn.edu/humanrts/arab/a003-2.html>

As shown above, the same technique is used in example 1 above where there is a rephrasing of the ST modal expression لا يجوز (it is not allowed) to a prohibition in the TT 'shall not'. The verbal noun حرمان (deprivation), is rendered as 'be deprived' following a structure and voice shift of a noun to a passive verb. Below are more examples:

Examples 3 and 4

.3 لا يجوز تنفيذ حكم الإعدام فيمن يقل عمره عن ثمانية عشر عاماً أو في امرأة حامل حتى تضع حملها أو على أم مرضع إلا بعد انقضاء، عامين. (AChHR, article 28)	3. The death penalty shall not be inflicted on a person under 18 years of age, on a pregnant woman prior to her delivery or on a nursing woman.
.4 لا يجوز أن يفرض من القيود على ممارسة أي من هاتين الحريتين إلا ما تستوجبه دواعي الأمن القومي أو السلامة العامة أو حماية حقوق الآخرين وحرياتهم. (AChHR, article 28)	4. No restrictions shall be placed on the exercise of this right unless so required by the exigencies of national security, public safety or the need to protect the rights and freedoms of others.

<http://www1.umn.edu/humanrts/instree/arabhrcharter.html>
<http://www1.umn.edu/humanrts/arab/a003-2.html>

In examples 3 and 4, the Arabic modal is negated, but translation of it differs; in the first instance, it is the modal which is negated 'shall not' but in example 4, the proposition is negated 'no restrictions'. The ST passive structure: لا يحوز أن يُفرض (it is not allowed to be placed on) is adhered to in the TT. Such adherence to the ST syntax, one can argue, is rare in the translation of the whole text.

6.3.2.2 Translation of less frequent modal expressions

Example 5

ولها استناداً لهذا الحق أن تقرر بحرية نمط كيانها السياسي. (AChHR, article1:a)	. . . and, accordingly, have the right to freely determine the form of their political structure.

<http://www1.umn.edu/humanrts/instree/arabhrcharter.html>
<http://www1.umn.edu/humanrts/arab/a003-2.html>

Example 5 above represents one of the less frequent forms of modal expression, لها . . . أن تقرر بحرية (it is permissible for them to freely decide). This is rendered as 'have the right to freely decide' by shifting from a modal expression of permissibility into a lexical verb of possession. This, however, has not affected the meaning intended in the ST.

Example 6

ومن الواجب إدانة جميع ممارساتها والعمل على إزالتها. (AChHR article 1:b)	There is a need to condemn and endeavour to eliminate all such practices.

<http://www1.umn.edu/humanrts/instree/arabhrcharter.html>
<http://www1.umn.edu/humanrts/arab/a003-2.html>

'من الواجب إدانة – it is a must (it is compulsory) to condemn' is rendered as 'there is a need to condemn'. Thus, translation of a modal expression of necessity in the ST has been shifted to a lexical noun denoting need or demand. It does not convey the meaning intended in the ST as expressed by the modal expression. A suggested better translation can be 'it is necessary (a must) to condemn'.

6.4 TRANSLATION OF THE PASSIVE IN ENGLISH–ARABIC DOCUMENTS

This part investigates how the passive is translated from English into Arabic in the ChUN. As noted before in our analysis of the modal auxiliaries when translating from English into Arabic, most of the modal structures occurred in combination with the passive. I will analyze such structures as well as other normal passive structures. My discussion, however, will be concerned with the passive not the modals. I will start with a statistical analysis then follow with a critical analysis of some examples.

6.4.1 Quantitative analysis of passive in English–Arabic documents

In the following table we attempt to give the frequency of the different forms of the passive structure in the ST and their counterparts in the TT with reference to the ChUN.

Table 6.5 Frequency analysis of the passive structure in the ChUN

Cases of passive	Number of occurrences	Proportion of cases of passive found (%)
Shall + passive	51	60.00
May + passive	18	21.18
Will + passive	03	3.53
Normal passive	13	15.29
Total	**85**	**100.00**

As shown from the table, the total number of passive structures in the ChUN is 85 the greatest number of which comes in conjunction with modals (for example shall + passive, 60.00 percent; may + passive, 21.18 percent; and will + passive, 3.53 percent). Normal passive comes in third place with an overall percentage of 15.29 percent. This information can be illustrated by Figure 6.4.

It is interesting to see how these structures are translated into Arabic. Representation of such information is given in Table 6.6 and Figure 6.5.

The table shows that the TT rendition of the ST passive structure comes in two cases: active is used in place of passive with an overall percentage of 58.82 percent; passive is adhered to in the TT with a general rate of 41.18 percent.

The most obvious first impression from the table and the figure is that Arabic uses considerably fewer passive forms than English. This can justify the fact that legal Arabic favours the active. In fact it is not only legal drafters who favour the active structure to passive; MSA generally prefers the use of the active. In this context, Al-Najjar

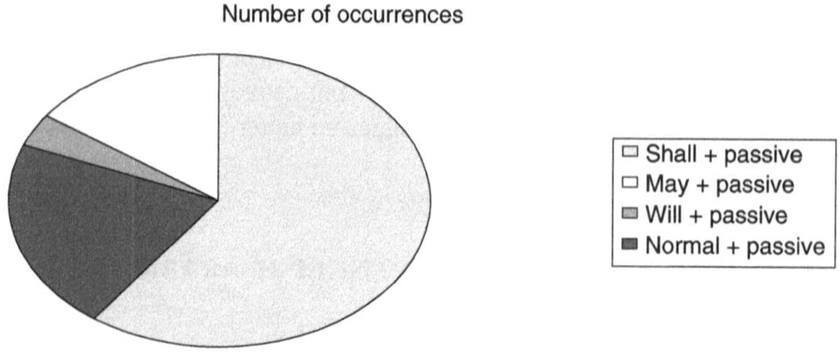

Figure 6.4 Frequency of the passive structure in the ChUN.

Table 6.6 Frequency analysis of the translation of the passive structure into Arabic in the ChUN

ST passive → TT	Number of occurrences	Proportion of ST → TT tense changes (%)
passive → active	50	58.82
passive → passive	35	41.18
Total	**85**	**100.00**

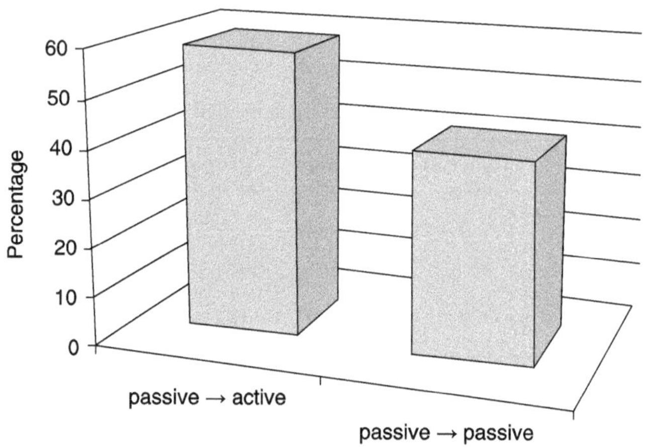

Figure 6.5 Frequency of the translation of the passive structure into Arabic in the ChUN.

(1984:150–151) comments: ‘it is intuition that pushes or motivates speakers of MSA to translate English passive sentences into active’.

6.4.2 Qualitative analysis of passive in English–Arabic documents

In this section, I will show how translation of the English passives into Arabic varies. The use of either structure is motivated by the linguistic system of the TT. I will discuss some of the representative ST passive examples and explain the different ways of rendering them into the TT active, then into passive.

6.4.2.1 Passive → active

The first case of passive forms occurs with a modal verb plus the passive. It is rendered into Arabic as an imperfect verb denoting modality plus a clause initiated with أن (that). To illustrate this, consider the following example:

Example 1

A Member of the United Nations against which preventive or enforcement action has been taken by the Security Council may be suspended from the exercise of the rights and privileges of membership by the General Assembly upon the recommendation of the Security Council. (ChUN, article 5)	يجوز للجمعية العامة أن توقف أي عضو اتخذ مجلس الأمن قِبَله عملاً من أعمال المنع أو القمع، عن مباشرة حقوق العضوية ومزاياها، ويكون ذلك بناءً على توصية مجلس الأمن.

<http://www.un.org/en/documents/charter/index.shtml>
<http://www.un.org/ar/documents/charter/index.shtml>

In the above example, there are two examples of the passive structure which are rendered into active: 'has been taken' is translated as اتخذ (took) and 'may be suspended' is rendered as يجوز أن توقف (it is allowed that (agent) suspend). Thus, the ST passive is translated as the TT active. In both cases the active is used because the ST 'by-phrase' is better rendered into the TT by using the agent or the subject of the verb. It becomes common, however, to see the by-phrase rendered by certain linguistic Arabic phrases such as من قِبَل (on the part of). If the passive is adhered to, the meaning will not change but the TT will be redundant and wordy. The change to passive is underlined below:

يجوز أن يُوقف أي عضو من قِبَل الجمعية العامة اتُخذ قِبَله عملًا من أعمال المنع أو القمع من جانب مجلس الأمن، عن مباشرة حقوق العضوية ومزاياها، ويكون ذلك بناءً على توصية مجلس الأمن.

Example 2

Nothing in this Chapter shall be construed in or of itself to alter in any manner the rights of any states or any peoples, (ChUN, article 80:1)	لا يجوز تأويل نص أي حكم من أحكام هذا الفصل ولا تخريجه تأويلاً أو تخريجاً من شأنه أن يغير بطريقة ما أية حقوق لأية دول أو شعوب،

<http://www.un.org/en/documents/charter/index.shtml>
<http://www.un.org/ar/documents/charter/index.shtml>

In example 2 above, the passive verb (construed) is rendered into Arabic as a verbal noun (تأويل – interpretation). This voice shift as well as verb-noun 'transposition' is done for stylistic reasons. The reason why we claim so is that the same structure has been rendered differently in another example, viz. in example 3 below, the English passive structure 'interpreted' is translated into Arabic as passive (أن تؤول – to be interpreted). Thus, the passive is adhered to and also there is no verb-noun 'transposition':

Example 3

Paragraph 1 of this Article shall not be interpreted as giving grounds for delay or postponement of the negotiation. (ChUN article 8:2)

لا يجوز أن تؤول الفقرة الأولى من هذه المادة على أنها تهيئ سبباً لتأخير أو تأجيل المفاوضة .

<http://www.un.org/en/documents/charter/index.shtml>
<http://www.un.org/ar/documents/charter/index.shtml>

The same passive structure can be translated into a prepositional phrase plus a clause initiated with أن (that) as underlined in the example below:

Example 4

The exercise of these rights and privileges may be restored by the Security Council. (ChUN, article 5)

ولمجلس الأمن أن يرد لهذا العضو مباشرة تلك الحقوق والمزايا.

<http://www.un.org/en/documents/charter/index.shtml>
<http://www.un.org/ar/documents/charter/index.shtml>

Again the passive is changed into active through the occurrence of a clause initiated with أن (that).

Example 5

Any such question on which action is necessary shall be referred to the Security Council by the General Assembly. (ChUN, article 11:2)

وكل مسألة مما تقدّم ذكره يكون من الضروري فيها القيام بعمل ما، ينبغي أن تحيلها الجمعية العامة على مجلس الأمن .

<http://www.un.org/en/documents/charter/index.shtml>
<http://www.un.org/ar/documents/charter/index.shtml>

The above sentence represents an English passive structure: subject + V passive + *by* NP agent. Such a structure is rendered into Arabic as: object + verb + subject (OVS) as illustrated below:

ST	Any such question Grammatical subject (theme)	shall be referred to V (passive)	by the General Assembly *by* NP agent (rheme)
TT	كل مسألة Foregrounded object (theme)	ينبغي أن تحيلها Modal imperfect active verb + (‘*an* clause: imperfect active verb (attached to an object pronoun))	الجمعية العامة Subject (rheme)

From the above analysis, although the translator shifts to the active voice, he/she has preserved the message structure of the ST breaking the normal VSO order of the Arabic sentence, choosing to foreground the object and use an attached pronoun in the verb phrase to refer back to it. By doing so, the translator kept the 'informational organization' (Abdul-Raof, 1998:94) through form and meaning. On this point El-Yasin (1996) holds that 'English passives should be translated into Arabic topic–comment (or theme–rheme) structure in order to capture both form (word order) and meaning'. However, the translator has undertaken some minor reordering of the TT by phrase (the General Assembly – الجمعية العامة) and the prepositional phrase (to the Security Council – على مجلس الأمن). Such a change of the word order is motivated by the syntactic and semantic interrelationships of sentence structure.

In example 6 below, the translator has chosen to stick to the Arabic normal sentence order VSO:

Example 6

The expenses of the Organization shall be borne by the Members as apportioned by the General Assembly. (ChUN, article 17:2)	يتحمّل الأعضاء نفقات الهيئة حسب الأنصبة التي تقرّرها الجمعية العامة.

<http://www.un.org/en/documents/charter/index.shtml>
<http://www.un.org/ar/documents/charter/index.shtml>

In the above excerpt, there are two passive structures, the first of which is 'shall be borne': 'modal auxiliary plus passive' which is rendered into Arabic as the active form of the verb in the imperfect: يتحمّل ((they) bear). In the second part of the example, (as apportioned by the General Assembly – حسب الأنصبة التي تقرّرها الجمعية العامة), there are two syntactic changes in this example: first, translating the English passive verb (apportioned) by paraphrasing it into the active voice (according to the amounts which the General Assembly decide). The other change is mentioning the agent/doer of the action without using any agentive construction. In this example, the translator did not follow the same structure given in the ST, which may have been motivated by a stylistic preference.

All of the above examples as well as other examples mentioned in articles 88, 89, 92, 96, 98, to mention just a few of them, are rendered in the active. What is common among these examples is that all of them are 'agentive passives' the agent of which is animate. In Arabic, the translator has shifted to the active voice in order to mention the agent: 'if an Arabic speaker wants to mention the agent (doer) the only choice open to him is an active sentence' (Farghal, 1991:144). Other examples have been translated into active but the agent (*by* phrase) has been rendered into Arabic by using a prepositional phrase.

Example 7

Decisions of the General Assembly on important questions shall be made by a two-thirds majority of the members present and voting. (ChUN, article 17:2)	تصدر الجمعية العامة قراراتها في المسائل الهامة بأغلبية ثلثي الأعضاء الحاضرين المشتركين في التصويت.

<http://www.un.org/en/documents/charter/index.shtml>
<http://www.un.org/ar/documents/charter/index.shtml>

In the above example, the passive ('shall be made') is translated into Arabic as verb-initial sentence (VSO): تصدر الجمعية العامة قراراتها (the General Assembly issues its decisions). The agentive (*by* phrase) is rendered into Arabic as a prepositional phrase initiated by بـ (by) because it is inanimate or as Cantarino calls it an 'instrumental idea' (1974:53). Wright (1967:163–164) also gives the reasons for using this preposition: 'among its other uses, by is used for الاستعانة (*al-ist'anah*) to indicate the instrument of whose aid we avail ourselves and للسببية (*li-al-sababiyah*) or للتعليل (*li-al-ta'lil*) to express the reason or cause'.

6.4.2.2 Passive → passive

In this section, I will examine some examples which are rendered from the ST passive structure into TT passive:

Example 8

Such subsidiary organs as may be found necessary may be established in accordance with the present Charter. (ChUN article 7:2)	يجوز أن يُنشأ فقاً لأحكام هذا الميثاق ما يُرى ضرورة إنشائه من فروع ثانوية أخرى .

<http://www.un.org/en/documents/charter/index.shtml>
<http://www.un.org/ar/documents/charter/index.shtml>

The ST gives two passive structures that adhere in the TT to 'may be established'. The first is rendered into a verb denoting modality plus a clause initiated with أن (that): يجوز أن يُنشأ (it is allowed to be established). The other example is 'may be found necessary' which is rendered into a TT passive: ما يُرى ضرورة إنشائه (what is seen necessary for establishing). There is an adaptation of the meaning of the verb 'found' plus an 'addition' of the verbal noun إنشائه (its establishing) to complete the meaning given in the clause and to relate it back to the main verb of the sentence.

Example 9

The non-permanent members of the Security Council shall be elected for a term of two years. In the first election of the non-permanent members after the increase of the membership of the Security Council from eleven to fifteen, two of the four additional members shall be chosen for a term of one year. (ChUN, article 23:2)	يُنتخب أعضاء مجلس الأمن غير الدائمين لمدة سنتين، على أنه في أول انتخاب للأعضاء غير الدائمين بعد زيادة عدد أعضاء مجلس الأمن من أحد عشر عضواً إلى خمسة عشر عضواً، يُختار اثنان من الأعضاء الأربعة الإضافيين لمدة سنة واحدة.

<http://www.un.org/en/documents/charter/index.shtml>
<http://www.un.org/ar/documents/charter/index.shtml>

In example 9, two ST passive structures are adhered to in the TT: 'shall be elected' is rendered as يُنتخب (is elected) and يُختار (is chosen). Translation in both examples adapts to the TT syntactic system which uses the imperfect to denote a mood of obligation. As clear from the above examples, the ST passive is rendered into TT passive when the agent is not specified.

6.5 TRANSLATION OF PASSIVE IN ARABIC–ENGLISH DOCUMENTS

This section discusses how Arabic passive structures are rendered into English. To achieve this, we investigate the parallel Arabic and English versions of the Decree of the Establishment of the National Council of Women. The reason why this document has been chosen is that it offers a good number of examples to be analyzed which are given in the table below.

No	Arabic	English
1	يُنشأ مجلس يُسمى " المجلس القومي للمرأة يتبع رئيس الجمهورية تكون له الشخصية الاعتبارية، ويكون مقره مدينة القاهرة.	A National Council for Women shall be established under the President of the Republic. It shall have a moral character and its seat shall be in Cairo. (article 1)
2	تُشكل بالمجلس لجان دائمة لممارسة اختصاصاتها المبينة في المادة الثالثة.	The Council establishes the following Standing Committees in order to carry out its functions as stipulated in Article Three: (article 5)
3	و يُنشأ حساب خاص لحصيلة هذه الموارد في أحد بنوك القطاع العام التجارية ويراعى ترحيل الفائض من هذا الحساب في نهاية كل سنة مالية إلى موازنة السنة التالية.	A special account shall be set up to collect these resources in a public sector commercial bank. The surpluses shall be carried forward at the end of each fiscal year to the budget of the following year. (article 10)
4	يُنشر هذا القرار في الجريدة الرسمية.	This Decree shall be published in the official Journal. (article 12)

<http://www.portsaid.gov.eg/magals/women/decision.aspx?ID=2> <http://www1.uneca.org/ngm/NCWAnnex1.aspx>

As discussed in the previous section, the translation of the ST passive into TT passive is due to the unspecificity of the agent. The above table gives examples of the passive structures in Arabic, the agent of which is unknown. These passive structures are adhered to in 1, 3 and 4. In these sentences, the imperfect mood of Arabic passive verbs is rendered as 'shall plus passive'. Only in example 2 a voice shift occurs when the ST passive is rendered into active (the present tense). In the next few lines, we will consider the translation of example 3 in the above table.

The ST has the passive structure ويُراعى ترحيل الفائض (it should be considered that the surpluses are carried forward). In this, the translator has opted for an 'omission' and a 'structure shift' (Catford, 1965:76). For the former, he/she has omitted the ST passive verb يُراعى (is considered (should be considered)). For the latter, there is a shift of the ST verbal noun ترحيل (carrying forward) for the TT passive verb in conjunction with the necessity modal 'shall'.

6.6 EXERCISES AND DISCUSSIONS

Exercise 1: Analyze the Arabic translation of the English text below on the syntactic level (for example modal auxiliaries, passive).

English	Arabic
No one shall be presumed guilty of a criminal offence before a judgment of conviction has entered into force with regard to him or her.	لا يجوز افتراض إدانة أي شخص بارتكاب جريمة ما قبل نفاذ حكم الإدانة في حقه
It is the case when somebody gives authority to another to act in his name as his agent.	إنها الحالة التي يمنح فيها شخص السلطة لشخص آخر للتصرف باسمه كوكيله
If a provision is not included therein, then reference shall be made to the Civil Code, otherwise provisions of commercial practice and guidance by judicial, jurisprudent interpretation and equality principles shall be applied.	فإن لم يوجد فيه حكم يتناول هذا الأمر يرجع إلى القانون المدني و إلا فتطبق أحكام العرف التجاري و الاسترشاد بالاجتهادات القضائية و الفقهية ومبادئ المساواة
Every fault which causes damage to another obliges that who has committed this fault to repair it.	كل خطأ يسبب ضرراً للغير يلزم من ارتكبه بالتعويض
So long as the Loan Agreement is in effect the warranties herein shall be true and correct.	طالما ان اتفاقية القرض سارية المفعول فإن الضمانات الواردة في هذا الإتفاق صحيحة
The contractor shall not assign the Contract or any part thereof or benefit or interest therein without the prior consent of the Employer.	يتعهد المقاول بعدم التنازل عن العقد أو أي جزء منه أو أي منفعة أو مصلحة فيه أو بموجبه بدون موافقة مسبقة من صاحب العمل

<http://www.eajournals.org/wp-content/uploads/The-Translatability-of-English-Legal-Sentences-into-Arabic-by-Using-Google-Translation.pdf>

Exercise 2: Translate the following text into Arabic, pay particular attention to mood phrases.

> If the Security Council deems that the continuance of the dispute is in fact likely to endanger the maintenance of international peace and security, it shall decide whether to take action under Article 36 or to recommend such terms of settlement as it may consider appropriate. (ChUN, article 37:2)
>
> <http://www.un.org/en/documents/charter/index.shtml>

Exercise 3: Consider the parallel translation from the ChuN in the table below and answer the following questions:

1. What is the type of modality in the underlined English phrases?
2. What is the technique of translating these underlined phrases into Arabic?
3. In pairs comment on this translation and suggest changes, if any.

English	Arabic
A Member of the United Nations against which preventive or enforcement action has been taken by the Security Council may be suspended from the exercise of the rights and privileges of membership by the General Assembly upon the recommendation of the Security Council (article 5)	يجوز للجمعية العامة أن توقف أي عضو اتخذ مجلس الأمن قِبَله عملاً من أعمال المنع أو القمع، عن مباشرة حقوق العضوية ومزاياها، ويكون ذلك بناءً على توصية مجلس الأمن،
The exercise of these rights and privileges may be restored by the Security Council. (article 5)	ولمجلس الأمن أن يرد لهذا العضو مباشرة تلك الحقوق والمزايا.
A member of the United Nations may be expelled from the organization . . . (article 6)	إذا أمعن عضو من أعضاء "الأمم المتحدة" في انتهاك مبادئ الميثاق جاز للجمعية العامة أن تفصله
Such subsidiary organs as may be found necessary may be established in accordance with the present Charter. (article 7:2)	يجوز أن يُنشأ فقاً لأحكام هذا الميثاق يُرى ضرورة إنشائه من فروع ثانوية أخرى .

Exercise 4: Comment with examples on the translation of the modal 'shall' into Arabic with reference to the parallel translation of the Universal Declaration of Human Rights.

Exercise 5:

1. 'Drafting modality in legal documents can sometimes be indeterminate.' Discuss this statement and provide examples from different Arabic and English legal text types to support your arguments.
2. Comment on the translation of the underlined modal phrases in Examples 1 and 2. Is modality unbinding in both texts? Could you suggest a better drafting for the ST and a better translation for these underlined phrases?

Example 1

وعدم جواز تكرار المحاكمة عن ذات الفعل وشرعية الجرائم والعقوبات.
(AChHR, article 4: c)

the inadmissibility of retrial for the same act and the legal status of crime and punishment.

<http://www1.umn.edu/humanrts/instree/arabhrcharter.html>
<http://www1.umn.edu/humanrts/arab/a003-2.html>

Example 2

ومن الواجب إدانة جميع ممارساتها والعمل على إزالتها. (AChHR, article 1:b)

There is a need to condemn and endeavour to eliminate all such practices.

<http://www1.umn.edu/humanrts/instree/arabhrcharter.html>
<http://www1.umn.edu/humanrts/arab/a003-2.html>

Exercise 6: Translate the following part of a Partnership Agreement into Arabic; pay particular attention to the negated modal expressions; and compare your translations in pairs.

Partnership Agreement

Forbidden acts

- No Partner may do any act in contravention of this agreement.
- No Partner may permit intentionally or unintentionally, the assignment of express, implied or apparent authority to a third party that is not a Partner in the Partnership.
- No Partner may do any act that would make it impossible to carry on the ordinary business of Partnership.
- No Partner may confess a judgment against the Partnership.
- No Partner will have the right or authority to bind or obligate the Partnership to any extent with regard to any matter outside the intended purpose of the Partnership.
- Any violation of the above Forbidden Acts will be deemed Involuntary Withdrawal of the offending Partner and may be treated accordingly by the remaining Partners.

<http://www.lawdepot.co.uk/contracts/partnership-agreement/?ad=business-plan_related>

Exercise 7:

1. Translate the following two texts into English.
2. In pairs, discuss the difficult areas in the texts (for example modals).
3. What are the procedures you used to translate these areas?

Text A

الشروط الخاصة:

1. يجب على المورد إحضار شهادة المنشأ للمواد التي تتطلب ذلك.
2. يحق لوزارة الصحة رفض أي مادة كاملة أو أي جزء منها في حال مخالفتها للمواصفات التي تم الاتفاق عليها.
3. يتم استلام المواد الموردة من قبل لجنة استلام مختصة مُشَكلة لهذا الغرض وفقاً للمواصفات والشروط العامة والخاصة للتعاقد الواردة في دعوة العطاء وقرار الإحالة وأمر التوريد والعينات المعتمدة والتي يتم فحصها وإجراء التجارب عليها بالطريقة التي تحددها الجهة المستفيدة أو لجنة الاستلام بموجب لجان فنية

تُشكل لهذا الغرض لمعرفة مدى مطابقتها للمواصفات المطلوبة ويجب كذلك إرفاق الشهادات الصحية والمخبرية اللازمة من قبل المورد و تؤخذ العينات بنسبة 1-2 في الألف حسب المادة الموردة و بناءً على طلب من المختبر عند كل توريد .

4. يجب على المورد العلم بأن ما يقدمه من عرض سعر ساري المفعول لمدة ستون يوماً من تاريخ إغلاق المناقصة.

5. على المورد الالتزام بتوريد المواد المتعاقد عليها في الخدمات المساندة بوزارة الصحة بغزة أو الجهة التي تحددها الوزارة طبقًا للشروط والمواصفات الواردة في المناقصة متضمنا النقل والتحميل والتنزيل وما يترتب على عمليات التوريد من نفقات بالغة ما بلغت أو مصاريف على نفقته الخاصة.

<www.mof.gov.ps>

Text B

خامساً : التزامات المتعهد أو المورد :

1. على المتعهد الذي أحيل عليه العطاء استكمال إجراءات العقد الخاص بقرار الإحالة وتوقيع الاتفاقية وما يلحقها من أوراق ومستندات بما فيها (أوامر الشراء).
2. يلتزم المتعهد بالتوريد خلال شهر من تاريخ استلامه لأمر التوريد.
3. . لا يجوز للمتعهد أن يتنازل لأي شخص آخر عن كل أو أي جزء من العقد دون الحصول على إذن خطي من لجنة العطاءات التي أحالت العطاء.
4. لا يحق للمناقص أو المورد الرجوع على لجنة العطاءات بأي خسارة أو ضرر ناشئ عن تقديمعرضه في حالة إذا ما رفضت لجنة العطاءات كل العروض المقدمة إليها أو إذا لم تحل العطاء علىمقدم أقل الأسعار أو إذا ألغت لجنة العطاءات دعوة العطاء في أي وقت أو أي مرحلة دون ذكر الأسباب.
5. يلتزم المورد بتسليم اللوازم وفقًا للمواصفات والشروط المتفق عليها والواردة في قرار الإحالة وكذلك العينات المعتمدة والمذكورة فيه.

<www.mof.gov.ps>

Exercise 8: Translate the following two texts into Arabic:

Text A

3.5.4 The two parties agreed that the Account Holder shall pay to the bank on a regular basis the fees for the SAMBA Collection & Reconciliation Services by hereby authorizing the Bank to debit its designated account directly. However, the Bank's fees may change from time to time depending on the service provided by the Bank. Please note that fees will be charged on each transaction conducted by the Account Holder even if the transaction is subsequently reversed, cancelled or proven ineffective for some reason pertaining to the Account Holder.
3.5.5 Either the Account Holder or the Bank may terminate this service at any time, by giving the other party 90 days' written notice. Additionally, either party may terminate this agreement on 30 days' notice if the other party have not complied with the terms and conditions of the service.
(Account Opening Form: 3.5.4 and 3.5.5)

Text B

3.9.1 Access to use the Platform shall be provided by the Bank through any communication or delivery system that the Bank may specify from time to time, which includes the internet. The Account Holder understands and acknowledges the confidentiality and other risks associated with use of the internet. The Account Holder accepts these risks inherent in the use of the internet and agrees that the Bank shall not be responsible to the Account Holder for any damages that it may suffer which are caused by the third party.

3.9.3 Authorized Users: The Account Holder has identified to the Bank (by completing the Bank's relevant forms) those individuals who will be authorized to use the platform on the Account Holder's behalf, and those individuals who will verify (when required) the users and transactions performed. The level of authority, usage ability, and security level for each Authorized User will be defined in the application form. The Bank will rely on these authorizations unless it receives a written notice from the Account Holder changing the identity of any Authorized User.

(Account Opening Form: 3.9.1 and 3.9.3)

Exercise 9: Below are two texts: The English ST in text A and the Arabic TT in text B. Identify the major lexical, syntactic and textual errors in the TT. Rewrite the TT paying particular attention to sentence and text cohesion without distorting the accuracy of the text.

Text A

Statement of Tenancy Terms

Your landlord by law must provide you with a Statement of Tenancy Terms free of charge, within 28 days of the start of the tenancy.

Repairs

You and your landlord can agree the responsibility to repair, with the exception of gas and electrical appliances and furniture safety which are the responsibility of your landlord. Where the Statement of Tenancy Terms is not clear as to who has responsibility for repairs the law will impose 'default terms' for landlord and tenant repair responsibilities. You may be able to get some help from your local district council for some items of disrepair.

Tenancies for a term certain

If you do not have a tenancy agreement or the tenancy agreement does not state when the tenancy will end, under the law you have a right to a tenancy that will run for six months initially and after this period it will become a periodic tenancy (for example month to month).

<http://www.nihe.gov.uk/rent_book.pdf>

Text B

بيان شروط الإيجار

ملك العقار بموجب القانون يجب أن توفر لك مع بيان شروط الإيجار مجانا، في غضون 28 يوما من بداية الإيجار.

تصليحات

يمكن أنت و مالكك توافق مسؤولية إصلاح، باستثناء غاز والأجهزة كهربائية والأثاث الامن التي هي من مسؤولية مالك العقار . حيث قانون شروط الإيجار ليس من الواضح من الذي يتحمل المسؤولية لإصلاح القانون سوف فرض " شروط فرضية " لمك العقار المستأجر وإصلاح المسؤوليات. قد تكون قادرة على الحصول على بعض مساعدة من المجلس البلدية المحلي لبعض البنود من العطب .

التأجير لمدد معينة

إذا لم يكن لديك عقد الإيجار أو لا ينص عقد الإيجار عند وسوف ينتهي عقد الإيجار ، وفقا للقانون لديك الحق في الإيجار الذي سيتم تشغيله لمدة ستة شهر في البداية و بعد هذه الفترة سوف يصبح الايجار الدورية (مثل شهر لآخر).

Exercise 10: Compare the translation of the ST in the table below with the two translated versions given in TT (1) and TT (2):

1. How was the ST passive structure rendered in the TT (1) and TT (2)?
2. What are the problems of each translation if any?
3. What changes would you suggest to deal with these problems?

ST	TT (1)	TT (2)
المادة الأولى: يُعمل بأحكام القانون المرافق بشأن نظام استثمار المال العربي والأجنبي والمناطق الحرة.	Arab and foreign investment and free zones are governed by the attached law.	The provisions of the attached law shall govern the Arab and foreign investment.
المادة الثانية: تُطبق أحكام القوانين واللوائح المعمول بها في كل ما لم يرد فيه نص خاص في القانون المرافق.	Matters not covered by this Law are subject to the applicable laws and regulations.	The provisions of the laws and regulations applicable in each unless it is specifically provided in the attached law.
يُلغى القانون رقم 65 لسنة 1971 في شأن استثمار المال العربي والمناطق الحرة. يُلغى بذلك كل نص آخر يخالف ما ورد في هذا القانون. ويستمر تمتع المشروعات التي سبق إقرارها في ظله بما تقرر له من الحقوق والمزايا المنصوص عليها في هذا القانون.	Art IV: Law No. 65 of 1971 on Arab Capital Investment and Free Zones is hereby repealed. Any provision contrary to what is stated in the present law is also repealed. Projects approved under said law shall continue to enjoy the rights and privileges specified thereunder (under that law).	Art IV: Law No. 65 of 1971 on Arab Capital Investment and Free Zones shall hereby be repealed. Any provision contrary to what is stated in the present Law shall also be repealed. Projects approved under said law shall continue to enjoy the rights and privileges specified thereunder (under that law).

(*Continued*)

(Continued)

ST	TT (1)	TT (2)
يتم تحويل المال المستثمر إلى جمهورية مصر العربية وإعادة تصديره وكذلك تحويل الأرباح المحققة إلى الخارج وفقًا لأحكام هذا القانون وذلك بأعلى سعر معلن للنقد الأجنبي القابل للتحويل بواسطة السلطات المصرية المختصة.	Investor money is transferred to the Arab Republic of Egypt and the re-export as well as the transfer of profits earned abroad and in accordance with the provisions of this law, and that the highest rate of foreign exchange declared convertible by the Egyptian authorities competent.	Invested capital shall be duly transferred to, and repatriated from, the Arab Republic of Egypt, and profits generated therefrom shall be duly transferred in foreign currency abroad in accordance with the provisions of this Law, at the highest rate prevailing and declared for free foreign currency by the competent Egyptian Authorities

ST: http://2daya.blogspot.co.uk/2012_07_08_archive.html
TT (1) and TT (2) are adapted from:
<http://englisharabictranslators.blogspot.co.uk/search/label/Legal%20Translation>

Exercise 11: Translate the following text into Arabic:

Founding Principles

1. The Constitution of the Federal Republic of Somalia is based on the foundations of the Holy Quran and the Sunna of our prophet Mohamed (PBUH) and protects the higher objectives of Shariʿah and social justice.
2. The Federal Republic of Somalia is a Muslim country which is a member of the African and Arab Nations.
3. The Federal Republic of Somalia is founded upon the fundamental principles of power sharing in a federal system.
4. The Constitution of the Federal Republic of Somalia promotes human rights, the rule of law, general standards of international law, justice, participatory consultative and inclusive government, the separation of powers between the legislature, executive and an independent judiciary, in order to ensure accountability, efficiency and responsiveness to the interests of the people.

Article 35. The Right of the Accused

1. The accused is presumed innocent until proven guilty in a final manner by a court of law.
2. Every person arrested or detained has the right to be informed promptly of the reason for their arrest or detention in a language which the person understands.
3. Every person arrested or detained shall have the right for his or her family and relatives to be informed of his or her situation.
4. Every person may not be compelled to self-incriminate, and a verdict may not be based on evidence acquired by means of coercion.
5. Every person who is arrested has the right to be brought before a capable court within 48 hours of the arrest.

6. Every person who is arrested or detained has the right to choose, and to consult with, a legal practitioner and if he or she cannot afford one, the government must appoint a legal practitioner for him or her.
7. Every person brought before a court of law for an alleged criminal offence is entitled to a fair trial.
8. The accused has the right to be present at their trial.
9. The accused has the right to challenge the evidence presented against him or her.
10. The accused has the right to an interpreter if the accused person does not understand the language being used in the court.

<http://www.constitution.org/cons/somalia/120708_ENG_constitution.pdf>

Exercise 12: Translate the following texts from a Power of Attorney (A) and from an Acknowledgement (B) into Arabic:

Text A

Power of Attorney

Know all men by these present by this power of attorney That I Mr .. . . DOB . . . of Derby, United Kingdom, holder of British Passport No . . . and citizen of the United Kingdom.

I through this POWER OF ATTORNEY hereby authorize, appoint and constitute Mr. . . . Residence permit No: . . . Jeddah, Somali national as my true and lawful General Attorney in respect of registering my son's birth and to do following acts, deeds & things on my behalf:

. . .

IN WITNESS WHERE OF Mr. . . . executed this deed on the day first above written
Signed and delivered by the said Principal Mr. . . .
In presence of:
Witness: **Solicitor's Stamp**

Text B

Acknowledgement

I hereby acknowledge that all the data and information herein above stated are valid and that all documents and instruments submitted are valid and legal. I also declare liability for the programs, database and contents thereof and that same do not infringe upon the intellectual rights of others. I declare full liability if any or part of the above mentioned information is proved to be invalid with no liability whatsoever on part of the Intellectual Rights Protection Office and staff thereof.
Name:
Signature:

7 Conclusion and recommendations

This book sheds light on legal translation from English to Arabic and vice versa. It analyzes the features of legal English and Arabic; investigates the techniques of translating certain elements of difference between English and Arabic on the lexical and the syntactic levels. To analyze the features of legal Arabic and legal English, the chapters have referred to a corpus of authentic legal texts covering various legal subtypes compiled from the internet, solicitors and legal and translation books. Such analysis has come up with some conclusions that are highlighted in what follows.

Legal English is unique in terms of its lexical features. It involves 'terms of art' with a highly technical meaning, terms with a semi-technical meaning as well as general everyday vocabulary. Legal English also includes Latinisms, French and archaic terms, all of which continue to exist in legal texts in spite of the plain language campaign. Analysis of English legal discourse has shown that lexical features such as archaic and Latin terms tend to occur more frequently in one legal subtype than another; they are more common in official documents in general and in contracts in particular. Formality, which is another distinctive feature of legal English, is expressed by fixed linguistic aspects such as speech acts, modals and enactment formulas.

Legal English is characterized by many syntactic features such as complex sentences, nominalization, passivization, performative verbs, modal auxiliaries, conditionals, doublets and triplets and double negatives. Some of these features are more common than others such as nominalization and modal verbs whereas some others are more common in one legal subtype than another (for example passive, conditional and prepositional phrases).

As for the textual features, cohesion, and in particular lexical repetition, is a common cohesive device expressed through reiteration (for example synonyms, near synonyms, superordinates, etc.) or lexical chains. Due to the complexity of English legal texts, subordinating or coordinating conjunctions are also a common feature in legal texts: 'and', 'or' and the hybrid conjunction 'and/or', which suggests a degree of uncertainty. Generally, English avoids recurrence, viz. the occurrence of the same word several times in a text, but it is common in English legal discourse.

In analyzing the features of Legal Arabic, this research has come up with some considerable findings about the characteristics of legal Arabic discourse. Like English, 'terms of art' exist in legal Arabic but they are more common in official documents. Highly formal expressions and figurative language are common in legal Arabic. Such formality is expressed through first person plural pronouns, the use of formulas and honorific titles. Arabic tends to use the gender-biased terms in which there is a preference for the masculine element in writing, which can be considered a tradition in Arabic stylistics. Arabic legal discourse uses a lexical category, common in official documents, called the 'template terms and phrases'.

Unlike in English, some of these template terms have disappeared, whereas a few others have continued to exist such as السالف/ المذكور/ الوارد (the previously mentioned, the above-mentioned, mentioned/contained, subsequently).

There are some commonalities between legal Arabic and other Arabic registers such as political Arabic, diplomatic Arabic, media Arabic in terms of lexis and style. It can be argued that boundaries between legislative and international (for example UN) Arabic legal documents on the one hand and diplomatic Arabic discourse on the other are fuzzy. Furthermore, there is a degree of similarity between Arabic legal discourse and news and diplomatic discourse in relation to some lexical items such as highly decorative expressions; grammatical elements such as nominalization, passivization and negation as well as textual features such as parallelism and repetition (for example lexical repetition, be it morphological, word, phrase, or clause repetition). The repetition is employed for different functions in various Arabic registers. For example, it is informative in legal texts, whereas it is used for purposes of persuasion and emotiveness in political discourse.

Legal Arabic is characterized by many syntactic features, the most common of which are nominalization, modal expressions, doublets and triplets and complex sentences. Although the passive exists in legal Arabic, it is less preferred and less common than the active voice. Regarding the textual features, generally speaking Arabic legal discourse employs many of MSA stylistic features: mainly parallel structures, root repetition, patterns (synonyms, antonyms). Techniques such as suffix repetition and parallel structures are sometimes used for rhetorical purposes and for achieving cohesion of the text. Lexical density and lexical chains or listings are among the distinctive features of legal Arabic. Thus, one can argue that the Arabic textual features are to be considered regular or universal among different Arabic text types, the legal type being one of them. This emphasizes the hybridity principle I have assumed when discussing the lexical features of Arabic legal discourse.

Our analysis has shown that punctuation marks do not follow a well-defined rule in MSA in general and in legal Arabic in particular. In legal discourse, the analysis shows the ungrammaticality of the punctuation system in Arabic, its fluidity and the lack of reference rules to be followed (if any exist, they are general and highly prescriptive). We can also deduce that legal Arabic uses the period and the comma more often whereas frequency of other punctuation marks, namely the colon and the quotation marks depends on the legal subtype.

In spite of the existence of such punctuation marks, conjunctions such as و (and), ف (and), كما (also, in addition), هذا (this), إن (and), قد (indeed / verily) and و ذلك (and that) still play a major role in the Arabic punctuation system 'to compensate for the lack of adherence to a strict system of punctuation and sentence division' (Al-Qinai, 1999:248).

Legal English compared to legal Arabic, keeps within the confines of register, whereas the latter has a higher tolerance such that the cutting edge is not so clear between different Arabic registers. The features of legal Arabic partially prove what has been stated by Hatim's seminar (2008, see endnote 30) about the register of legal Arabic: 'Arabic has no legal register'. Hatim's statement might refer to the textual features of legal Arabic, most of which are common in other Arabic registers. But in the case of Arabic official documents (for example contracts), they are like English ones, unique and it can be argued that they are representative of legal Arabic whether lexically, syntactically or textually.

Discussion of the features of legal English and Arabic, it can be argued that there are a number of similarities between them. These include the formulaic nature of both registers (for example archaic and template terms and expressions) on the lexical level. Nevertheless, one cannot claim that legal Arabic exhibits such a large number of these lexical items as legal English.

Formality is another common feature of legal English and Arabic, but it is expressed differently in the two languages. In English, it is expressed through modal auxiliaries, speech acts and formulas. It is used through the medium of decorative language in Arabic, for example through different forms of address and honorary titles.

There are some areas on the syntactic level that are common to both English and Arabic legal language. These include *nominalization, complex structure, doublets and triplets* and *parallel structures*. However, translation of these elements varies and does not follow the same syntactic structures. On the textual level, both English and Arabic legal language use *lexical chains* and *lexical repetition* which add to the semantic load of the sentence and demand an effort as to their degree of translatability.

It can also be argued that there are several differences between English and Arabic legal language. The first of these differences is in the domain of *religious*, *culture-specific* and *system-based* terms. Due to the difference between the legal systems in both Arabic and English on the one hand and the cultural systems on the other, both languages use totally different terms to express these aspects as was demonstrated in Chapters 3 and 5. *Gender-based terms* present another area of difference between English and Arabic legal language. There is inconsistency both in the ST representation of gender elements and the translation of such elements into the TT. In Arabic, for example, sometimes neutral words are used while at other times the gender-marked masculine is used. The fact that Arabic prefers the masculine element in writing has a close relation to the Arabic cultural and social background. That is, if a choice is to be made in writing about both sexes it will be made in favour of the masculine and not the feminine. This attitude needs to be adapted in legal language as otherwise there may be serious legal consequences.

There are also some differences between English and Arabic legal language on the syntactic level. Firstly, *the passive* in Arabic is flexible and constructing it is much easier than in English. Arab authors, however, tend to prefer the use of the active to the passive for linguistic reasons or for stylistic preferences. With regard to translation, Arabic uses both structures but the active is often used more. *Modals* are different in both English and Arabic legal language, because modality is lexically realized in Arabic, whereas it follows a grammatical and syntactic system in English. The difference between the two systems has been reflected in the translation of these modals from and into Arabic. The *absolute object* is a syntactic structure in Arabic which does not have an equivalent in English; hence it is translated communicatively in English, using one of the intensifying adverbs, such as effectively, completely, etc. *Punctuation marks* are less standardized in Arabic than in English and the only defined punctuation mark is the full stop at the end of a long sentence. In the following lines, the outcomes of analysis of the techniques of translating some areas of difference between English and Arabic legal language on the lexical and syntactic levels will be discussed. On the lexical level, two lexical areas have been investigated: *religious, system-based and culture-specific terms and archaic terms*. On the syntactic level, the translation of *modal auxiliaries and passive structures* have been analyzed.

In terms of religious, system-based and culture-specific terms, from Arabic into English, we have noticed that documents that are subject to Shariʿah Law use certain religious formulas such as the '*basmala*' and reference to God. These formulas are translated through 'domestication' of the term 'Allah' to correspond to 'God' in the TT. Other forms referring to God have been rendered 'denotatively' as they are; thus neither interpretation nor vagueness has been represented in the TT.

Analysis of the official documents cited in Hatim, Shunnaq and Buckley (1995) and in Mansoor (1965a and b) has shown that techniques such as 'omission', 'adaptation', or 'transposition' are used in rendering religious terms such as الشرعي and المعروف ('legal' or 'religious', 'equity' or 'good act'). In translating terms related to marriage, the translator has opted for 'cultural adaptations' as in the translation of the term المهر (dowry); unjustified 'addition' in translating the conditions of marriage, as in translating the term الإبراء (absolution). In translating the terms related to 'divorce', the translator has used different strategies such as 'borrowing', 'expansion' and 'unjustified omission'.

In the translation of the UIDHR, 'omission' comes in first place, especially in religious references. Other techniques such as 'borrowing', 'literal translation' and 'adaptation' are also used in the translation of this document. It should be noted that the translation of this document as it stands is problematic and it should be retranslated.

It is clear from the analysis that 'literal translation' is the most common technique in translating the system-based and culture-specific terms and other relevant synonyms from English into Arabic such as 'partner' or 'dissolution of partnership'. Other techniques such as 'adaptation' and 'expansion' have also been used in translating terms relating to the topic of civil partnership.

As for English *archaic terms* which are considered part and parcel of the English legal language, they do not have a direct equivalent in Arabic; translation of them into Arabic varies. They are sometimes rendered into Arabic template terms or conceptually explained, for example into non-archaic Arabic words or phrases. 'Addition' is another technique used in the translation of such terms into Arabic where the translator opted for making the reference of the archaic term in the TT clear.

Arabic template terms and phrases are used to refer to the names of persons or to a piece of information rather than repeating them. These are more common in Arabic official documents than any other legal subtypes. They are rendered into English archaic terms. It is also worth pointing out that English archaic terms can replace Arabic demonstrative pronouns or prepositional phrases in which case 'transpositions' are employed.

Concerning the translation of *modal auxiliaries from English into Arabic and vice versa*, as in the ChUN and the AChHR, it does not follow well-defined semantic and syntactic rules. This can be attributed to the difference between the modal systems in English and Arabic and the lack of correspondence between the English modals and the Arabic modal expressions. For example, English prefers the use of imperative *shall* in legislative commands to the present indicative or the future tense, whereas the Arabic translation of imperative *shall* or *may* uses normal verbs in the imperfect tense or lexical verbs denoting modality such as يجب (must), ينبغي (should). The modal meaning of the latter, however, is not decisive and so is subject to many interpretations, hence avoiding it in legal documents is recommended. Not only this, but drafting of the ST sometimes uses modals that are not decisive in their deontic meaning, such as using *should* to denote obligation rather than *shall* or *must*, or using لايجوز (it is not permissible/it is not allowed) to express prohibition where لا يجب (must not) could have been used to sound more binding.

In the case of translating *modal expressions from English into Arabic* as in the ChUN, the most common modal auxiliaries are *shall* and *may*. The analysis shows that the translation of *shall* does not follow a systematic pattern. The variation in translating it depends on its structure in the ST, whether active or passive. Also, translation of *may* into Arabic varies: sometimes a lexical verb is used; a shift in the tense is also used, or a preposition is used instead of the lexical verb denoting possibility or permissibility. I have found the techniques that Abdel-Fattah (2005:42–45) has established to be helpful in translating modals from English into Arabic.

In the case of translating *modal expressions from Arabic into English* as in the AChHR, the most frequent modal verbs are the negative form of the verb يجوز (it is allowed); لا يجوز (it is not permissible). Translation of this structure into English varies; shifting to a more binding prohibition expressed by 'shall not', or to 'transpositions' of a noun to a verb or active to passive. A suggested solution for this inconsistency could be making the ST wording of modal expressions could be more binding.

The translation of *passive structures from English into Arabic* varies. Sometimes the passive shifts to active as in the case of translating agentive passive (*by* phrase). The active is used in both animate and inanimate agents, but the translation of the (*by* phrase) itself varies, viz. it is represented as a subject in the case of animate agents, whereas it is represented as an agentive phrase in Arabic using the preposition بِ (by) and sometimes لِ (for). The translator sometimes sticks to the order of the ST, when the TT syntactic structure allows him / her to do so, to keep the organizational structure of the ST message. In some other cases, however, the translator changes the word order in the TT.

Arabic also adheres to the English passive structures mostly in cases where the agent is not specified. Although the gap is not so wide between the active and the passive, the fact that the TT shifts to active structures in translation validates the claim in Chapter 3 that Arabic legal documents favour the active over the passive. In the case of the Arabic–English document analyzed, the passive was adhered to most of the time. This may be attributed to the fact that English uses the passive when the agent is not identified in the sentence.

As shown from the above discussion, legal translation presupposes a solid knowledge of the linguistic structures of the SL and the TL and the strategies of analyzing translationally-parallel legal texts such as transposition, modulation, equivalence and adaptation. Not only that but experience on the part of the translator and knowledge of the cultural and legal systems are also important. These enable the translator to locate texts in their social and legal contexts. We can also argue that legal translation has always been related to general translation theory, but theorists and lawyers have realized the specific nature of it and the importance of looking at it as a discipline in its own right.

FUTURE PROJECTS

Further contrastive corpus-based analysis of modal auxiliaries in English–Arabic–English legal texts is recommended. A further important aspect for future research is the investigation of gender differences between Arabic and English legal language. Translation of other areas such as doublets and triplets which are common in both English and Arabic are also interesting to investigate because rendition of them into English varies; sometimes they are adhered to, while on other occasions they are reduced. Another pressing need is for an analysis of the textual features of different Arabic text types so as to compare them to those of legal texts and thus to check the regularities existing among them. This quest for regularities can be approached through corpus-based translation studies, based on a larger scale of electronic data, in order to arrive at more reliable and comprehensive results in terms of regularities. Some restrictions will be on the horizon, however; these include the lack of a well-defined legal corpus based on purely legal texts.[70]

Investigation of certain textual features, namely the lexical repetition on the word or the phrase level in detail is also recommended. This can be done through corpus-based analysis.

It will also be very beneficial to undertake some research that looks beyond the language of a text, through looking at legal translation from different perspectives. This can be conducted through the interface between critical legal studies, critical linguistics and translation theories. In this way, semiotics, gender, race, hegemony and ideology are all highlighted, where the views of Saussure, Bourdieu and Foucault come into play. This means understanding the ideological relations of meaning which affect the interpretation of texts. In general, the breadth of Arabic–English–Arabic legal translation offers a vast amount of material for future studies, including the sociolinguistic and cultural aspects of legal translation.

Notes

1 The reason why I will focus on some areas and leave others out is because some of the areas of difference between English and Arabic – which can have an impact on English/Arabic legal translation – such as the gender differences, complexity of sentences on the syntactic level or the different forms of repetition and punctuation on the textual level will require more detailed investigations and can invariably be done in separate studies.

2 Full details of these documents will be given in chapter 4 of this book.

3 It is also known as the *Code of Justinian*, which is a compilation of Roman Law in Latin. It forms the foundation of the *Civil Law*. For more information, refer to this website: <http://www.princeton.edu/~achaney/tmve/wiki100k/docs/Corpus_Juris_Civilis.html>

4 For information on the history of translation in the Arabic tradition, consult Guttas (1998).

5 For more information, see Shaltout (1987:119).

6 For more information about Arabic translation activities and projects in the twentieth century, refer to Baker and Hanna (2009:337).

7 According to Reiss (2000), texts serve four functions: informative (e.g. legal), expressive (e.g. literature), operative (e.g. adverts) and audiomedial (e.g. film). The informative function involves communicating facts, information or opinions, e.g. legal documents; the expressive function is concerned with the composition of the message, the sender and the message addressed, e.g. literature; the operative function focuses on how the text is appealing, e.g. persuading, requesting such as the language of adverts or 'a barrister's concluding statement' (Munday, 2012:112). Finally the audiomedial function stresses the audio and visual elements of the text, such as that in films and music. Boundaries between Reiss's text typology are fuzzy because each of the above categories can serve more than one function. For instance, the ST of كليلة و دمنة (Kalilah and Dimnah) is meant to be an operative text but the function of the TT is obviously an expressive one.

8 Inner-state speeches refer to those addressed to the people of a particular state (e.g. concerning a domestic issue) and they are not addressed to the international community. If they are addressed to the International Community, they are described as inter-state speeches. For example, Obama's speech about the Healthcare plan is meant to be an inner speech addressed to the American people only. But if he speaks about the Egyptian Revolution 2011, it is an inter-state speech. Some speeches can be both, For example, Gadafi's speech at the beginning of the Libyan revolution in February 2011 was meant to be addressed to the Libyans and the international community.

9 Among the main pre-twentieth century theorists are Cicero, Horace, Jerome, Luther, Dolet, Dryden, Tytler, Pope, Schegal, Humboldt and Schleiermacher. For more information on them, refer to Munday (2001).

10 By this is meant translating word-for-word, following the same syntactic structures and the word order of the ST, though sometimes some transformations are made to respect the rules of the TT.

11 Pym (2011:81) argues that equivalence is a 'widespread term for a relation that many believe in and no one can prove beyond the level of terminology. We should accept that equivalence has no ontological foundation, since translation problems allow for more than one viable solution.' This means that, in the field of translation problems, equivalence is always: 'belief in the translation as equivalent of an ST.'

12 A gloss means 'an explanation or translation of a difficult word or phrase, usually added to a text by a later copyist or editor . . . When placed between the lines of a text, it is known as an "interlinear

gloss", but it may appear in the margin, or as a footnote, or in an appendix, and may form an extended commentary' (Baldick, 2001:106).

13 Metalanguage means 'any use of language about language, as for instance in glosses, definitions, or arguments about the usage or meaning of words. Linguistics sometimes describes itself as a metalanguage because it is a "language" about language . . . Roman Jakobson describes the "metalingual" (or metalinguistic) function as that by which speakers check that they understand one another' (Baldick, 2001:152).

14 Full Arabic and English versions of the *Iraqi Constitution* are available from:
<http://www.pogar.org/publications/other/constitutions/iraq-a.pdf>
<http://www.pogar.org/publications/other/constitutions/iraq-e.pdf>

15 According to Venuti (1995:20), foreignization is 'an ethno deviant pressure on [target-language culture] values to register the linguistic and cultural difference of the foreign text, sending the reader abroad'. It is 'a non-fluent or estranging translation style designed to make visible the presence of the translator by highlighting the foreign identity of the ST and protecting it from the ideological dominance of the target culture' (Munday, 2001:147).

16 For more information about these theories, refer to Jakobson (1959): 'On Linguistic Aspects of Translation' in which he maintains that 'equivalence in difference is the cardinal problem of language and the pivotal concern of linguistics' (1959:135). He distinguishes between three ways of translating a verbal sign: intralingual (within one language), interlingual (between two different languages) and semiotic (between two different sign systems). Other theorists such as Vinay and Darbelnet (1995) propose their contrastive stylistic analysis of translation; Catford (1965), Levy (1967) and Blum Kulka (1986) have discussed shift theory. Leuven-Zwart (1989, 1990) has adopted Vinay and Darbelnet's and Levy's theories into a study of shifts through the micro and the macro structural level of the text. In chapter 4. we will discuss Vinay and Darbelnet's approach in more detail.

17 Halliday's systemic functional analysis (1985) is one of the widely applicable models to translation from the 1980s and it is still forming a basis for many translation studies. In this model, Halliday focuses on the sociocultural environment of translation for which he introduces many concepts such as genre, register (field, tenor and mode), discourse semantics and lexicogrammar.

18 Function-based theories involve the text type theory led by Reiss (2000), the skopos theory introduced by Vermeer (2000) and the text analysis model by Nord (1997).

19 Microlinguistics and macrolinguistics are the two main levels of linguistics. The former 'refers to phonetics, phonology, grammar and semantics'. The latter 'covers sociolinguistics, discourse analysis and other related disciplines. In sociolinguistics, the micro level is often equated with variation and face-to-face communication, whereas macrosociolinguistics involves language planning and sociology of language' (Johnson and Johnson, 1999).

20 Nord (1997) has developed the skopos theory into a more detailed theory of text analysis. She has provided basic concepts such as intention, function and effect. The hallmark of Nord's approach is 'text organization at or above sentence level' (Munday, 2001:81). She classifies translation into two main types: documentary and instrumental. The former 'serves as a document for the source culture communication between the author and the ST recipient, i.e. food items' (Nord, 1997:72). The latter allows for the TT reader to get the same function that the ST reader has got as in the case of a computer manual (ibid.). That is, the translation 'acts as an instrument in its own right' (Chesterman and Wagner, 2002:50).

21 This corpus is available from: <http://smlc09.leeds.ac.uk/query-ar.html>

22 The former refers to the period prior to the Norman Conquest (fifth century to 1066). In this period, the Celts, Anglo-Saxons and Christians loaded the language of law with archaic terms such as 'hereafter' and 'herein'. Middle English covers the period from after the Norman Conquest (1100–1500).

23 Kocbek (2008:64) comments on the translation of 'bona fide' into English: 'When for instance the continental concept *bona fide* is translated into English, most frequently the expression *good faith* is used, which, however, does not fully render the continental notion. The English concept of *good faith* excludes negligence, while the continental understanding of *bona fide* often regards gross negligence as the equivalent of bad faith. Moreover, the continental concept covers a wider semantic field and includes confidential relationships and a minimal standard of conduct expected of the parties engaging in commercial transaction'.

24 The formula for announcing the elections results in the UK is: ‘I, *name*, The Acting Returning Officer for the *name of seat*, hereby give notice that the total number of votes given for each candidate at the election *date* was as follows, *list of candidates and the number of votes received.* And that *name of winning candidate(s)* has been duly elected to *name of democratic body* for *name of seat* (as *name of office*).’
<http://www.electoralcommission.org.uk/>
25 This is the code of the document from the UN Official Document System (ODS). The document is entitled: ‘Committee on the Elimination of Discrimination against Women Consideration of Reports Submitted by States Parties under Article 18 of the Convention on the Elimination of All Forms of Discrimination against Women Sixth Periodic Report of States Parties United Kingdom of Great Britain and Northern Ireland’.
26 This is the code of the document from the UN (ODS). The document is entitled: ‘Implementation of the International Covenant on Economic, Social and Cultural Rights Fifth Periodic Reports Submitted by States Parties under Articles 16 and 17 of the Covenant United Kingdom of Great Britain and Northern Ireland.’
27 Addition of ‘shall’ is mine.
28 Permissibility in English can be expressed by lexical items, such as the adverbials ‘duly’, ‘likely’, ‘possibly’; and the verbs such as ‘to be’ plus ‘entitled to’ or ‘free to’ (Bhatia, Candlin and Gotti, 2003:106–7).
29 For a detailed account of these elements, consult Mellinkoff (1963:305–330).
30 For more information about cataphoric and anaphoric reference, see Halliday and Hasan (1976).
31 Hatim is quoted from a lecture for the Centre of Translation, University of Leeds (March 2008).
32 Hatim commented on the lack of specific features of Arabic legal discourse in the Third Conference of the Said Association of Translation and Arabization (28–30 December 2009).
33 Most of the work I have come across deals with Arabic–English–Arabic translation theory in general such as the works of Hatim (1990, 1994, 1997a, 1997b) among some others.
34 Metaphors are also said to occur in English legal discourse, examples of which are given by Alcaraz Varó and Hughes (2002:11) such as ‘to stand mute by visitation of God’ and ‘money laundering’. In this respect, they (ibid.:44) commented:

> Given the traditional and eminently conservative nature of legal phraseology, it is quite likely that the same or similar figurative usages will be found in many different languages. Whenever this is not the case, perhaps the wisest course is for the translator to choose the plainest possible rendering rather than run the risk of fanciful or highly coloured expressions at odds with the generally formal and even solemn tone of this type of text.

35 On the difference between English and Arabic use of formulaic expressions, Davies (2007:67) comments: ‘A comparison of the politeness formulas used in Arabic and English, for example, soon reveals that literal translations of these will often be communicatively disastrous; where functionally similar formulas exist in the target culture, an equivalent effect can often be achieved by substituting these, but in many cases there is quite simply no equivalent to be found and omission may then be a reasonable solution’.
36 Some of these terms have been known to be used in the masculine because persons who are doing the job are males such as القاضي ، الحاجب ، الكاتب (the judge, the bailiff and the clerk). However, the situation might have been changed and females can undertake these jobs.
37 Translations of Qur’anic verses are cited at ‘The Meanings Of The Holy Qur’an’ by Abdullah Yusuf Ali [online]:
<http://www.islam101.com/quran/yusufAli/> [accessed 05/09/2013]
38 ‘The passive participle is a morphological form derived from the verb to refer to the person or thing that undergoes the action denoted by the verb. In Classical and Modern Standard Arabic grammars, it is called */ism-u l-maf‘ul* / noun of the patient’ (Gadalla, 2010:1).
39 For more information about the passive participle, its definition and functions refer to Gadalla (2010:1–4).
40 I have investigated a considerable corpus compiled in the Ottoman Empire in the seventeenth century. The texts are void of any punctuation marks apart from a period at the end of the text. In discussing the lexical density earlier in this chapter, we have noted that each word in the lexical string is separated from the other by means of و (and) which functions as a punctuation marker.

This has been a continuation of the old tradition, which used it in exactly the same way as in the case of the Ottoman texts.

41 In order for me to provide examples, I need to present a big excerpt if not the complete document to investigate the different types of commas and this can be done in a separate study.

42 For more information about the use of و (and) as a conjunction, refer to Hassan (2005b).

43 For examples on this, see Alcaraz Varó and Hughes (2002:185).

44 The textual level requires a separate study which will be one of my future projects. Similarly, not all the areas of difference on the lexical and syntactic levels will be covered in this book. For example, on the syntactic level, we are not going to discuss gender differences and their impact on the accuracy of legal translation. That is only because it requires separate research where we can apply a different methodology and use a different corpus.

45 Epistemic modality is 'concerned with the speaker's assumptions or assessment of possibilities and, in most cases, indicates the speaker's confidence (or lack of confidence) in the truth of the proposition' (Coates 1983:18). An example of this category is presented by the phrase 'I think' in: I think *that Manchester United plays better in this game.*

46 An example of deontic modality is represented in the modal 'must' in '*The United Nations* must *interfere to end the conflict in the region*'.

47 Dynamic modality 'is concerned with the disposition of certain empirical circumstances with regard to the occurrence of some event' (Perkins, 1983:34). Palmer (1990:7) notes that it 'is concerned with ability and volition of the subject of the sentence, and is not, perhaps, strictly modality at all'. Thus, according to Palmer: dynamic modality represents (ability) not 'judgements (epistemic) or attitudes (deontic) of the speaker' (Palmer, 1990:83). An example of dynamic modality is represented by 'can' in: *I* can *swim.*

48 Volition means intention, for example *I promise I* will *say the truth, nothing but the truth.* For more information about volition modality, refer to Nuyts (2006).

49 Intrinsic 'shows some human control' whereas extrinsic 'not the result of human control but of human judgment' (Dury: *Brief Glossary of Modality*) Online
<http://dinamico2.unibg.it/anglistica/slin/modgloss.htm>

50 Refer to Nuyts (2006) and Dury: *Brief Glossary of Modality* online:
<http://dinamico2.unibg.it/anglistica/slin/modgloss.htm>

51 Alethic modality refers to logical modality and ranges from logical impossibility, possibility to logical necessity (von Wright, 1951:1–2); 'it relates to the notion of truth itself: it is necessarily true or false that p; it is possibly true or false that p' (Anchimbe, 2012: 32).

52 For information on the meaning of epistemic, deontic, alethic modality refer to (4.5.2.2) and the above endnotes.

53 Boulomaic modality refers to desire (Anchimbe, 2012:32). It 'can be paraphrased as *it is hoped/desired/feared/regretted that*. . . It ranges from not-wanting through not-opposing to wanting' (Dury: *Brief Glossary of Modality*) Online:
<http://dinamico2.unibg.it/anglistica/slin/modgloss.htm>
For more information on boulomaic modality, refer to Perkins (1983).

54 Temporal modality is one of Rescher's (1968) eight modal categories: alethic, epistemic, temporal, boulomaic, deontic, evaluative, likelihood and causal (quoted in Perkins, 1983:9). It 'relates to time' (Anchimbe, 2012:32) and ranges from 'never' through 'sometimes' to 'always'. 'Like existential modality this refers to the target of description' (quoted in Dury: *Brief Glossary of Modality*) Online. Anchimbe (2012:32) comments on the other modalities: 'epistemic (relating to knowledge and belief); boulomaic (relating to desire); deontic (relating to duties); evaluative (for example 'it is good thing that p'); likelihood (for example 'it is likely that p') and causal (for example 'the existing state of affairs will bring it about that p').

55 For more information on the passive voice, its constraints, consult Svartvik (1966) and Quirk et al. (1985).

56 Periphrastic is defined as 'combination of words rather than by inflection (such as did go and of the people rather than went and the people's)' Oxford Dictionaries online:
<http://www.oxforddictionaries.com/definition/english/periphrastic>
Thus, periphrastic agents in Arabic passive describe a phrase of more than one word, normally initiated by a preposition.

57 The two terms refer to the process of separation between married couples. Yet, there is a difference between both concerning the procedures of performing it in the Arabic and English cultures. For

example, *talaq* in Shariʿah Law is viable verbally or via written certificate issued from the court upon the request of the husband. A copy of this certificate is sent to the divorcee's home address to sign. In the UK, for instance, marriage is considered a 'civil contract' the dissolution of which is subject to the evaluation of the magistrates' court based on the circumstances of preaching the vows of marriage and whether or not the two parties are guilty.

58 This is a purely cultural situation that does not exist in the TT culture.

59 Details of the exact time of ʿ*iddah* in the Qurʾan have been mentioned in Sura 2, J.2 verses 232–234 which is available from:
<http://www.noblequran.com/translation/>
This term ʿ*iddah* is also mentioned in the Qurʾan in Sura 65 verse: 4 which is available from the following website:
<http://corpus.quran.com/translation.jsp?chapter=65&verse=4>

60 A copy of the ST is available from:
<http://www1.umn.edu/humanrts/arab/UIDHR.html>
The TT is available from:
<http://www.barrypearson.co.uk/articles/gods/islam_universal.htm>
© Barry Pearson 2008.

61 This is the correct way of pronouncing this term as a derived noun from the verb (*khalaʿa*).

62 'I pledge to share my life openly with you. I promise to cherish and tenderly care for you, to honour and encourage you. I will respect you as an individual and be true to you through all the good and bad times.' For exchanging rings these words are uttered: 'I give you this ring as a token of my love and a sign of the promises I make to you today.' Civil partnership ceremonies, available online from: <http://www.bracknell-forest.gov.uk/your-civil-partnership-ceremony-choices.pdf>

63 For information on civil partnership and the differences between it and civil marriage and/or marriage, refer to the Civil Partnership Act 2004 or the Civil Partnership Guide available from: <http://www.civilpartnershipinfo.co.uk/>

64 These documents have been selected through a term-based search from the UN official document database. They have been introduced in Chapter 4 (section 4.6.1). Thus, we will only refer to them by the symbol of the document as given by the database, and the article number will also be included.

65 The two examples are obtained from the BBC English and Arabic websites in an article about the resignation of David Laws, the British Treasury Minister, after his expenses scandal. Links to the English and Arabic articles are given below:
<http://news.bbc.co.uk/1/hi/uk/10192614.stm>
<http://www.bbc.co.uk/arabic/multimedia/2010/05/100530_hs_uk_laws_resign_cabinet.shtml>

66 This article is available from:
<http://www.express.co.uk/news/uk/184647/Gay-couple-set-to-christen-children>

67 This example is quoted from the article about David Laws, the British Treasury Minister mentioned earlier in section 5.4.3.

68 We have highlighted that the function of these archaic words in Chapter 3 (section 3.3.2.4) is to be used for reference. I believe that this function is employed here by using the demonstrative pronoun هذه (inanimate plural) – 'these' and the prepositional phrase – فيها (in them).

69 The difference between لا/*la* (not) and ليس/*laysa* (not) is that the former occurs before a verb while the latter occurs before a noun or a noun preceded by a preposition.

70 The only Arabic legal corpus available from the University of Leeds Centre for Translation Studies website, compiled by Dr Serge Sharoff and myself, is not purely legal as all data is derived from the internet, hence includes many irrelevant web pages.

References

Abdel-Fattah, Mohamed (2005) 'Translating Modal Auxiliaries from English into Arabic and Vice Versa'. *Babel*, vol. 51 (1): pp. 31–48.

Abdul-Raof, Hussein (1998) *Subject, Theme and Agent in Modern Standard Arabic*, Surrey: Curzon.

—— (2001) *Arabic Stylistics: A Coursebook*, Wiesbaden: Harrassowitz.

Aixela, J. (1996) 'Culture Specific Items in Translation'. In Alvarez, R., and Vidal, M. C. (eds), *Translation, Power, Subversion*, Clevendon and Philadelphia: Multilingual Matters: pp. 52–78.

Al-Bainy, Ramez H. (2002) *Additions and Omissions in Translation With Special Reference to Literary and Legal Translated Texts*, Unpublished Ph.D. thesis, UK: University of Portsmouth.

Alcaraz Varó, Enrique (2009) 'Isomorphism and Anisomorphism in the Translation of Legal Texts'. In Olson, F., Lorz, R. A. and Stein, D. (eds), *Translation Issues in Language and Law*, London/New York: Palgrave Macmillan, pp. 182–192.

Alcaraz Varó, Enrique and Hughes, Brian (2002) *Legal Translation Explained*, Manchester: St. Jerome.

Al-Karooni, Dhia M. (1996) *The Transfer of Modal Content in Translation.* Unpublished Ph.D. Thesis, Glasgow: University of Glasgow.

Al-Khafaji, Rasoul (1996) 'Arabic Translation Alternatives for the Passive in English'. *Papers and Studies in Contrastive Linguistics*, Poznan: Adam Mickiewicz University, vol. 31: pp. 20–36.

—— (1999) 'Punctuation Transfer in Translated Arabic Texts'. *Turjuman*, vol. 8 (2): pp. 71–97.

—— (2001) 'Punctuation Marks in Original Arabic Texts'. *Zeitschrift für Arabische Linguist*, vol. 40: pp. 7–24.

—— (2006) 'In Search for Translational Norms: the Case of Shifts in Lexical Repetition in Arabic–English Translations'. *Babel*, vol. 52 (1): pp. 39–65.

—— (2007) 'Translation-Specific Language Universals: The Case of Arabic Translated Texts'. *Turjuman*, vol. 16 (2): pp. 69–90.

Al-Khudrawi, Deeb (1995) *A Dictionary of Islamic Terms*, Beirut and Damascus: Alyamamah for Printing and Publishing.

Al-Najjar, Majed F. (1984) *Translating as a Contrastive Meaning*. Unpublished PhD Thesis, Bloomington: Indiana University.

Al-Qinai, Jamal (1999) 'Explication vs. Implication in English–Arabic Translation'. *Theoretical Linguistics*, vol. (25): pp. 235–255.

Al-thaʿaliby, Abu Mansoor (2000) *Fiqh al-lughah* (2nd edition), Beirut: Awlad Sherif Al-Ansary Ltd.

Alvarez, R., and Vidal, M. C. (eds) (1996) *Translation, Power, Subversion*, Clevedon, Philadelphia and Adelaide: Multilingual Matters.

Alwazna, Rafat Y. (2013a) *Translating Ḥanbalī Sharīʿa Code from Arabic into English*, LAP Lambert Academic Publishing.

—— (2013b) 'Testing the Precision of Legal Translation: The Case of Testing Islamic Legal Terms into English', *International Journal of Semiotics of the Law*, vol 26 (4): pp. 897–907.

Anchimbe, Eric A. (2012) *Language Contact in a Postcolonial Setting: The Linguistic and Social Context of English and Pidgin in Cameroon*, Berlin: De Gruyter Mouton.

Anghelescu, Nadia (1999) 'Modalities and Grammaticalization in Arabic'. In Suleiman, Yasir (ed.), *Arabic Grammar and Linguistics*, London: Routledge.

Austin, J. L. (1962) *How to Do Things with Words*, Oxford: Clarendon.

Bach, A. C. and Cable, T. (2002) *A History of the English Language* (5th edition), London: Taylor and Francis.

Badawi, E., Carter, M. G. and Gully, A. (2004) *Modern Written Arabic: A Comprehensive Grammar*, London and New York: Routledge.

Bahumaid, S. A. (1994) 'Terminological Problems in Arabic'. In Beaugrande, R. de, Shunnaq, A. and Heliel, M. H. (eds), *Language, Discourse and Translation in the West and Middle East*, Amsterdam and Philadelphia: Benjamins Publishing Company, pp. 133–140.

Baker, Mona (1992/2011) *In Other Words*, London and New York: Routledge.

Baker, Mona and Hanna, S. F. (2009) 'Arabic Tradition'. In Baker, Mona, and Saldanha, G. (eds), *The Routledge Encyclopaedia of Translation Studies* (2nd edition), London and New York: Routledge, pp. 328–337.

Baldick, Chris (2001) *The Oxford Dictionary of Literary Terms* (2nd Edition), London: Oxford University Press.

Bassnett, S. and Lefevere, A. (1990) *Translation History and Culture*, London: Pinter.

Beveridge, Barbara J. (2002) 'Legal English, How it Developed and Why it is Not Appropriate for International Commercial Contracts'. In Mattila, Heikki E. S. (ed.), *The Development of Legal Language*. Papers from an international symposium held at the University of Lapland, September 13–15, 2000, Helsinki: Kauppakaari, pp. 55–79.

Bhatia, V. K. (1993) *Analyzing Genre: Language Use in Professional Settings*, London: Longman.

Bhatia, V. K., Candlin, C. N. and Gotti, M. (eds) (2003) *Legal Discourse in Multilingual and Multicultural Contexts: Arbitration Texts in Europe. (Linguistic Insights)*, vol. 6, USA: Peter Lang Publishing.

Black's Law Dictionary (2009) (9th edition), London: West Group.

Blum-Kulka, S. (1986) 'Shifts of Cohesion and Coherence in Translation'. In House, J. and Blum-Kulka, S. (eds), *Interlingual and Intercultural Communication: Discourse and Cognition in Translation and Second Language Acquisition Studies*, Tubingen: Gunter Narr Verlag, pp. 17–35.

Bowers, Frederick (1989) *Linguistic Aspects of Legislative Expression*, Vancouver: University of British Columbia Press.

Cantarino, Vicente (1974) *Syntax of Modern Arabic Prose: The Simple Sentence*, (vol. 1), Bloomington and London: Indiana University Press.

Cao, Deborah (2007) *Translating Law*, Clevedon: Multilingual Matters.

Catford, J. C. (1965) *A Linguistic Theory in Translation: An Essay in Applied Linguistics*, Oxford: Oxford University Press.

Charrow, V. R., Crandall, J. A. and Charrow, R. P. (1982) 'Characteristics and Functions of Legal Language'. In Kittredge, R., and Lehrberger, J. (eds), *Sublanguage: Studies of Language in Restricted Semantic Domain*, Berlin and New York: Walter de Gruyter, pp. 175–190.

Chesterman, A. (ed.) (1989) *Readings in Translation Theory*, Helsinki: Finn Lectura.

Chesterman, A. and Wagner, Emma (2002) *Can Theory Help Translator?: A Dialogue Between the Ivory Tower and the Wordface*, Manchester: St. Jerome.

Clanchy, M. T. (1993) *From Memory to Written Record: England 1066–1307* (2nd edition), London: Blackwell Publishers.

Coates, J. (1983) *The Semantics of Modal Auxiliaries*, London: Croom Helm.

Conley, J. M. and O'Barr, W. M. (1998) *Just Words: Law, Language and Power*, Chicago: The University of Chicago Press.

Crystal, D. and Davy, D. (1969) *Investigating English Style*, London: Longman.

Danet, B. (1976) 'Language and the Construction of Reality in the Courtroom 1'. *Semantic Issues in the Trial of Kenneth Edelin, Working Paper No. 3, Law and Language Project*, NSF Grant SOC-74-23503, Boston University.

Danet, B. (1980) 'Language in the Legal Process'. *Law and Society Review*, vol. 14 (3): pp. 447–564.

—— (1985) 'Legal Discourse'. In van Dijk, T. A. (ed.), *Handbook of Discourse Analysis*, vol. 1, pp. 273–291.

Davies, Eirlys E. (2007) 'Leaving it out: On Some Justifications for the Use of Omission in Translation'. *Babel*, vol. 53 (1): pp. 56–77.

Delisle, Jean and Woodsworth, Judith (1995) *Translators Through History*, Amsterdam and Philadelphia: John Benjamins.

Dickins, J., Hervey, S. and Higgins, I. (2002) *Thinking Arabic Translation: A Course in Translation Method, Arabic to English*, London and New York: Routledge.

Dodds, J. M. (1985) *The Theory and Practice of Text Analysis and Translation Criticism*, vol. 1 Literary Prose, Udine: Carnpanotto Editore.

Dury, Richard (no date available) *Brief Glossary of Modality*, Available from: <http://dinamico2.unibg.it/anglistica/slin/modgloss.htm> [Accessed on 23 April 2014].

Ebeid, R. Y. and Young, M. J. L. (1976) *Some Arabic Legal Documents of the Ottoman Period*, Leiden: E. J. Brill.

Edzard, Lutz (1996) 'Stylistic Elements in the Use of Arabic as Language of Diplomacy: Recent Developments in United Nations Context'. *Die Welt des Islams*, vol. 36 (1): pp. 25–58.

—— (1997) 'Language as Medium of Legal Norm: The Topics "War and Peace" and "Human Rights" in Bi- and Multilateral Treaties with Arab States and Organizations'. In Edzard, Lutz and Szyska, Christian (eds), *Encounters of Words and Texts: Intercultural Studies in Honor of Stefan Wild on the Occasion of His 60th Birthday, March 2, 1997, Presented by His Pupils in Bonn*, Olms: Hildesheim.

Elmgrab, Ramadan A. (2011) 'Methods of Creating and Introducing New Terms in Arabic: Contributions from English–Arabic Translation'. *Proceedings from the International Conference on Languages, Literature and Linguistics, IPEDR* vol. 26, Singapore: IACSIT Press.

El-Yasin, M. K. (1996) 'The Passive Voice, A Problem for the English–Arabic Translator'. *Babel*, vol. 42 (1): pp. 18–26.

Emery, Peter G. (1989) 'Legal Arabic Texts: Implications for Translation'. *Babel*, vol. 35: pp. 1–11.

—— (1990) 'Lexical Incongruence in Arabic–English Translation'. *Babel*, vol. 37 (3): pp. 129–137.

Esposito, John L. (1998) *Islam: The Straight Path* (3rd Edition), UK: Oxford University Press.

Fareh, Shehdeh (2006) 'Some Textual Problems in Translating Arabic into English'. *Turjuman*, vol. 15 (2): pp. 99–115.

Farghal, M. (1991) 'Evaluativeness Parameter and the Translator from English into Arabic and Vice-Versa'. *Babel*, vol. 37 (3): pp. 138–151.

Faruqi, Harith S. (1983) *Faruqi's Law Dictionary: Arabic–English*, Beirut: Librairie du Liban Publishers.

—— (2008) *Faruqi's Law Dictionary: English–Arabic*, Beirut: Librairie du Liban Publishers.

Foley, Richard (2002) 'Legislative Language in the EU: the Crucible'. *International Journal for the Semiotics of Law*, vol. 15 (4): pp. 361–374.

Fowler, R. (1991) *Language in News: Discourse and Ideology in the Press*, London: Routledge.

Gadalla, Hassan, A. H. (2010) 'Syntactic Classes of the Arabic Passive Participle and How they Should be Rendered into English'. *Babel*, vol. 56 (1): pp. 1–18.

Garre, Marianne (1999) *Human Rights in Translation: Legal Concepts in Different Languages*, Denmark: Copenhagen Business School Press.

Garzone, Giuliana (1999) 'The Translation of Legal Texts. A Functional Approach in a Pragmatic Perspective'. *Textus*, vol. XII (2): pp. 391–408.

—— (2000) *Legal Translation and Functionalist Approaches: A Contradiction in Terms?* [online]. Available from: <http://www.Tradulex.org/Grazone.pdf> [Accessed on 18 July 2013].

—— (2003) 'Arbitration Rules across Legal Cultures: An Intercultural Approach'. In Bhatia, V. K., Candlin, C. N. and Gotti, M. (eds), *Legal Discourse in Multilingual and Multicultural Contexts: Arbitration Texts in Europe*, vol. 6. Antwerp: Linguistic Insights pp. 177–220.

Goodrich, Peter (1987) *Legal Discourse: Studies in Linguistics, Rhetoric and Legal Analysis*, London: Palgrave Macmillan.

Gu, Sharron (2006) *The Boundaries of Meaning and Formation of Law: Legal Concepts and Reasoning in the English, Arabic and Chinese Traditions*, Montreal and London: McGill-Queen's University Press.

Gustafsson, M. (1975) *Binomial Expressions in Present-day English: A Syntactic and Semantic Study*, Turku: Turun Yliopisto.

Guttas, D. (1998) *Greek Thought, Arabic Culture: The Graeco–Arabic Translation Movement in Baghdad and Early Abbasid Society (2nd–4th/8th–10th Centuries)*, London: Routledge.

Haigh, Rupert (2004) *Legal English*, London: Cavendish Publishing.

Halliday, M. A. K. (1985) *An Introduction to Functional Grammar*, London: Edward Arnold.

Halliday, M. A. K., and Hasan, Ruqaiya (1976) *Cohesion in English*, London: Longman.

Hassan, Aboudi J. (2005a) 'Repetition as a Means of Disambiguation', *Turjuman*, vol. 14 (1): pp. 85–111.

—— (2005b) 'The Unilateral Arabic Connector When Translating into English'. *Turjuman*, vol. 14 (2): pp. 89–114.

Hatim, B. (1990) 'A Model of Argumentation from Arabic Rhetoric: Insights from a Theory of Text Types'. *British Society for Middle Eastern Studies Bulletin*, vol. 17 (1): pp. 47–54.

—— (1994) *English–Arabic–English Translation: A Practical Guide*, Morocco: The King Fahd School of Translation.

—— (1997a) *Communication Across Cultures: Translation Theory and Contrastive Text Linguistics*, UK: T. J. Press Ltd.

—— (1997b) *English–Arabic/Arabic–English Translation: A Practical Guide*, London: Saqi Books.

Hatim, B., Shunnaq, A. and Buckley, R. (1995) *The Legal Translator at Work: A Practical Guide*, Jordan: Irbid: Dar Al-Hilal for Translating and Publishing.

Hatim, B. and Mason, I. (1997) *The Translator as Communicator*, London and New York: Routledge.

Hiltunen, R. (1990) *Chapters on Legal English: Aspects Past and Present of the Language of the Law*, Helsinki: Suomalainen Tiedeakatemia.

Hoffman, T. R. (1976) 'Past Tense Replacement and the Modal System'. In McCauley, J. (ed.), *Syntax and Semantics*, vol. 7, New York: Academic Press, pp. 86–100.

Holes, Clive (2004) *Modern Arabic: Structures, Functions, and Varieties*, Washington DC: Georgetown University Press.

House, Juliane (1997) *Translation Quality Assessment: A Model Revisited*, Tübingen: G. Narr.

Huddleston, Rodney D. (1988) *English Grammar: An Outline*, Cambridge: Cambridge University Press.

Ḥunayn ibn Isḥāq. *Encyclopædia Britannica* [online]. Available from: <http://www.britannica.com/EBchecked/topic/276461/Hunayn-ibn-Ishaq> [Accessed on 18 July 2012].

Jakobson, Roman (1959) 'On Linguistic Aspects of Translation'. In R. A. Brower (ed.), *On Translation*, Cambridge: Harvard University Press, pp. 232–39.

Jawad, Hisham A. (2009) 'Repetition in Literary Arabic: Foregrounding, Backgrounding and Translation Strategies'. *Meta*, vol. 54 (4): pp. 753–69.

Jenkins, L. (1972) *Modality in English Syntax*. MIT Dissertation (distributed by Indiana Linguistic Club).

Johannesson, Nils-Lennart (1976) *The English Modal Auxiliaries: A Stratificational Account*, Stockholm: Almqvist and Wiksell International.

Johnson, Keith and Johnson, Helen (eds) (1999) *Encyclopedic Dictionary of Applied Linguistics: A Handbook for Language Teaching*, London: Wiley Blackwell.

Johnstone, Barbara (1991) *Repetition in Arabic Discourse: Paradigms, Syntagms and the Ecology of Language*, London: John Benjamins.

Khalil, A. (1993) 'Arabic Translation of English Passive Sentences: Problems and Acceptability Judgments'. *Papers and Studies in Contrastive Linguistics* (vol. 27), Poznan: Adam Mickiewicz University, pp. 169–181.

Kittredge, Richard and Lehrberger, John (1982) *Sublanguage: Studies of Language in Restricted Semantic Domain*, Berlin and New York: Walter de Gruyter.

Kocbek, Alenka (2008) 'The Challenges of Intercultural Legal Communication'. *International Journal of Euro-Mediterranean Studies (IJEMS)*, vol. 1 (1): pp. 53–71.

Kurzon, Dennis (1986) *It is Hereby Performed: Explorations in Legal Speech Acts*, Amsterdam and Philadelphia: John Benjamins Publishing Company.

—— (1989) 'Language of the Law and Legal Language'. In Lauren, C. and Nordman, M. (eds), *Special Language: From Humans Thinking to Thinking Machines*, Clevedon and Philadelphia: Multilingual Matters, pp. 283–290.

—— (1997) 'Legal Language: Varieties, Genres, Registers, Discourse'. *International Journal of Applied Linguistics*, vol. 7 (2): pp. 119–139.

Leech, G. and Svartvik, J. (1975) *A Communicative Grammar of English*, London: Longman.

Lefevere, A. (1992) *Translation, Rewriting and the Manipulation of Literary Frames*, London and New York: Routledge.

Leuven-Zwart, K. M. van (1989) 'Translation and Original: Similarities and Dissimilarities', *Target*, vol. 1 (2): pp. 151–81.

—— (1990) 'Translation and Original: Similarities and Dissimilarities', II. *Target*, vol. 2 (1): pp. 69–95.

Levy, Jiri (1967) 'Translation as a Decision Making Process'. *To Honor Roman Jakobson* vol. 2, The Hague: Mouton, pp. 1171–1182.

Maley, Yon (1994) 'The Language of the Law'. In Gibbons, John (ed.), *Language and the Law*, London and New York: Longman, pp.11–50.

Mansoor, M. (1965a) *Legal and Documentary Arabic Reader* (vol. 1), Leiden: E. J. Brill.

—— (1965b) *Legal and Documentary Arabic Reader* (vol. 2), Leiden: E. J. Brill.

Mattila, Heikki E. S. (2006) *Comparative Legal Linguistics*, Translated by Christopher Goddard, UK: Ashgate.

Matulewska, Alexandra (2007) *Lingua Legis in Translation*, Europaischer Verlag der Wissenschaften: Peter Lang.

Mayoral Asensio, Roberto (2003) *Translating Official Documents*, Manchester: St. Jerome.

—— (2007) 'Specialized Translation: A Concept in Need of Revision'. *Babel*, vol. 53 (1): pp. 48–55.

Mellinkoff, David (1963) *The Language of the Law*, Boston: Little Brown.

Menacere, M. K. (1997) 'Basil Hatim, Abdullah Shunnaq, Ron Buckley (eds): The Legal Translator at Work: Arabic–English Legal Translation. A Practical Guide'. *Babel*, vol. 43 (1): pp. 82–85.

Meredith, Clive, R. (1979) 'Some Notes on Legal English'. *Meta*, vol. 24 (1): pp. 54–67.

Montgomery, Scott L. (2000) *Science in Translation: Movement of Knowledge through Cultures and Time*, Chicago, London: The University of Chicago Press.

Morley, David G. (2000) *Syntax in Functional Grammar: An Introduction to Lexico-Grammar in Systemic Linguistics*, London and New York: Continuum.

Morris, Marshall (1995) *Translation and the Law*, Amsterdam and Philadelphia: John Benjamin.

Munday, Jeremy (2001/2012) *Introducing Translation Studies: Theories and Applications*, London: Routledge.

Newmark, Peter (1981) *Approaches to Translation*, Oxford and New York: Pergamon.

—— (1982) 'The Translation of Authoritative Statements: A Discussion'. *Meta*, vol. 27 (4): pp. 375–391.

—— (1988) *A Text Book of Translation*, New York and London: Prentice Hall.

Nida, Eugene A. (1964) *Towards a Science of Translating*, Leiden: Brill.

—— (1993) *Language, Culture and Translating*, Shanghai: Shanghai Foreign Language Education Press.

—— (2001) *Contexts in Translating*, Amsterdam and Philadelphia: J. Benjamins.

Nord, Christiane (1997) *Translating as a Purposeful Activity: Functionalist Approaches Explained*, Manchester: St. Jerome.

Nuyts, Jan (2006) 'Modality: Overview and Linguistic Issues'. In Frawley, William (ed.), *The Expression of Modality*, Berlin: De Gruyter Mouton, pp. 1–26.

O'Barr, William M. (1982) *Linguistic Evidence: Language, Power and Strategy in the Courtroom*, New York: Academic Press.

Osborne's Concise Law Dictionary (2001) (9th edition), London: Sweet and Maxwell.

Oxford Dictionaries [online]. Available from: <http://www.oxforddictionaries.com/definition/english/should> [Accessed on 13 September 2012].

Palmer, F. R. (1974/1987) *The English Verb*, London: Longman.

—— (1986) *Mood and Modality*, Cambridge: Cambridge University Press.

—— (1990) *Modality and the English Modals*, London and New York: Longman.

Perkins, M. R. (1982) 'The Core Meaning of the English Modals'. *Journal of Linguistics*, vol. 18: pp. 245–73.

Perkins, M.R. (1983) *Modal Expressions in English*, London: Pinter.

Pym, Anthony (2010) 'Translation Theory Today and Tomorrow—Responses to Equivalence'. In Zybatow, N. (ed.) *Translationswissenschaft Stand and Perspektiven*, Frankfurt aM: Peter Lang, pp. 1–14.

—— (2011) 'Translation Research Terms: A Tentative Glossary for Moments of Perplexity and Dispute'. In *Translation Research Projects* 3 (ed.), Tarragona, pp. 75–110. Available from <http://isg.urv.es/publicity/isg/publications/trp_3_2011/index.htm> [Accessed on 23 April 2014].

Quirk, R. et al. (1985) *A Comprehensive Grammar of the English Language*, London/New York: Longman.

Reiss, K. (2000) 'Type, Kind and Individuality of Text: Decision Making in Translation'. In Venuti, L. (ed.), *The Translation Studies Reader*, New York: Routledge, pp. 160–71.

Rek-Harrop, Joanna J. (2008) *Polish and English Translation of Jurilinguistic Discourse: Key Aspects and Problem Areas in the Translation of Certain Forms of Legal Contracts in Terms of Terminology Transfer Between Two Different Legal Systems: Polish and English*. Unpublished Ph.D. Thesis. [online]. Available from: <http://www.harroptranslations.com> [Accessed on 11 August 2010].

Rescher, N. (1968) *Topics in Philosophical Logic*. Dordrecht: Reidel.

Rosenhouse, J. (1988) 'Occurrences of the Passive in Different Types of Texts in Engish, Hebrew and Arabic'. *Babel*, vol. 34 (2): pp. 90–103.

Ryding, Karin C. (2005) *A Reference Grammar of Modern Standard Arabic*, Cambridge: Cambridge University Press.

Sager, Juan (1993) *Language Engineering and Translation*, Amsterdam and Philadelphia: Benjamins.

Salama-Carr, Myriam (2006a) 'Translation into Arabic in the Classical Age'. In Hermans, Theo (ed.), *Translating Others* (vol. I), Manchester: St. Jerome Publishing, pp. 121–130.

—— (2006b) 'Translation and the Creation of Genre: The Theatre in Nineteenth-Century Egypt'. In Hermans, Theo, *Translating Others* (vol. II), Manchester: St. Jerome Publishing, pp. 314–324.

Šarčević, Susan (1997) *New Approach to Legal Translation*, London and Boston: Kluwer Law International.

Schäffner, Christina (1997) 'Strategies of Translating Political Texts'. In Trosborg, A. (ed.), *Text Typology and Translation*, Amsterdam and Philadelphia: John Benjamins Publishing Company, pp. 119–144.

Schäffner, Christina and Adab, Beverly (eds) (2000) *Developing Translation Competence*, Amsterdam and Philadelphia: John Benjamins Publishing Company.

Schleiermacher, F. (2004) 'On the Different Methods of Translating'. In Venuti, L. (ed.), The Translation Studies Reader (2nd edition), New York: Routledge, pp. 43–63.

Shaltout, Mahmud (1987) 'Islamic Beliefs and Code of Laws'. In Morgan, Kenneth W. (ed.), *Islam the Straight Path: Islam Interpreted by Muslims*, Delhi: Motilal Banarsidass, pp. 87–143.

Shiyab, Said M. (2006) *A Textbook of Translation: Theoretical and Practical Implications*, Antwerp and Apeldoorn: Garant.

Shunnaq, Abdullah T. (1994) 'Semantic Redundancy and Translation from Arabic into English'. *Turjuman*, vol. 3 (2): pp. 103–120.

—— (2000) 'Arabic–English Translation of Political Speeches'. *Perspectives: Studies in Translatology*, vol. 8 (3): pp. 207–228.

Smith, S. A. (1995) 'Culture Clash: Anglo-American Case Law and German Civil Law'. In Morris, M. (ed.), *Translation and the Law*, Amsterdam and Philadelphia: John Benjamin, pp. 179–197.

Snell-Hornby, M. (1988) *Translation Studies: An Integrated Approach*. Amsterdam: John Benjamins.

Steiner, G. (1998) *After Babel: Aspects of Language and Translation* (3rd edition), London and New York: Oxford University Press.

Suleiman, Yasir (1999) *Arabic Grammar and Linguistics*, London: Routledge.

Svartvik, Jan (1966) *On Voice in the English Verb*, The Hague and Paris: de Gruyter Mouton.

Sweetser, E. E. (1982) 'Root and Epistemic Modality: Causality in Two Words'. *Berkeley Linguistic Society Papers*, vol. 8: pp. 484–507.

Tessuto, Girolamo (2003) 'Legislative Discourse in Arbitration Language: The English 1996 Arbitration Act and the UNCITRAL Model Law'. In Bhatia, V. K., Candlin, C. N. and Gotti, M. (eds) *Legal Discourse in Multilingual and Multicultural Contexts: Arbitration Texts in Europe. (Linguistic Insights)*, vol. 6, USA: Peter Lang Publishing.

Tiersma, Peter M. (1999) *Legal Language*, Chicago: University of Chicago Press.

Tomášek, M. (1991) 'Law – Interpretation and Translation'. *Translatologica Pragensia V*, Acta Universitatis Carolinae Philologica 4–5: 1991, Prague: Karolinum, pp. 147–157.

Totter, William (2000) *Translation Salience: A Model of Equivalence in Translation (Arabic/English)*. Unpublished Ph.D. Thesis, University of Sydney: Department of Semitic Studies.

Triebel, Volker (2009) 'Pitfalls of English as a Contract Language'. In Olson, F., Lorz, R. A. and Stein, D. (eds), *Translation Issues in Language and Law*, London/New York/UK: Palgrave Macmillan, pp. 147–181.

Trosborg, A. (1995a) 'Introduction: Special Issue on Laying down the Law-Discourse Analysis of Legal Institutions'. *Journal of Pragmatics*, vol. 23 (1): pp. 1–5.

—— (1995b) 'Statutes and Contracts: An Analysis of Legal Speech Acts in the English Language of Law'. *Journal of Pragmatics*, vol. 23 (1): pp. 31–53.

—— (1997) *Rhetorical Strategies in Legal Language: Discourse Analysis of Statutes and Contracts*, Tübingen: Gunter Narr Verlag Tubingen.

Vázquez-Ayora, Gerardo (1977) *Introducción a la Traductología*, USA: Georgetown University Press.

Venuti, L. (1995) *The Translator's Invisibility: A History of Translation*, London and New York: Routledge.

—— (2000) (ed.) *The Translation Studies Reader*, New York: Routledge.

Vermeer, H. (2000) 'Skopos and Commission in Translation Action'. In Venuti, L. (ed.), *The Translation Studies Reader*, New York: Routledge, pp. 221–32.

Vinay, Jean-Paul and Darbelnet, Jean (1995) *Comparative Stylistics of French and English: A Methodology for Translation*, Amsterdam and Philadelphia: John Benjamins.

von Wright, G. H. (1951) *An Essay in Modal Logic*, Amsterdam: North-Holland.

Watt, W. (1972) *The Influence of Islam on Medieval Europe*, Edinburgh: University Press.

Webster's Online Dictionary [online]. Available from: <http://www.merriam-webster.com/dictionary>. [Accessed 4 December 2009].

Weisflog, W. E. (1987) 'Problems of Legal Translation'. *Swiss Reports Presented at the XII International Congress of Comparative Law*, Zurich: Schultthess, pp. 179–218.

Williams, M. P. (1989) *A Comparison of the Textual Structures of Arabic and English Written Texts: A Study in the Comparative Orality of Arabic*, unpublished Ph.D. thesis, University of Leeds.

Wright, William (1967) *Grammar of the Arabic Language* (3rd edition), Cambridge: Cambridge University Press.

Yusuf Ali, A. *Translations of the Qur'an* [online]. Available from: <http://www.islam101.com/quran/yusufAli/> [Accessed 21 June 2014].

Index

Please note that page numbers relating to Notes will have the letter 'n' following the page number. References to Figures or Tables will be in *italics*

For Product Safety Concerns and Information please contact our EU
representative GPSR@taylorandfrancis.com
Taylor & Francis Verlag GmbH, Kaufingerstraße 24, 80331 München, Germany

www.ingramcontent.com/pod-product-compliance
Lightning Source LLC
LaVergne TN
LVHW080810011026
849160LV00015B/1586
* 9 7 8 0 4 1 5 7 0 7 5 3 4 *